GAOKAO

A Personal Journey Behind
China's Examination Culture

Published in the United States of America by

Sinomedia International Group
China Books
360 Swift Avenue, Suite 48
South San Francisco, CA 94080

Library of Congress Cataloging-in-Publication Data

Gong, Yanna.
Gaokao : behind China's examination culture / by Yanna Gong.
pages cm
Includes bibliographical references and index.
ISBN 978-0-8351-0062-5 (pbk. : alk. paper) 1. Universities and colleges--China--Entrance examinations. 2. Colleges & Universities--Entrance examination system--China. I. Title.

LB2353.8.C6G66 2013
378.51--dc23

Printed in the USA

For Sinomedia International Group
Editorial: Chris Robyn, Nina Wegner
Cover Design: Tiffany Cha
Text Design: Thomas White

GAOKAO

A Personal Journey Behind China's Examination Culture

BY
YANNA GONG

China Books
San Francisco

CONTENTS

Preface

As a high school student born of Chinese immigrant parents and raised in the United States, I straddled the fence of two dramatically different educational approaches every day. My normal high school life consisted of taking the bus to my suburban school, where I attended regular classes in science, humanities, social studies, and fine arts, as well as advanced-placement classes in American history, chemistry, calculus, and comparative politics. I participated in class discussions, group studies, and course projects. Over the summer, I read (and enjoyed) assigned books like *The Grapes of Wrath*, *The Jungle*, *The Color of Water*, and *Fast Food Nation*, and turned in book reports to my history and English teachers at the beginning of fall quarter. For my US history class, I learned about major historical events and their impacts on the course of US history. I didn't memorize the specific dates of those events because my teacher said it was not required. For my chemistry class, I grasped all the major concepts and principles, but I didn't memorize every detail about the 118 elements in the periodic table, as my teachers said that was unnecessary. I attempted to accomplish every requirement the school or my teachers asked of me, to the best of my ability. I believe I am a good student. But this was my life at school—it was not my whole educational experience. When I got home, my parents were waiting on the other side of the fence.

Every time I came home with the results of a quiz, midterm, or final, I needed to report my performance to my parents. They always wanted to know my grade or my score, even if it was just a quiz. Then they went further, asking me how my performance ranked in my class. My mom was happy only when I performed at the very top of my class. She was upset when I said I didn't know much about the other students' performances. When I said my teacher didn't require us to memorize the specific timelines of historical events such as the Revolutionary War, the Civil War, or the civil rights movement, I saw confusion on my father's face. He would question me, and then tell me I needed to memorize those dates and events. It seemed that to him, history was meaningless without a clear chronology. When I prepared for a major test, my mom insisted I do more practice tests than my teachers required. In other words, my parents were always *there*, always involved in the smallest details of my schoolwork, and always treating my school life like it was a competitive event. My mom and dad have different personalities and frequently see the world from different perspectives, but in the area of my education they are on the same page.

My parents immigrated to the United States from mainland China in 1989, when they were in their late twenties. They are both products of the Chinese higher education system, trained as professionals. They adapted to a new country, learned to speak fluent English, and built successful careers. But in their home life, and in the way they raised their children, they kept many of their traditions from China, including their devotion to education. When my brother and I started school, we brought the culture and educational values of the U.S. into the house. One can only imagine a household where two totally diverse cultures and educational systems intersect.

In a way, I should have known what to expect when I started high school, since my brother had the same experience with our parents. But I am seven years younger than my brother, and when he was in high school I didn't understand the extent to which he was living in two different worlds. (Also, my brother is much more patient than I am, and he never seemed to be especially annoyed about our parents' constant monitoring.) Sometimes I find it frustrating to communicate with my parents about how certain things are done in the United States, whether it's etiquette or curriculum. But in the end we always find some common ground.

Over the years, my parents have taken my brother and me on many trips across the United States and around the world. I have traveled to more than 100 cities, forty-eight of the fifty states, and countless national parks and historical monuments. I've walked on the battlegrounds of the Civil War, touched artifacts from our past, stood where heroic deeds have been done, and seen a copy of the Magna Carta in England. But these were not intended to be fun-filled vacations: they were designed to be educational tours. My parents expect me to cement the dates and figures of these historical sites and events into my brain. They ask me to read every display panel at a historical site and connect it to the lessons in my history class. I'm supposed to write down twenty new words every time we visit a national park. Whenever we visit my brother in Boston, my father takes me on a side trip to Ralph Waldo Emerson's mansion, Henry David Thoreau's graveyard, Nathaniel Hawthorne's home, or Louisa May Alcott's cottage. Most people go to Key West for rest and relaxation. But after we came back from a visit to Ernest Hemingway's Key West home, I had to read five of Hemingway's major works. After we visited Thomas Wolfe's home in Ashville, North Carolina, my father bought all of Thomas Wolfe's very thick books for me. Before I attended a creative writing summer camp at Stanford University, my parents and I stayed in Salinas for one day, and I was tested on John Steinbeck's writings after we came out of the Steinbeck Center.

No matter where we go, there is always an educational purpose. I not only have to read every sign we come across, but sometimes I'm also asked to memorize them, whether it's a brief summary of the area, an in-depth description of how glaciers are formed, or the sequential events leading to John Brown's execution. I clearly remember the time we went to the Lincoln Memorial in Washington, DC, for a winter-break vacation. While my dad was asking me to recite the Gettysburg Address from memory, I received a text from a friend who said she was currently lying on the beach at Sanibel, Florida. I began to ask my parents when I could have a vacation like that. There are times when I feel like I've had enough education.

In my daily life at home, conversations with my parents continue to focus on the subject of education: school, homework, tests and grades, along with educational aspects of my extracurricular activities. When my dad returns in the evening from a day of work, he always brings me a "present" (at least that's what he calls it): an article from that day's newspaper, or from a magazine or book he read in his college library. The topics vary: sometimes it has to do with science, or maybe it's the latest book review. He always starts off with the same line, "Yanna, I got a good article for you today." Sometimes when he's had a really busy day at work he'll forget, and I'll poke my head into his study and ask him if he has anything for me. There are evenings when we spend time watching television, playing in the yard, or going for a family walk, but soon enough the topic of education, news, articles, or books will come up. Because my life is so strongly impacted by my parents' obsession with education, it made me wonder about education in China, and how it shaped my parents.

I finally had the opportunity to explore this question directly, beginning with a visit to China with my parents in 2005, and on a few trips after that. If I needed any further evidence that education is a big deal in China, it turned out that even our travel plans and arrival dates were dictated by the Chinese educational system. Every time we tried to schedule a trip, we were warned not to come between June 6th and 8th because the whole country would be on lockdown for the *gaokao*, China's national college entrance examination. Every year during the gaokao, major roads are blocked to create quiet zones around testing sites, and taxi drivers ignore paying customers to provide rides to gaokao students. Doctors are busy prescribing sleeping pills and anti-anxiety medications to both students and parents. Parents and grandparents abandon their regular jobs to provide special care to their gaokao students.

"For three days China is on lockdown. I wouldn't advise you to come until afterward, when things quiet down," my aunt told me. "It'll be too inconvenient for you to travel here." Thus, we arranged our travels so that they wouldn't clash with China's "three-day panic," as I like to call it. With each trip to China, as I talked to people involved in the system, I gained more insight into the culture and historical background of education in China. I was truly astounded by some of the things I saw, and I was touched by many of the stories people told me. I hope to convey some idea of what I learned to those who are looking at the Chinese system from the outside. I also hope to show that people everywhere have the same goals and dreams for their children. Americans who have read this book say, "Wow, that's extreme!" But for the Chinese, it's just the way things are.

By the time I finished writing this book, I finally understood that my parents were not picking on me. They were only repeating the behavior of *their* parents, and were heroically upholding the standards and values of the society they grew up in. For me, this book is not just an academic investigation into the Chinese educational system—it is personal. It helped me understand why my brother and I were raised the way we were, and enabled me to glimpse the cultural forces that shaped my parents' approach to the world.

CHAPTER 1
The High Test

June 7, 2011, was the first day of China's annual three-day national test called the gaokao. On that day, more than ninety-three million high school students walked into classrooms across the country to take the largest test in China—probably the largest test in the world. At 9:00 a.m. across the vast land of China, every high school senior began to take the test: the subject was Chinese language and Chinese literature proficiency.

Every person in China is aware of the gaokao (meaning "high test"), also known as the National Higher Education Entrance Exam; everyone knows someone who is taking the test. It is difficult to adequately convey how important the gaokao is to the Chinese, and what a large part it plays in the culture of China. But think about it this way: almost every high school senior in China has spent the previous three years preparing intensively for this test, knowing that the results of the test have a profound effect on the potential future of each test taker. The roots of gaokao go far back in Chinese history, to the days of the Sui dynasty, when achieving the highest score in a national test meant a life of power and prestige.

With such high pressure upon this one test, who exactly are the victims of this challenge? The seniors in high school, whether they're farmers' sons, factory workers' daughters, princelings of the communist elite, offspring of capitalist entrepreneurs, taxi drivers' sons, or rural migrants' daughters. It doesn't matter if you live high in the Himalayan Mountains or in the center of Beijing. Students enter classrooms in developed coastal provinces, impoverished inland regions, medial cities, mountaintop villages, the

Qinghai-Tibet plateau, the Mongolian steppes, crowded communes, and isolated deserts. Inequalities prevail in every area in China, but when it comes to the gaokao, most people still believe that everyone has an equal chance to succeed.

June 7, 2011, began with a cool morning but soon developed into a hot, overcast day. The temperature climbed to 97°F in Beijing, the hottest day so far that year. On the second day of the test, it cooled slightly, but it was still hot and humid. In spite of the stifling heat, parents and grandparents maintained a vigil outside the test sites, waiting for their children to emerge from the classrooms.

On gaokao days in Beijing—a city of eighteen million people—public transportation systems are not allowed to sound their horns and sirens, especially when they pass through the 113 test locations in the nineteen test districts during testing hours; the testing hours were from 9:00AM to 4:00PM with an hour break at 12:00PM for lunch. All construction sites within half a mile of these test locations must maintain silence. It is a national social responsibility to shield the examinees from distractions. Proctors are not allowed to wear high-heeled shoes or perfume, or wear thin or low-cut blouses. Every effort is made to avoid distracting the test takers.

In Qingdao, a scenic coastal city in Shandong Province, taxi drivers volunteered their services to transport gaokao students. They placed signs on their cabs labeled "sweetheart taxi," and wherever taxi drivers saw students walking to school, they offered free rides. The cab drivers understood very well that each student's future was riding on the outcome of the gaokao. Maybe giving a student a free ride to a test site would give that student an edge. The Qingdao taxi drivers did not want to see students in their city relegated to a life of menial work if they did poorly on the gaokao—they offered their services in the hope that the children would not have to be taxi drivers in the future, a possibility if the students were late to the test, or if a mishap occurred while walking to the test center. People in all aspects of life in China recognize the gaokao as the only fair access to social mobility.

In Yunnan, one of China's southernmost provinces, 220,000 students entered more than eight thousand test locations on the morning of June 7. Entertainment facilities such as karaoke TV halls, ballrooms, and game stations in the vicinity of these test sites were under injunctions to keep quiet. Public security departments in cities and towns were mobilized to monitor these temporary regulations. In Kunming, the capital city of Yunnan, trucks and buses were detoured around test sites. Yunnan is one of the poorest, most underdeveloped provinces, and contains the largest number of minorities (non-Han people) in China. Local governments in Yunnan were watching out for their students' futures and their province's development.

In Tianjin, the third-largest metropolis in China, some construction projects were suspended for the duration of the testing, out of concern that the clangs and booms might stand in the way of a good night's sleep for the 64,600 test takers, who were randomly assigned to testing sites by computer, according to their school districts and selected majors.

This is how extreme the response to gaokao testing can be: it was even reported that doctors prescribed birth control pills to female students whose parents feared that an untimely period would be too distracting to the young women during the tests. My mother still remembers clearly that her parents brought her to a doctor for Chinese herbal prescriptions to delay her period when she sat for the gaokao more than thirty years ago.

In Wushan County, Chongqing Municipality, in the central-west region, 500 students from the town of Dachang needed to cross the Tianning River to reach their testing site, while 400 students from the town of Guandu needed to cross the Yangtze River to get to theirs. To meet the needs of its students, Wushan County assigned special ferries to transport the students, calling it the "green passage." For many of these students, this might be the only time they ever left their remote mountains and valleys and the undeveloped Three Gorges Dam area, where generations of their ancestors had lived for a thousand years. The natural landscapes in this area are stunningly beautiful, but the people are isolated and economically deprived.

The preparation for the gaokao, as well as the ordeal of the test days, is all-consuming for the participants. The importance of this one test creates a great deal of anxiety for many families. A student's score on the gaokao has the power to forever change the life path and future of that student. A good score spells success; a poor showing can relegate a person to a life with few opportunities. In every test location across China, parents and grandparents wait anxiously outside the classrooms to comfort their children as they emerge. Some have booked hotel rooms near the test sites to be on hand. Government employees and employees of private companies are frequently permitted to take time off so they can support their children on this make-or-break day. For the sake of this single test, many parents have often spent much of their income and savings over the previous three years, paying for tutors, review sessions, and special coaching.

The test itself consists of three required sections, math, Chinese, and another language—usually English, but this can be substituted with Japanese, Russian, or French. A fourth section is a choice of either humanities or science.

My father still vividly recalls his "big test" day in 1978. Even small details of the preparation process have not been erased from his memory. Mark Twain once said, "When opportunity knocks, shake it by the lapels." My dad assimilated that approach, even though he had never heard of Mark Twain when he was young.

While my father pursued his individual dreams, his generation experienced many of China's most dramatic historical moments firsthand. He started elementary school during the height of the Cultural Revolution in China, and went to high school during its last years.

During the Cultural Revolution (1966-1976) China closed its colleges and universities. All school activities were affected by national political developments. Only political propaganda and Chairman Mao's books were available: *Chairman Mao's Little Red Book*, his four volumes of selected works, and some booklets extracted from Lu Xun's essays and novels. Other books were burned. Professors were sent to labor camps. Teachers were "re-educated" by farmers and workers.

During my father's two years in high school, he was desperate to study and absorb academic subjects. But he was forced to spend a year doing soil analysis on communal farms, and another year in Chinese medicine with his Chinese language and Chinese literature class teacher, who also had training in Chinese medicine. The amount of time my father was able to devote to mathematics, physics, chemistry, and Chinese-language studies was limited and minimal. Under pressure from his instructors, my father committed the Chinese Communist Party Constitution to memory, word for word.

There was only one bookstore in the town my dad lived in, and he had already purchased or read every single book they carried, including books on how to raise rabbits and how to harvest corn. After he memorized all the main essays from Chairman Mao's books, it seemed to my father that rabbits and corn would accompany him for the rest of his days. His hunger for knowledge and longing for books remained a driving force in his life. But his desire to continue his education and attend college was little more than a hopeless dream at that point. When he graduated from high school in 1977, shortly after the death of Chairman Mao, China was enveloped in political turmoil and on the brink of an economic collapse.

On October 12, 1977, a few months after Deng Xiaoping resumed the leadership of China, China's only news channel, *Xinhua News Agency*, made the momentous announcement that Mr. Deng's leadership coalition had decided to reopen the colleges and universities and resume the national exam. My dad was working in the fields when he heard the news on the radio. After a moment of stunned silence, he joined in the uproar and excitement that followed the official declaration. People hardly dared to believe it was true at first, but it was.

After ten years without a national exam, or any regular system of education, a huge influx of students from the countryside, the factories, the armies, and the cities registered for the test. So, on December 5, 1977, my father sat in a classroom, taking the national exam. Alongside him sat many of his teachers, who had never been able to take the gaokao themselves in the years lost to the Cultural Revolution.

Many of those first test takers, including my father, were bitterly disappointed after the 1977 gaokao, because their education had been so impoverished that they did not have the academic background to do well in the test. Because of this, a second gaokao was held six months later, in the summer of 1978. To prepare for the second test, my father joined review classes and systematically studied math, chemistry, physics, Chinese, and politics. In order to find enough study questions, he visited every school and classroom in his town, asking for review materials, which were usually a few handwritten problems on a piece of scratch paper. Ten years of catastrophic political disruption had created a scarcity of academic materials. Almost all of them had been burned during the previous decade. The 1977–78 national college entrance examinations, with a combined total of 11.4 million participants, set an all-time record for students taking one exam. (About 9 million students now take the test annually in China, despite the population in China being much higher.) Even though only 4 percent of the test takers were accepted into colleges from that year's test, the first gaokao after the Cultural Revolution was a landmark event in China's history, indicating that a renaissance in education was coming.

When the results of the second exam were announced, the names of students who were accepted into colleges were posted in every town. My father's name was at the top of the list. He had received the top score in his county. He told me, "This was the most significant turning point in my life." My dad was accepted into the mathematics department at Shandong University. He took up his long-delayed dreams along with hundreds of other newly-minted university students who had been released from the nightmarish decade of the Cultural Revolution.

As the era of reconstruction began, a lost generation of students reacted against the extreme politics and culture wars of the previous decade by turning to science and technology. They threw themselves into their studies with an intensity that can only be understood by people who have been denied their heart's desire for a long time.

Along with his classmates, my father found that his new life was defined by a simple triangle. The three points in the triangle were the classroom, the dining hall, and the dormitory. All time not spent eating and sleeping was devoted to study. My father's classmates ranged from a boy of fifteen to a thirty-seven-year-old man with two children. Those who attended middle school or high school during the Cultural Revolution, like my parents, were just beginning to get married and have kids. One can only imagine the stresses experienced by those trying to make up for lost time by condensing ten years of their lives into a few hectic years.

To American readers, the gaokao may seem like the equivalent of the SAT (Scholastic Aptitude Test) or the ACT (American College Testing), but perhaps on a larger scale. But to students, parents, and teachers in China, the gaokao is a thousand times more significant. In the United States, a student's SAT or ACT score is one of a number of factors that are taken into consideration by a college when deciding whether or not to grant admission. Even if a student is rejected by his or her first-choice college based on a poor SAT score, the student can always apply to other colleges.

In China, students cannot apply to colleges based on their personal preference or choice. The gaokao score is the *sole* determining factor that decides not only which college the student may attend, but also whether or not the student can even apply to go to college at all. And the gaokao is offered only once a year. The student has one make-or-break chance to achieve a respectable score. For this reason, the impact of the gaokao radiates beyond the test takers themselves, to their parents, teachers, and entire communities.

In the United States, when students apply for college, there are many aspects that play into whether or not they will be accepted: grades, clubs, sports, recommendation letters, college essays, etc. But in China, when students apply for college, there is only one thing universities and schools look at: the outcome of the gaokao. For certain schools in China, students can apply before taking the test for the option of early action, where the score computed is immediately sent to the college, while for other schools, students apply after taking the test and receiving the score. Each college releases the score that they require in order to be accepted; if the student's score is above their score requirement, the student is accepted.

When my family planned our trip to China for the summer of 2011 (for my father, my brother, Dan, and me), one objective was to schedule meetings with students—not only high school students, but also middle school students who were my age at the time. We received the same response from each of the high school students we contacted: "We can meet after June 9." We were not surprised, knowing that June 9 was the final day of the gaokao.

We received a similar reply from the middle school students and their families: "We will meet after June 20." June 20 was the day middle school students finished their version of the gaokao, called the zhongkao, a high-school entrance exam that determines which high school they would attend. The zhongkao is almost as important as the gaokao, because being accepted into the "right" high school is a strong determinant of how one will do on the gaokao. The best high schools have the best teachers, the best curriculum, the best environment, and provide the best chance of doing well on the gaokao.

When we visited schools in Shandong, Sichuan, Beijing, and Shanghai, a common topic of discussion was the "star" teachers from those schools. The basis of their reputation was the number of their students who had been accepted into college, especially into the most elite colleges. In Huantai County, Shandong Province, if a student was accepted into Beijing University or Qinghua University, that student's teachers—especially the *ban zhu ren* (the chief advisor) for the class—were accorded high honors.

In the place where my father was born, the villagers never tired of discussing gaokao results: how many college students were accepted from the village, which family's son or daughter was accepted into college, who did worse than expected, which family is thriving because of the number of family members who have been accepted into colleges, etc.

By now, a Western reader may be asking, "What kind of a system puts children under such intense pressure in which their entire future lives are at stake? Is it necessary? Is it worth it?"

The answer for most Chinese students, teachers, and families is "Yes."

In the summer of 2011 Wang Jiayi was a rising freshman in the Affiliated High School of Shanghai Jiaotong University in Shanghai. We met for an interview during the week before he was due to take his zhongkao. Wang Jiayi was a year older than me, skinny, and unusually tall. He had thick-framed glasses (a popular fashion trend in China), and wore an Adidas-brand shirt. When I asked him about the gaokao, he explained, "The gaokao is a necessity. With the enormous population in China, it seems like the only solution right now. There are so many students to deal with, and such limited resources and time. Even though people criticize the gaokao as unfair, it's probably the most practical system at this point. Sure, I would love to get into college by writing an essay or sending in an application some day, but . . . " He ended his thought there, and looked up at me. I knew what he was thinking: it was just impossible.

The population of China is close to 1.4 billion, more than quadruple that of the United States. If all the potential college students in this achievement-driven society applied for the available openings, the number of applications, essays, and grade reports would be overwhelming. The amount of time it would take college administrations to evaluate all the students' applications would be inconceivable.

When I asked Chen Haiyan, an English teacher at Beijing Fifth High School, for her opinion on the subject of gaokao, her response reflected the same dilemma: "It's just that there are too many people! In China, if the system were to be altered, schools would have to change their ways of teaching and their curricula. The thousands of gaokao programs and tutoring services, which amount to a secondary industry in education, would go out of business. The transition would result in a catastrophe. Parents who spent so much time and money preparing their children for the test that would determine their fate would feel it was all for nothing, and students who had been training for months and years would have no sense of direction. I'm not saying I don't support the application system itself," she explained, "but I just don't believe it would be the most efficient thing to do."

For now, it seems that all we can do is mourn for students in China whose fate is to take the grueling gaokao. The amount of pressure that piles up on these students is greater than one might easily imagine. Parents not only mark the gaokao date on the calendar, but some families have even posted their child's testing date on the wall years beforehand. The impending event hangs over students' heads from the time they are in grade school, as they begin preparing years in advance for their zhongkao and gaokao. Some high schools devote the last year, or even the last two years, of their schooling to full-on study and preparation for the gaokao. Some parents believe that enrolling their children in review programs is a necessity, while others believe that hardcore drilling should be constantly practiced at home, in addition to the usual school workload.

In China, school is in session for approximately 220 days of the year (180 is the average number of school days in the U.S.). Chinese children attend classes six days a week. School starts at 6:30 or 7:00 in the morning from Monday through Friday, and runs until noon. After a two- or three-hour lunch break, when students traditionally go home to eat a hot lunch and rest, they return to the classroom until 9:00–10:00 p.m. Saturday classes are held from about 8:00 a.m. to 8:00 p.m. The summer break is a little less than two months, much of it consumed by summer school classes and review sessions. Parents in China are afraid that if their children take a longer break, they will forget what they have learned, thus they enroll them in summer programs to maintain the scholastic momentum.

Sitting in math class my sophomore year in high school, as the bell rang for my last period, my teacher told the class, "Remember, during summer many students lose about one-third of the knowledge that they have accumulated during the previous school year." He chuckled and added, "Good luck." Many students in China go to summer school willingly, in order to prepare for more advanced studies during the school year. And always, whether it is a school day or a vacation day, students are assigned hours and hours of homework and mental exercises in order to keep the blood flowing in their brains.

Sometimes I wonder if this is some kind of chicken-and-egg situation. Did the Chinese mania for studying create the gaokao? Or did the gaokao spawn this unceasing drive to study, study, study? Why *do* Chinese students spend all those hours devoted to academic pursuits?

"The results of gaokao determine their future!" answered Gao Daquan, principal of Huantai Second High School. Months before the gaokao, it is rare to find high school seniors wandering around in the streets. They voluntarily assign themselves hours of practice questions and tests. They make their parents quiz them on every single possible concept that might appear on the test. And when the new school year starts, they will likely find out that the student across the street has done more practice tests than they have!

Loudi is a third-tier city, designated by its population and administrative level in China's Hunan Province, with six public high schools. There is quite a bit of competition and tension between the six high schools. Students compete to do well in the gaokao, and to get into good colleges. Loudi First High School has a sister-school relationship with Eden Prairie High School in the Minneapolis suburbs, where I study. In the summer of 2011 the principal of Loudi First High School, Gong Maolin, visited Eden Prairie as part of the annual student/teacher exchange program, and I had the opportunity to speak with him. Because Principal Gong has a strong Hunan accent, I could understand very few words of his dialect. I had to rely on Mr. He Yixin, an English teacher who accompanied him on his visit, to translate Principal Gong's Hunan dialect into Mandarin Chinese for me.

"We value the reputation of our school," said Principal Gong. "We work hard to improve our school, and whenever some important event happens, news spreads like wildfire through the entire city. From what I see, the life of a student is easier in the United States. In China, the life of a student is hinged on the gaokao."

"Is a better system than gaokao possible for students in China?" I asked.

"I can't imagine it now," said Principal Gong.

"Why?"

"Think of one million applications being sent to Beijing University or Qinghua University every year. How could that be managed? Who can manage that? The top universities in the United States only receive twenty or thirty thousand applications each year. Those numbers are not applicable to China," explained Principal Gong.

In Loudi, students and teachers are up at 6:00 a.m., Monday through Sunday. In other words, every day of the week! At Loudi First High School, Mr. He Yixin is the chief adviser for the Exchange Class—the most competitive senior class in the school. Mr. He brings the Exchange Class out for a run every morning before school, about two to three miles each day. Although getting up at 6:00 a.m. and running three miles might sound like punishment, Mr. He does this because he cares deeply about his students, and wants to make sure they remain strong and healthy while they study.

From 8:15 a.m. to 12:00 p.m., the Exchange Class has four forty-five-minute class sessions, with a fifteen-minute break between each class. From 12:00 p.m. to 3:00 p.m. students and teachers go back home for lunch, and most of them take a nap. Students are not allowed to wander on the streets during this break time. If they were caught on the streets by their teachers, they would be called into the office and given a warning. Afternoon classes run from 3:00 p.m. to 6:00 p.m. Students return home for dinner with their family from 6:00 p.m. to 7:30 p.m., and then it is back to school from 7:30 p.m. to 10:00 p.m. for evening review sessions and homework time.

It is not only the students who endure these long days—their teachers are there with them the entire time, devoted to their work and their students. Teachers remain at their desks and are available to any student who has questions about the homework, previous lectures, or whatever they may need. The teachers wake up with the students and leave the classrooms only after all the students have left for the evening. Most of the teachers live in on-campus apartments, and many have families who live there with them.

The intensity of the educational system breeds competition at every level. Students, parents, teachers, schools, and entire communities are competitive when it comes to the gaokao. Teachers who devote themselves to their jobs in such an all-consuming way can earn significant rewards in this atmosphere of nonstop competition. A teacher who exemplifies excellence in education by improving the test scores of his class, or by sending off a large number of her students to top colleges, can earn a well-deserved bonus. For example, a bonus of RMB 50,000 (about US$8,000) is collectively awarded to the teachers of every student who is accepted into Beijing University or Qinghua University. The RMB 50,000 reward is divided among the teachers who taught those top students. In 2011 four students from Loudi First High School were accepted by either Beijing University or Qinghua University, and Mr. He was awarded a total of RMB 40,000 for his part in educating those students. That amount is equivalent to Mr. He's yearly salary.

Parents are also willing to subordinate their lives for the sake of the gaokao and a brighter future for their children. When I interviewed Principal Gong, I asked if there were cases where parents relocated the entire family to support their test taker. Principal Gong nodded his head vigorously. The apartments on or near the campus for the convenience of the teachers are very hot properties. Eager parents are willing to rent them at a high premium so they can be completely involved in their child's educational experience. To take advantage of this market, some teachers will buy a second home farther from campus, and then sublet their campus apartment to students' families. This practice is especially common around China's most elite high schools, which I will say more about later.

Back in the Shanghai classroom with student Wang Jiayi, I asked more about what he thought of the gaokao. "Do you think the gaokao is a good way to determine your future?"

He pushed his heavy glasses higher on his nose.

"Yes and no," he replied. "If you put all of your effort into it, it will be worth it in the end. Gaokao is a test of ability. It tests your heart, your will, your strength, and your passion. It is not a test of curriculum, but a test of what you can truly accomplish."

There is another twist to the process of gaokao testing that adds even more pressure to the already-stressful proceedings. Once the testing dates have been decided—even years in advance—they are set in stone, with no chance of rescheduling them due to bad weather, personal illness, or circumstance. It doesn't matter if there's a blizzard, a flood, or a tornado in your town; the test goes on. It doesn't matter if you have stomach flu, a broken wrist, or can't even get out of bed; that is your only chance to take the test. The only time in recent history that the gaokao has been rescheduled was in the wake of the catastrophic earthquakes in Sichuan Province in May 2008. In addition to the tragedy of thousands of people killed by the quakes, many school facilities were devastated or completely destroyed, collapsing on the students within. On that occasion, the test date for students in the affected areas of Sichuan was rescheduled.

One of my cousins was a senior in Huantai First High School, where she was scheduled to take the gaokao in the summer of 2012. She finished her requirements for mathematics and physics during her junior year and spent her entire senior year reviewing for the gaokao. My cousin is a very good student and ranked in the 200s out of 1,800 students in her class. Her parents had no real cause for worry, but they remained completely absorbed in the testing process, anxiously monitoring the results of every quiz and test my cousin had to take. For every test that moved her up in the ranking, her parents were elated. If she moved down in the ranking, her parents became nervous. To increase her odds of obtaining good scores, her parents sent her to review classes in Jinan on the fourth of January in the lunar calendar. The Spring Festival was not yet officially over. This represented a sacrifice because, for Chinese, the Spring Festival is similar to America's Christmas. Traditionally, it is every family's major gathering holiday.

Although I work hard in my AP (advanced placement) classes, I need to prepare for my SAT or ACT test in my school in Minnesota. I feel extremely lucky that I don't have to study for and take China's intensive gaokao.

Visiting the Beijing Wangfujing Bookstore located in a bustling commercial district, I saw that each floor of the store was comparable in size to a medium-to-large Barnes & Noble. The entire second floor was filled with all kinds of student review materials for gaokao testing. The saleswoman told me that gaokao review books are the best-selling books, year after year. The buyers are parents.

One survey showed that 80 percent of the parents whose children are preparing for the gaokao suffer from anxiety.[1] They have put years of effort and a significant amount of their family's resources toward their child's gaokao performance. Their anxiety about their child's gaokao results often affects their own work performance.

Though at a basic level the gaokao can be described as an academic aptitude test for high school students, I have come to see it as a test for the whole society of China, involving the majority of citizens at

1 "Over Eighty Percent of Parents Whose Children Are Preparing for the Gaokao Suffer From Anxiety." *News Noon Daily*. May 18, 2006.

recurring points in their lives—as schoolchildren, as parents, and as grandparents. Considering the power of this "test" and its profound and pervasive influence on the Chinese family, gaokao appears to be China's largest national love/hate affair.

CHAPTER 2
Glamorous Zhuangyuan

Once the dreaded gaokao test is over, attention immediately refocuses on the *results* of the gaokao, which are released in July. Students, parents, college admissions officers, and teachers feverishly await the all-important test scores. How did I do? How did my child do? How did my students do? How did our town do? Of course, high-scoring students are relieved and happy because they now stand a good chance of achieving a successful future. But the stars of the show are the zhuangyuan. These are the fortunate few—two from each province—who achieve the highest gaokao scores in their province. After years of grinding work and incredible stress, these students suddenly become overnight celebrities. Interviews and photographs are released in the news media, and everyone is interested in which universities they will choose to attend.

The word "zhuangyuan" comes to modern China from the imperial examinations of dynastic China. The basic translation of zhuangyuan is "number one in the national examination," but the designation has a much more extended and complex meaning in Chinese culture. Eras of Chinese history are typically designated in terms of the name of the dynasty that was in power at the time. In four thousand years of dynastic history, there have been about five hundred emperors. In the 1,300 years of the imperial examination system, which ended in 1905, only 504 zhuangyuan were produced.[1] Under the imperial system, the national test was given once

1 Xiao Hua, "How Many Zhuangyuan There Were in China's History." *Xian Feng Dui*, No. 18, 2005. http://www.cnki.com.cn/Article/CJFDTotal-ZBJZ200518042.htm

every three years, and only one person from the entire country was named the zhuangyuan from that test.

From 1905 to 1949, China was in the smoke of civil wars and Japanese invasions. The college entrance examinations were administrated by individual universities and colleges, which continued until 1952. After 1952 the national examination system (the gaokao) replaced the imperial system that ended in 1905, along with ending the individual universities' and colleges' administration of entrance exams. After the administration of the gaokao was disrupted by the Cultural Revolution from 1966 to 1976, the national examination system was reinstated. The prestige of being designated "zhuangyuan" also returned.

Another modification made in modern times is that there are now two zhuangyuan selected from each province every year: one in the science division and one in the humanities division. Students who major in the humanities and social sciences are separated from those who major in mathematics and the hard sciences during the first year of high school. Each student choses his or her own path to pursue for the rest of high school until the gaokao where he or she takes the test corresponding to the subject chosen. There can even be more than two zhuangyuan from a province, if two or more students happen to achieve the identical highest score in their division, but this is rare. Two or more zhuangyuan chosen from each province or municipality in China thereby expanded the number of zhuangyuan considerably.

Every year approximately seventy zhuangyuan become the focal point of national attention and adulation, especially among students whose gaokao is coming up. One of the privileges a zhuangyuan enjoys is the ability to choose his or her dream school in China. Wang Duo, a zhuangyuan from Jilin Province in 2009, decided that out of all the choices, he would only go to Beijing University or Qinghua University. Another zhuangyuan, Ling Hu, passed up other schools that would have gladly accepted him and went to school for another year so that he could get into Qinghua University.

A pink qipao (or cheongsam, the body-hugging one-piece Chinese dress) was the first thing I noticed about Annie Jiao when I invited her to visit my house in Eden Prairie, Minnesota. At the time, Annie was a rising senior at Breck School, a private school in Minneapolis. Her glowing complexion added some warmth to the atmosphere as we introduced ourselves. After being on the Breck student-exchange program, she decided to stay for another year to finish her studies here and apply for college in the United States. She received her acceptance letter from the Massachusetts of Institute of Technology on Pi Day[2]—March 14.

"My dad was the zhuangyuan in Hebei Province. My uncle was the zhuangyuan in Heilongjiang Province," Annie Jiao said proudly.

"Do they expect you to be the zhuangyuan in Beijing?" I asked her.

"Of course," she said, "but I came to the United States to finish high school. I gave up my chance to take the gaokao. My cousin will probably be the zhuangyuan in Beijing when she takes the gaokao next year. She always ranks in the top twenty students there. There is a good chance for anyone in the top twenty to become zhuangyuan. Every year, the Beijing zhuangyuan almost always comes from my alma mater, Ren Da Fu Zhong (The Affiliated School to China People's University)." Ren Da Fu Zhong is one of the top public schools in Beijing, even in all of China.

"Four years ago, my brother Dan co-authored a book with Lin Qian, the Beijing zhuangyuan," I said.

"I know about Lin Qian," Annie said. "Lin Qian was the Beijing zhuangyuan in 2007. She was accepted by both Beijing University and Hong Kong University. Hong Kong University offered her a scholarship worth 560,000 Hong Kong dollars. Instead, she went to Beijing University to study mathematics."

The fact that Annie knew about a zhuangyuan from four years before shows how well known the zhuangyuan becomes. Each zhuangyuan is the envy of millions of students who participate in the gaokao each year.

I was very curious about the cultural phenomenon of zhuangyuan,

---

2 Pi Day was founded in 1988 by physicist Larry Shaw to honor the mathematical constant, 3.14 (March 14 is also the birthday of Albert Einstein). In 2009 the US Congress, in HRES244, officially named March 14 as a national day of Pi.

so I was happy when a visit to Shandong Province allowed me to visit the China Zhuangyuan Culture Museum in Qufu, located just behind the Confucius Temple and Confucius Mansion (which are also well worth seeing).

Our tour guide, Ms. Liu, gave us additional information about the historical development of the imperial examination structure, called the Keju system, and expanded on the cultural aspects of Keju and zhuangyuan. The Keju system was initiated in AD 605 and ended in AD 1905, lasting thirteen hundred years. It was a fairly complex system, which involved testing at the local, provincial, and national levels.

The local test, called the *yuanshi*, was administered by the provincial minister of education, and was a qualifying test for the subsequent tests. Men who passed the yuanshi gained the title of *xiucai*, and were then candidates for the provincial examination called the *xiangshi*, which was offered once every three years.

Provincial-level examinations tested candidates on their knowledge of the Confucian classics and their ability to compose poetry on given subjects using set poetic forms and calligraphy. Anyone who passed the provincial-level exam was titled *juren*, and was then eligible to take the ministerial-level examination, called the *huishi*, which was administered by the imperial Department of Rituals in the spring following the provincial examination.

At the ministerial level of examination, candidates were tested on their ability to analyze contemporary political problems in addition to the usual examinations based on the classics. Candidates who passed the huishi were called *gongshi* and could sit for the final level of examinations, the *dianshi*, which was administered directly by the emperor or by a special delegate of the emperor. Those who passed this final hurdle were titled *jinshi*, and the one with the very highest score earned the designation zhuangyuan.

Ms. Liu explained, "In the zhuangyuan culture, the great prize was the fact that anyone who became a zhuangyuan by succeeding in the imperial examination could step into the imperial courtyard overnight. This was the sweetest dream of young students and scholars."

China is generally credited with inventing the idea of a civil service system staffed on the basis of merit. The Keju testing system was the mechanism used to select the best potential administrators in the country. This merit-based administrative structure supported the Chinese imperial dynasties for more than a thousand years. Japan adopted and used a similar system for hundreds of years. Many scholars believe that China's civil service structure had a significant influence on the civil service system that helped imperial Great Britain project its power around the world.

Ms. Liu continued, "Under the Keju system, anybody, regardless of economic or social background, could acquire a high-ranking government post by passing the imperial examination, and in some cases, even become the son-in-law of the emperor. Since studying for the examination was very time consuming and expensive, most of the candidates came from relatively wealthy and powerful families. However, there are a handful of cases in Chinese history of individuals who moved from humble obscurity to great scholarly and political prominence through success in the imperial examinations."

Ms. Liu's comments about zhuangyuan came alive for me during a taxi ride in Beijing. As we drove down Changan Road and crossed Tiananmen Square, I chatted with Mr. Wang, a middle-aged taxi driver, and watched as his heavily marinated tealeaves sloshed around in a glass bottle as he wove in and out of traffic on the way to Beijing Airport. I tried to entice him in a conversation about Beijing's new buildings, and the trendy fashions we saw all around us. But highrise buildings and fancy hotels were not stimulating to Mr. Wang. The only thing that made Mr. Wang excited was when he began talking about his niece, who was engaged to a zhuangyuan, and his own life story.

The life of a taxi driver is not glamorous. Mr. Wang told me that most of the taxi drivers in China have some type of chronic health problem.

For example, it is almost impossible for taxi drivers to drink a healthy amount of fluids every day, because they never know when they will have the opportunity to go to the bathroom. They might be stuck in traffic, or waiting at the airport, or driving on a long crosstown trip.

Eating healthy meals is just as hard. Taxi drivers need to eat something fast and cheap, and this is true for all three meals. Obviously, getting an adequate amount of exercise is out of the question. After a few years of this daily routine, it is no wonder their health begins to deteriorate.

The average income of taxi drivers in Beijing, including Mr. Wang himself, is about RMB 3,500 per month, or approximately US$560. When his daughter was preparing to take her high-school entrance examination (the zhongkao test), Mr. Wang spent RMB 2,800 every month to pay for her after-school review sessions, which is about 80 percent of his income. His daughter, he explained, just took the zhongkao a few days before and would be attending Beijing Sixty-Fifth School, an "average" high school in Beijing.

After listening to Mr. Wang talk about his twelve-hour workdays, I was surprised to learn that he owns two houses. Together, the houses are worth at least RMB 7 million, or the equivalent of US$1.1 million; and he has no debt. He and his wife purchased one of the houses; the other was inherited from his parents.

When I asked Mr. Wang why he didn't just sell one house and keep the other, instead of working so hard day and night, he exclaimed, "Then what will I give to my daughter when she grows up? I don't have anything else to give her. Can she afford to buy a house in Beijing after she graduates from college? No way!"

But Mr. Wang's pessimistic view of his life was definitely improved by the news he got from his sister, a few weeks earlier, when she called and told him that his niece just became engaged to a Beijing University student. The student was a farmer's son from a village in Tianshui City, Gansu Province, and he was a zhuangyuan. "A zhuangyuan!" Mr. Wang exclaimed. "My niece is going to marry a zhuangyuan! I'm so proud of her."

Mr. Wang seemed to be expressing both relief and exhilaration, and I think it was because he believed that his niece and her fiancé were on the brink of escaping from China's class system. People who become zhuangyuan are judged by that achievement, rather than by their family or social background. When you're in elementary school, middle school, or high school, social background is a large factor in your life. But when you go to college in China, it doesn't matter where you came from or who you were back home.

I listened as Mr. Wang poured out his dreams in an animated monologue. "I understand myself to be a very humble man in our society," he said. "I could send my daughter to the same school some central government ministers send their kids to; but while they are being brought to school by limousines, I would be pulling up to the curb in a dirty old taxi to drop off my daughter. But when it's time for college, she'll be like a zhuangyuan, with as many possibilities as anyone else, and that's the day I'm looking forward to. The only way for my daughter to get out of the old Beijing Hutong (the narrow alleys or streets between the traditional courtyard residences) is to do a good job in the national entrance exam and be accepted into a good college. She might even marry a zhuangyuan in college, like her cousin."

Then Mr. Wang calmed down and spoke in a more somber tone. He said he couldn't dream too much, because he was getting old and was not able to work hard enough to earn a decent income. He said most of the taxi drivers he competed with were coming in from the suburbs and countryside around Beijing, and they worked twenty-hour days. If he could sustain that type of schedule, he might be able to earn closer to RMB 10,000 per month, but it just wasn't possible. But he would still try as hard as he could to support his daughter all the way through college. "She is my only hope."

The fact that Mr. Wang, and millions of other fathers in China, pin all of their hopes on a daughter shows one huge difference between imperial China and modern China: the increasing status of women on a social and economic level. In the world of Confucius, Mencius, Zeng Zi, and Zhu Xi, only men could be scholars and zhuangyuan. Only men could hold political or economic power. Traditionally, a woman's main function was to serve her husband and children and care for her father-in-law and mother-in-law. There is a traditional Chinese saying, *Nu zi wu cai bian shi de*, which means, "Women without talents, without intelligence, are a meritorious virtue."

The Communist Revolution that turned Chinese society upside down also changed the status of women. Mao Zedong declared, *Fu nu neng ding ban bian tian!* which means "Women can hold half of the sky!" For China to take its place in the modern world and build a glorious future, women had to come out of the shadows. Mao insisted that women can achieve anything that men can achieve.

The ability of women to hold up their half of the sky has become apparent in two high-visibility areas: sports and scholarship. In the 2008 Beijing Olympics, China earned fifty-one gold medals, twenty-seven of which were won by women athletes. A survey of students who achieved the title of zhuangyuan between 1999 and 2007 showed women steadily overtaking men. The survey, "1999 to 2007 Survey of China's Gaokao Zhuangyuan," conducted by China Alumni Network in 2008, revealed that while 34 percent of the 1999 zhuangyuan were female, by 2007 an incredible 63 percent of zhuangyuan were female.[1] In 2011 it was a little more equal, with 53 percent of zhuangyuan being female and 47 percent male.[2] In China there's a new saying: *Yin sheng yang shuai*, which means, "Women (yin) ascending; men (yang) descending."

Why is it that girls are outperforming boys in the national college entrance exam? Principal Gong explained his theory to me. He said that the nature of the exam questions has changed somewhat since 1999, and the range of topics covered in the test has expanded. Before 1999 in every

1 "1999 to 2007 Survey of China's Gaokao Zhuangyuan" Longwen Education, June 6, 2008.

2 "China's 2011 Gaokao Zhuangyuan" http://edu.sina.com.cn/gaokao/2011gkzy/

national college entrance exam, there were always a few extremely difficult problems, especially in the areas of mathematics, physics, and chemistry. Statistically, it appears that boys have some advantage over girls with this type of problem. After 1999 there were fewer problems at this difficulty level, and questions began to cover more and more of the curriculum compared to before. Fact-based questions that depend on memorization began to increase, while problem-solving questions began to decrease. Girls are generally considered to be very meticulous in memorizing and rehearsing facts, the basics and the fundamentals, and they also pay more attention to details. Therefore, the newer tests favor the skill sets of girls more than boys.

Hu Wenqi was a zhuangyuan from Shanghai Province in 2007. Her classmates nicknamed her the "Queen of Class Notes." For every essay taught in her Chinese class, she deconstructed the essay into paragraphs, sentences, and words or phrases. She wanted to apprehend every single element of the classical essay. She analyzed the essay word by word, making sure the key words were not replaceable. If any word or phrase could be substituted by another, the essay would lose its integrity. Hu Wenqi performed a research project on each classical essay, including its history and background, until she understood it inside and out. Using dictionaries and supplementary materials teachers provided, she was able to accomplish research projects for each of the essays.

Hu Wenqi applied her meticulous study techniques to mathematical problems as well. It is often the case with mathematical proofs in geometry, algebra, and trigonometry that the solutions found by students appear to be correct, but in reality are completely wrong. Any student can easily make these kinds of mistakes, even the top students of the class. In her notebooks, Hu Wenqi compiled hundreds of problems that were easy to make mistakes on, and analyzed each problem in detail. In understanding how and why mistakes were made, she gained knowledge from her own mistakes and from other students' mistakes as well.

From everything I learned about the Chinese culture of zhuangyuan, it seemed as if having this designation would be the most perfect thing that could happen to someone. There is no "luck" involved in becoming a zhuangyuan because it is based on extremely hard work. But it still seemed like finding a pot of gold at the end of the rainbow, until I heard the story of Lu Buxuan.

As Chinese society becomes more diversified and dynamic with market-oriented economic reforms and massive industrialization and urbanization, the traditional assumption that zhuangyuan sit at the apex of opportunity may be more questionable. In 2003 the misfortunes of a Beijing University graduate became front-page news across China and shattered the common perception about being a zhuangyuan. Lu Buxuan grew up in Chang'an County, Shanxi Province, in a suburb of Xi'an, famous for its army of terracotta soldiers. He graduated high school as a zhuangyuan of Chang'an County and entered Beijing University in 1985. When he graduated from Beijing University, he returned home to Chang'an County and was assigned an important management position with Chang'an Diesel Engine Manufacturers.

However, within a year, the company went bankrupt and Lu Buxuan was reduced to performing low-skilled maintenance repair work, and eventually ended up unemployed. By 2000 Lu Buxuan had become a meat cart vendor on the streets of Chang'an. He worked long hours but barely earned enough to pay his rent and utilities.

When this story was reported in 2003, it caused a huge sensation in China and is still widely discussed in the news media. Lu Buxuan's wife, Cheng Xiaolan, told the press, "I don't like him to sell meat on the streets. He's a graduate from Beijing University. He's a zhuangyuan of Chang'an County."[3]

His father said, "He was the only Beijing University graduate from our neighborhood, and also from his high school. Now he is making a living as a meat vendor. It is such a painful thing."

Lu Buxuan's high-school class advisor told reporters that Lu Buxuan always placed first or second in his class. "When he was accepted into Beijing University we were proud of him. The other students were

3 "Beijing University's Top Student Is Selling Meat on the Street" by Jiang Xue, *Hua Shang Bao* (newspaper), July 26, 2003.

encouraged because an alumnus of their school was attending Beijing University. He became a role model for all the students."

When the school's political science teacher heard about Lu Buxuan's problems, he said, "A zhuangyuan being a butcher? It's more like he is a butchered zhuangyuan! This is a waste of talent! The country spent so much money to have a student graduate from Beijing University. We need to protest this situation. How could this possibly happen?"

Expectations for Beijing University and Qinghua University graduates are incredibly high. Most Chinese would consider it shameful if a graduate of those elite schools did not enter, and succeed at, a prestigious profession such as a scientist, politician, or professor. A graduate who pursues a career that "ordinary" people can do is judged as someone who hasn't lived up to his or her potential. People who achieve the exalted status of zhuangyuan are expected to be extraordinary for the rest of their lives. The furor about Lu Buxuan's situation went on for so long that the administration of Beijing University felt embarrassed and tried to find ways to help him.

As a small businessman, Lu Buxuan had a good reputation with local residents for being honest, providing high-quality food, and serving the community. Although he had earned the respect of his neighbors, it is plain from the stories in the news media that most of China could not accept or respect Lu Buxuan's career path. A decade after the story broke, people are still murmuring about this situation. Now, after years of working hard on the street, he has started to think big. Some companies have offered him seed money to grow his meat business. These companies want to cash in on his zhuangyuan title and Beijing University prestige.

Lu Buxuan's story made me think of a Chinese-American named Tony Hsieh. Tony majored in computer science at Harvard and is the CEO of zappos.com, an online shoe store. While attending Harvard, Tony managed the Quincy House Grille, selling pizza to the students in his dorm. In the United States, people admire Tony for working his way through college and respect his success as an Internet entrepreneur. In

China, people would be horrified that a student at a major university was working at such a menial job, and would laugh at the idea of a Beijing University graduate selling shoes, unless it was as the CEO of a world-class company like Nike.

Americans are proud of stories about "self-made" entrepreneurs, even if they only wind up with modest success. The idea of trying something new, following your dream, and taking a risk with your life when you could play it safe engages the American spirit. Chinese love the idea that a student from a poor and humble background could become a zhuangyuan and a college graduate through hard work and discipline. But Chinese society degrades those who do not encapsulate success and good fortune. Chinese culture will only accept a narrow idea of "success" for the scholarly elite, and any zhuangyuan who fails to succeed in a culturally approved way will feel shame and embarrassment.

Historically, zhuangyuan profited from their status by climbing the social ladder and becoming part of the ruling class of China. Recently, some zhuangyuan have found a more direct way to market their celebrity: they sell their high-school notebooks to aspiring students. One zhuangyuan earned a six-figure income in two weeks by selling his class notes on an online bookstore. In Changsha, an enterprising college student collected the academic notes of zhuangyuan who had been accepted into Qinghua University, Beijing University, Tongji University, and Zhejiang University. He copied the notes and sold them online, making a good profit.

Most buyers of these notes are parents. They want to believe there are "secrets" in the zhuangyuan's notes that will promote the success of their own children. Traditionally, notes were shared among classmates and friends; now they've become a commodity. Some collections of notes have even become best sellers. Chinese teachers have debates about this phenomenon. Some teachers believe that zhuangyuan notes can be very beneficial for other students, especially in the humanities. Notes on history and geography, for example, are often well written and organize the material in a comprehensive and neat way. Other teachers are vehemently opposed to the sale of these notes. For them, notes can be copied, but zhuangyuan cannot be copied.

Yu Jun, a teacher from Changjun School in Changsha, says, "This is an opportunist's approach. You must create your own best method to study. Just copying or reviewing other student's notes is not creative; it impairs students' creativity. By copying notes, students begin to lose the ability to use inductive reasoning."

As I sit in my bedroom, studying for advanced placement tests, I sometimes daydream about selling my notes on eBay and making a fortune. Why not? Of course, we don't have zhuangyuan in the United States, but students who get into Harvard and Yale are widely envied and admired. Why wouldn't ambitious parents pay good money to buy their high-school subject notes for their own children? They would in China.

The founders of the China Zhuangyuan Culture Museum spent millions of dollars to acquire artifacts that were associated with China's zhuangyuan. The most valuable items in the museum were the essays written by zhuangyuan for the imperial test—the dianshi. These essays were preserved in imperial libraries and handed down by the zhuangyuan's families, and are part of the classical heritage studied and dissected by some contemporary scholars. In ancient times and in modern times, the mystique of the zhuangyuan is prevalent in Chinese society.

CHAPTER 3
Tiger Mom and Wolf Dad

In a time when the United States "as a culture has become a little soft and a little complacent and a little indulgent, and a lot of our kids don't have the kind of support that they need at home that says, you go to bed at a regular hour, you turn off the television set, you do your homework," remarked President Obama, "Tiger mom" Amy Chua stood out.[1] Chua's Chinese approach to parenting never allowed such things as "attend a sleepover, have a play date, be in a school play, complain about not being in a school play, watch TV or play computer games, choose their own extracurricular activities, get any grade less than an A, not be the number-one student in every subject except gym and drama, and play any instrument other than the piano or violin."

On January 8, 2011, *The Wall Street Journal* ran an article titled "Why Chinese Parents Are Superior." The article was derived from Amy Chua's soon-to-be-published book, *Battle Hymn of the Tiger Mother*. Chua is a Chinese-American law professor at Yale University.

This article stirred a sensational debate in the United States. Over eight thousand comments were posted on *The Wall Street Journal*'s website, making it one of the most commented on articles in *The Wall Street Journal*'s history. Amy Chua became a controversial celebrity with an equal number of supporters and detractors. A self-described tiger mom, Chua credits her Chinese parenting philosophy as the reason her daughter Sophia was accepted into Harvard. Following Amy Chua's *Battle Hymn of the Tiger Mother*, a

---

1 "Who's Best For Our Future? An Exclusive Interview with Barack Obama," *Reader's Digest*, September 2008, 123.

book called *So, Sisters and Brothers of Beijing University* was written by Xiao Baiyu, who claimed to be China's "wolf dad." The book was originally titled *Beat Them into Beijing University*. The book chronicles this father's application of "traditional" education methods that include "whippings." Xiao Baiyu credits his teaching technique for the "miracle" of sending three of his four children to Beijing University. In fact, his son Xiao Yao and his daughter Xiao Jun were accepted simultaneously. Never before had siblings been accepted into China's most famous university at the same time. All of his children were described as humble, intellectual, and excellent at doing household work. His sons were gentlemen; they loved reading classics, and they enjoyed calligraphy, playing piano, chess, and painting.

The disciplinary measures used by Mr. Xiao were harsh, particularly by Western standards. But he claimed that using the most aggressive, primitive, and ancient approach would prove to be the most effective, believing geniuses are produced by whippings. When his children were in kindergarten and elementary school, Mr. Xiao flogged his children if they made a mistake. When one child made a mistake, the other three had to stand by quietly and watch their sibling being punished. He contends that any punishment or reward his children receive should be based on their achievement or underachievement.

Mr. Xiao did not believe in the concept of a happy or joyful education. His view is that happiness has no place in the learning and training process; that is something reserved for the future—if children amass knowledge and skill, then they will be happy. Mr. Xiao says, "I don't have any religion. My whip is the rule of happiness; it is my bible."

Mr. Xiao considers his whippings and beatings a form of "baptism," and a way to express his "extreme love" for his children. He stresses that it is important to explain to children why they are being beaten, so that they understand that it comes from love. Mr. Xiao believes his approach is in keeping with the ultimate criteria of Confucianism: morality, intelligence, strength, loyalty, respect, and righteousness.

"Parents must have an education plan for their children," he emphasizes.

"You must have family rules. The children must understand the goal and the plan." This means that the parents set goals for their children and must be "consistent and persistent" role models for them in both their actions and their words, in their behavior and their morality. The children must show their respect for their teachers, be well behaved, and stay focused on learning. Children must know that there are consequences for breaking rules and for not following the plan that their parents have helped them design to meet the children's goals in life. The goals set should be placed a bit higher than they are likely to achieve. An example of a goal that Mr. Xiao required for his children was that they must achieve a ranking in the top three of each class.

Mr. Xiao set goals for all four of his children, as is common practice for Chinese parents. But he allowed his children some flexibility; they were allowed to choose their own field of interest. He told them, "Pursue it. Get to the highest degree in your field. Then return that to your society. Leave your mark on your society." His was a lofty expectation.

Although people call him "wolf dad," Mr. Xiao humbly admits that the success of his four children comes primarily from his wife's expressions of love for them. For twenty years, his wife always supported him in educating them. Theirs was a classic model of China's family education style: "harsh father, nurturing mother." She is convinced by the results achieved that the cooperation between them led to their children's success.

"As for loving children, persistence, patience, perseverance, and constant attention is a universal value for educating children," Xiao says. And he feels that his form of punishment, including beatings, is an effective way to convey that love.

Since 1978 in China, the Family Planning Policy has limited Chinese to one child per family. Each set of parents may have one child, meaning one grandchild for the four grandparents. For most families in China, these six adults place a great deal of attention and focus on that one child. The child in this situation is often referred to as "the little prince/princess" or "the little emperor."

Mr. Xiao is highly critical of the dynamic at work within the "little emperor generation." He insists that parents must take the role of "emperor" in the family and treat children with strictness—do not spoil them, do not give them so much freedom. Children must live with rules and restrictions. He believes that this generation has too much freedom, too much discretionary money to spend on whatever they choose. They have no discipline, don't know how to cook or do household chores, and they show no respect for their teachers. They "even have sex with others and get people pregnant," exclaimed Xiao. When they get to college, they "don't know even how to do the laundry. They were never trained." They were never taught survival skills. "They have truly become little emperors," Xiao says.

Though many families in China still uphold the traditional teachings and disciplining of their children, many families, especially urban families, fit the "little emperor" dynamic. There is a lot of pressure placed on one single child to live out the hopes and dreams of the parents and grandparents, and so much attention creates the possibility of being doted on to the extreme.

Ms. Tan Zilin was a classmate of my friend Annie. They were together in Ren Da Fu Zhong middle school from 2006 to 2009. She was going to high school in the fall of 2009. Traditionally, the high performers in middle school are recommended and contracted for acceptance into the top high schools. Ms. Tan was one of them. But she was recommended to the branch campus of Ren Da Fu Zhong, not the main campus. The main campus of Ren Da Fu Zhong is the most reputable high school in Beijing. The facilities and the faculty are top-notch. The school is equipped with a language lab, computer lab, and non-bacteria biology lab. Every year, the school sends 150 students to Beijing University and Qing Hua University. They encourage their students do research, which is published in top international journals.

Ms. Tan's mother, a physician in the medical school affiliated with

Beijing University, let her daughter turn down the early acceptance into high school, and instead take the zhongkao/high-school entrance exam in order to get into the campus of her choice. Though there were eight choices for school selection in Beijing's zhongkao, Ms. Tan's mother only allowed her daughter to choose the Ren Da Fu Zhong main campus, leaving blank the other seven selections on the form. Ms. Tan would either be accepted at Ren Da Fu Zhong main campus, or no school at all.

While her good friends, who were accepted early into high school, enjoyed an easier student life before graduation, Ms. Tan spent the next few months studying hard for the Beijing High School Entrance Examination. She scored 552 out of the 570 points, ten points above the acceptance line set by Ren Da Fu Zhong.

"Getting into a top high school is also one of the battlefields without gunpowder in China's education," stated a report in China's news media.[2]

A survey conducted by China Youth Daily Investigation Center[3] showed that 94.9 percent of parents think of themselves as tiger moms, or know other tiger moms in their neighborhood. More than half, 55.1 percent, of the parents agree with the tiger mom's extreme parenting approach.

Mr. Liu, a father whose children attend Ren Da Fu Zhong, said, "My daughter has studied violin and ballet since she was little. Sometimes she is reluctant to practice violin; her mother beats her." He described one occasion when his wife just threw their daughter's violin on the ground, shattering it to pieces. Mr. Liu believes that when children are young, they don't have a strong motivation to study. So the parents' guidance and disciplinary actions are absolutely necessary. He believes that all parents place high expectations on their children.

Wang zi cheng long (expecting children to be dragons) is a deeply rooted Chinese tradition. Dragons in China symbolize high status, power, and prestige.

---

2 "Battlefield without Gunpowder," *Da Chu Education*, No 27, May 26, 2012.

3 "Is Tiger Mom Education Normal? Survey Shows 55.1% Agree," *China Youth Daily*, April 14 2011.

Principal Gao observed this as well. "Parents put pressure on their children, expecting them to achieve the set goals, and to be the best. Parents expect to realize their own dreams and aspirations through their children. We understand this well."

Is China's education approach correct? What are the problems with the Chinese K–12 education system? A survey addressing this question[4] showed that 75.7 percent of parents say that the expectations of their children are too high; too much pressure is put on the children.

Professor Ma Jiansheng from Beijing Normal University believes that high expectations—even excessively high expectations—benefit the growth of children. But what to expect and how to guide the children toward meeting those expectations are the challenges for the parents' wisdom. Some parents believe that their children are the best, thus their expectations can be way higher than the reality, causing too much pressure on their children.

Professor Ma believes children's ability for self-control is weak, and that children are easily distracted by temptations from the outside world. Strict parenting helps children become successful. However, the survey also shows that 70.9 percent of parents emphasize the importance of test scores but neglect moral values and the nature of character.

Zheng Wenli, a graduate from Beijing University, studied electric keyboarding when she was young, going to classes and learning all about it. Interestingly, her mother always carried an electric keyboard to class with her, learning alongside her daughter. When Zheng Wenli went to middle school, she decided to give up electric keyboarding, since she had too much homework from her science and math classes. Her mother very sadly agreed, but said, "I respect your choice. But you must be responsible for your decision." Her mother's point indicated the beginning of Wenli's independence. By making the decision to quit electric keyboarding by herself, Wenli was also going to take the repercussions of her decision by herself. In this way Wenli learned about the roles of responsibility and

4 "Social Survey Center of China Youth Daily," *China Youth Daily*, April 2001.

independence from her mother.

Who is the best parent? What should one do to be the best parent? The *China Youth Daily* illustrates a difference between expectations and reality. A large number of parents, 82.7 percent, replied that nurturing their children's moral character is the most important aspect of parenting ranking it at 82.7% in significance. Communication with their children stands at 80.2% in significance.. Training rituals and habits ranked at 71.9% significance. Being a role model ranked at 64.7% significance. Intervening in their child's misbehaviors and wrongdoings stood at 57.5% significance. Companioning a child when they play, exercise, and travel ranked at 54.3% in significance, and strict parental guidance of the child's growth holds at 47.9% significance.

In China's education system, wherein test scores are so important that they can determine the fate of a child's future, parents often face the difficult conundrum of prioritizing what is needed in order to nurture the best child. This conflict can act as an obstruction to parents who are trying to decide what to focus on when raising a child, resulting in a state of oppression on the child due to so many factors.

The contrast between intent versus actual behavior is sometimes dramatic. And the difference between Chinese and Western culture on this matter is vivid.

A survey in China jointly conducted by Guangdong Women's Union and UNICEF (United Nations Children's Fund) revealed that 19.9 percent of students experienced violence from their parents and teachers. Violence by teachers was experienced by 51.1 percent of students, and the types of violence included disciplinary actions such as forced running or standing, single-leg standing, knee bends, push-ups, copying essays multiple times, and memorizing assigned texts. Degrading and abusive remarks such as "You are stupid" or "You are hopeless" from the teachers were experienced by 20 percent of the surveyed students. 18 percent said their teachers beat them in school; 17.6 percent reported that their teachers expressed anger toward them. The percentage of teachers who either threw books at students or tore up students' workbooks was at 10 percent.

More surprising, 60 percent of the students believed that all these teacher's behaviors were correct. Eighty percent of the parents surveyed did not consider these behaviors as acts of violence. Interestingly, all parents surveyed expressed the belief that all parents beat their children, and that these actions are "good" for students. These behaviors are considered reasonable disciplinarily actions toward students who are not performing well enough in school, and remain generally accepted as helpful for students' betterment.[5] A leading Chinese newspaper, the *Guangzhou Daily*, coined a phase for this phenomenon, calling it "benevolent violence."

This type of behavior is shockingly different from what is tolerated within the mainstream culture in the United States, where such actions can result in serious consequences. What happens when a teacher in the U.S. beats a disobedient student in front of the entire class? What if a professor tears a student's workbook into shreds? How do students, parents, the school, and the community react toward actions such as these? We know the answers. When a student is disciplined in violent, abusive, or inappropriate ways by teachers or parents in the U.S., legal action can be taken: schools can be sued, teachers can lose their jobs, parents can be prosecuted for child abuse, and educational programs and training sessions can be initiated to prevent such occurrences from happening again.

This Western response to the perceived mistreatment of children plays a large part in the widespread reaction to *Battle Hymn of the Tiger Mother* in the U.S. However, there is a long tradition in Chinese culture of respect for the mother who puts her child's education first. This goes back to the 300s BC, to the revered and admired mother of Mencius. She is most known in Chinese culture for her understanding of the importance of environment in raising children.

5 "Eighty Percent of Parents Believe Penalizing Is Non-Violent Behavior" by Huang Rongfang, *Guangzhou Daily*, May 26, 2011.

Mencius was a great sage and architect of China's Confucian-based civilization. His father died when Mencius was young, and he was raised by his mother, Madame Ni. They were poor and their living was dependent on Madame Ni's skill at weaving fabric. She was a hard worker and very insightful.

Madame Ni and Mencius lived in a quiet suburban neighborhood close to a cemetery. Mencius frequently observed the funerals in the cemetery, watching people on bended knees, crying for the dead. His childhood games included pretending some family member had died and imitating the mourners. Madame Ni was not pleased about this, and she decided they had to move away from this morbid influence.

Madame Ni and Mencius moved to a thriving neighborhood, to a home very close to a market. In the marketplace, butchers slaughtered hogs and sheep, businessmen bargained prices with each other, and blacksmiths forged knives and horseshoes out of iron on anvils. Accordingly, young Mencius quickly learned these skills. He used bricks to build an anvil and tree branches as hammers. Again, Madame Ni decided that this was not the neighborhood in which to raise her son. She wanted Mencius to grow up to become a learned man. Only learned men enjoyed the highest social status.

This time, Madame Ni and Mencius relocated into a neighborhood with a school. Mencius was now among people who valued scholarly learning. He was able to see enthusiastic students rehearsing ancient poems. Teachers came in and out attired as gentlemen. Students behaved with respect toward each other. Each month, government officials came to the nearby temple dedicated to scholars to pay tribute with rituals. Madame Ni was happy now. This was the environment most suited for her son to become a learned man. Mencius was enrolled in the school.

But one day, Mencius skipped school. Madame Ni was heartbroken. She called Mencius to her and told him that to miss school without a legitimate excuse was the same as tearing apart the fabric she worked so hard to weave. She lectured Mencius on the value of doing well in school to gain respect and standing in the world. As she spoke, she took scissors and briskly cut the cloth she was working on—dramatically illustrating what happens when you leave a task undone. All the fabric in her loom fell apart. Mencius was astonished by his mother's startling action. As a result, he was inspired to be a diligent student in school. From that point on, he grew to become a learned scholar. He was mentored by the grandson of Confucius, Zi Si, and became one of the greatest thinkers, philosophers, and representatives of Confucianism in China's glorious history.

The story about Madame Ni, *Meng Mu San Qian* ("Mencius' Mother Moving Three Times), was recorded in all the traditional textbooks in China. Madame Ni thus became the first tiger mom in China's recorded history, and she still remains a role model for parents heavily involved in their children's education.

How to handle the relationship between a child and a parent is a challenge for all involved. My friends and I often discuss these issues among ourselves.

My conversations with my friend Annie Jiao often focused on this struggle between a child and his or her parent.. Annie and her cousin Christina had been accepted to School Affiliated to China People's University, also known as Ren Da Fu Zhong, in 2009. Annie attended the school for her freshman and sophomore years, ranking 103 out of 700 students. Christina, ranking at 11, remained a top student at Ren Da Fu Zhong.

Annie told me, "My cousin and I talk to each other a lot, and we're really good friends; but our grades are just not something that comes up in our conversations. Christina is very humble; she never talks about what she gets on tests or her rankings. We were both placed in pretty top-ranking classes. I remember that after we had gotten our scores for a science test, I had gotten 67, and I was really happy because the next highest score in our class was a 62. My mom and Christina's mom call each other almost every night and gossip about us. Even though we don't talk about our grades to each other, our moms find out these things and tell us. The next morning I was awakened by my mom, and she said, 'Christina got an 83 on her science test. What did you get?' And the only thing I could think about at that moment was *oh crap, oh crap, oh crap*. When I told my mom my grade, she wasn't mad or anything, but it just got me so mad because I thought I did well! When in reality, I didn't."

Hearing that Annie's mom called her sister, Christina's mom, to talk about their daughters made me realize that Chinese families in the United States aren't much different. My friend told me that at a recent "Asian" gathering that occurs every so often, she could hear her mother asking other mothers how their children were doing in school. One mother gloated about her son who was doing extremely well in piano, and she kept asking what level all the other kids were at. Whether it's outside of school or during a music lesson, Chinese parents are super competitive about their children and where they are in the Kumon Learning Center program. With such a high level of competitiveness, students often feel like a show-and-tell object for their parents to flaunt around. Students are lead into a mindset of receiving the most awards or achieving the highest level. When the traditional Chinese goal of academic excellence morphs into a modern-day concept of competition, this can easily convey a misleading message to the students regarding what is important about education.

In both China and the United States, parents have certain expectations of their children. But the expectations are usually quite different. Parents in China expect their children to be the best of the best, to be number one, to always get 100 percent on tests and quizzes, to always get everything correct. But despite all the expectations, parents are still let down, their dreams are still crushed, and their hopes vanish.

Why? Because of their unrealistic expectations. Everyone can't be number one.

I find it interesting that Chinese parents are more likely to assume that any less-than-ideal performance (such as a poor test score) is the result of their child not working hard enough. In contrast, I've known

Western parents in the same circumstance to question the curriculum or the teacher's evaluation. In both China and in Western countries, grades become sensitive barometers for Chinese parents to pass judgment on their child's school performance. They are as focused on this barometer as a business focuses on profit and loss. The parents' satisfaction and expectations are attached to their child's academic achievement. And achievers who benefit from this tradition are probably more likely to single-mindedly appreciate their parents.

A magna cum laude graduate from Princeton University, Andrea Jung, was born in Ontario, Canada, and raised in Wellesley, Massachusetts. She was the chair of the board and the chief executive officer for Avon Products, Inc. Her father taught at MIT and was also a partner in an architectural law firm, while her mother was a chemical-engineer-turned-concert-pianist. She said, "My parents were always, and continue to be today, the single biggest influence in my life."[6]

Referring to how they raised her and her brother, Andrea said, "[We] were given all the opportunities of our American friends—the same schools, the same tennis lessons, the same piano teachers . . . but we had the wonderful advantage . . . of a cultural heritage that we were always taught to be proud of."

Suzanne Whang is an American actress and comedian who graduated from Yale and Brown University. Though she was raised in the United States, Suzanne upholds her Korean traditions, which follow Confucian traditions. She said, "In my opinion, Asians tend to succeed in the classroom because education is highly valued in Asian culture. . . . My parents instilled the value of education in me, and encouraged me to take it seriously, get good grades, and do my absolute best in school. Being good in school was fun, and it contributed to my self-esteem."[7]

High expectations of children and staunch support for their children's studies cross all economic and social strata in China. I had another

6 *Top of the Class,* Dr. Soo Kim Abboud. and Jane Kim, 2006.

7 Ibid.

sobering conversation with a taxi driver on the elevated highway between the Shanghai Bund and Pudong International Airport. Being a taxi driver is one of the toughest jobs in China. You don't need the advanced education that you need for other jobs, and many drivers are not well educated.

Mr. Wu drove my dad, my brother and I to the Shanghai International Airport in the drizzling rain. He didn't go to high school, and his wife didn't attend college. But their daughter, the darling of the couple, is currently attending Shanghai Jiaotong University. She is the first to go to college in his family. Mr. Wu earns about RMB 40,000 per year, and 16,000 goes toward his daughter's college tuition. Though you may think that seems like a lot of money for him to spend, this illustrates that money is not the key consideration. Regardless of how much education parents may have, their hopes and ambitions for their child will always be focused on obtaining the best possible education.

"What makes you invest 40 percent of your annual income into your daughter's education?" I asked.

"My RMB 40,000 income can only buy me one square meter if I want to buy a house in Shanghai. My entire lifetime income is not enough for me to buy an apartment. But 40 percent of my income for four years can help my daughter jump out of this trap. Without education, she would stay at the bottom of the society," Mr. Wu said.

"What do you want for your daughter's future?" I continued.

"To help my daughter finish college. If she can find a job, it is a relief for me. Otherwise, I will support her to continue graduate studies or to go abroad to study," Mr. Wu said.

"Would you expect her to stay in Shanghai, or come back to Shanghai?" I was curious.

"Either is fine. But Shanghai is not my Shanghai. Shanghai is the city for those who have money," said Mr. Wu.

"After your daughter obtains a good education, Shanghai will be her Shanghai," I remarked.

"That is the only light in my life. I don't see any other options," responded Mr. Wu.

Now it was raining so hard that it seemed the heavens were showing sympathy to Mr. Wu. Pudong International Airport appeared in front of us. The wave-shaped roof of this post-modern airport welcomes all guests, domestic or international. The extravagant airport is positioned like a flying bird toward the boundless Pacific Ocean.

Mr. Wu commented soberly as he pulled out our luggage from his trunk, "I drove customers to the airport for twenty years. I made over twenty thousand trips to the airport. But I have never flown anywhere from this airport."

I said goodbye to Mr. Wu. He was back on the rainy highway searching for his next customer, and continuing to carry his hope for his daughter.

No matter what their job or occupation, for parents in China, the number-one dream is for their child to go to the best college possible—to allow them to elevate their social status and become even more successful than their parents.

CHAPTER 4
Don't Lose on the Starting Line

The month of January is dedicated to the Spring Festival celebrated in China. In theory, China's most important holiday is the time for students to take a well-deserved break. But opportunities offered by course-review organizations for students have created a heated competition among elementary school students and their parents. The Spring Festival in 2012, like Spring Festivals in previous years, did not turn out to be a break at all for many students.

Parents of elementary school students in Beijing sent their kids to a program called Students Selecting School. And parents of elementary school students in Shanghai sent more than 20,000 fifth-grade students to the Olympic Mathematics Classes. Some students attended a class in the morning and another in the afternoon. They ate in the buses that transported them from one class to another.

The parents of these kids were convinced that middle schools, high schools, and colleges show preference to students who have attended the Olympic Mathematics Classes. A certificate from these classes is perceived as a strong credential for admission into good schools that favor students who are smart, analytical, and conscientious. Parents in Shanghai, the richest city in China, competed for the best Olympic Mathematics programs for their children, and the programs were filled to capacity.

Beijing operates the best public schools in China (maybe even in the world). Generally, students are expected to go to schools in their community or neighborhood if they so choose. But these high-quality schools in Beijing are permitted to take only a portion of their students from the neighborhoods, and the rest of the capacity remains open to students who want to, and can afford to, pay a fee to attend the school of their choice. This provides flexibility to the most reputable schools. This provides an opportunity for the highly reputable schools to obtain financial resources from wealthy families, as well as teach gifted students from the districts.

A good example of this is Jingshan School, which is well known as the school for children of the top Chinese leaders. The Affiliated Elementary School to Beijing University and the Affiliated Elementary School to Beijing Normal University are famous for being feeders for the top high schools and most elite colleges. Zhongguancun First Elementary School, Zhongguancun Second Elementary School, and Zhongguancun Third Elementary School are located in the heartland of China's academic elites, where China Academy of Science, China Academy of Social Science, Beijing University, Qinghua University, and many other famous universities are located. All these schools are public schools—and considered dream schools for parents in Beijing.

Parents want their children to be educated in these fantastic places. But how is this possible with such large demand? The answer is simple: sponsorship fees. And interested parents are willing to pay a sponsor fee. However, the actual fee is not a set price, but instead is voluntary, similar to a donation. Some families have paid as much as RMB 250,000 to assure their child's admission. That is almost US $40,000—five years' income for the average Beijing resident. And this amount does not include the tuition that must also be paid; it is only the sponsor fee. Though China's education law stipulates that nine years of elementary school and middle school education are offered for free in public schools, parents voluntarily pay for high-ticket sponsorships in order to have their choice of schools.

There is a famous saying that reflects a cultural attitude toward China's education system: "Don't lose on the starting line." It turns out that if you don't pay, you lose. Parents can't afford to lose on the starting line. Students may compete with their intelligence, but parents compete with their money.

In China's major cities, choosing a good school for a student is possibly the single most important thing in a parent's life. Whether it's elementary school, middle school, high school, or college, the pressure to do well is present throughout the student's entire school life—with increasing importance and tension in the later years.

During the summer season, finding the school principal or contacting the admissions office is an extremely arduous task. Summertime is when the admissions office is buzzing with decisions. For every school, the number of students to be accepted is decided by the bureaus of education, leaving the remaining quota for the school to decide—which is not always easy to administrate. Thus the many parents find it crucial to personally contact the school on behalf of their child to increase chances of acceptance.

A few years ago in Beijing, an affiliated school to a university had a few openings available at their middle-school and high-school campuses. Many parents came in to apply for the limited spaces for their sons or daughters, but it seemed as though all the parents involved had the desired social background—being rich or having power. The school administration was flummoxed by the vehement competition. The school principal found it hard to balance out the choices. In the end, the decision was made to hold an auction and offer the twelve openings in the school to the highest bidders. One parent who won a bid in the auction happily sent his son to this high school, paying a fee of RMB 80,000.

Is this fair? Is this right? Or is it blatant corruption to allow money to decide who will attend the best schools? For excellent students whose families cannot pay, admission is not a possibility. For students who do not excel, but whose families have money, admission to the school of their choice is attainable. One might argue the virtues of either side, but a willingness to pay such a high cost to get into a school demonstrates not only the privilge of these students, but the absolute desperation on the part of their parents to provide the best for their children. The parents don't participate in the auctions to boast about how much money they have; they do it because every Chinese parent wants their children to reach their utmost ability–which is only possible at a good school, with good students, good peers, good teachers, and a good principal.

Ms. Zhang's daughter attended an elementary school in the central district of Shanghai. She could have gone to the middle school in the same community, but that middle school was not ranked among Shanghai's top schools. Ms. Zhang decided to apply to the top schools, regardless of the cost. The application process was tedious and burdensome. She helped her daughter draft her resume, and supporting documents, which included a personal statement, certificates awarded, transcripts, documentation of her after-school activities, and letters of recommendation from teachers. Holding more than thirty pages of her daughter's application, Ms. Zhang felt funny thinking about how this huge pile of material compared to the application package she had created to apply for jobs after she graduated from college.

She selected five schools for her daughter to apply to, based on her strategic calculations. If she selected too few schools and the schools received too many applications, the chance for her daughter's acceptance would be slim. If she selected too many schools, her daughter wouldn't have enough time for the school interviews. After she submitted her daughter's applications, Ms. Zhang left her own cell phone number as her daughter's contact number. After all the planned applications were submitted, she waited anxiously for the schools to call for interviews. Whenever the phone rang, she answered immediately. She couldn't afford to miss any call from the schools.

Ms. Zhang had prepared a long list of prospective questions that the school interviewers might ask. She consulted everybody she knew whose child had been interviewed for acceptance into middle school. She quizzed her daughter on anything and everything that could possibly be asked. She was excited when she received the first call to arrange an interview.

She brought her daughter to the school as scheduled, but the results of that first interview were disappointing. Her daughter went home feeling defeated. It had been a group interview. She told her mother that she had to compete with other students to try to answer the questions she was asked, but other students answered faster.

"I didn't get many chances to present my answers," she said.

Ms. Zhang was disappointed, too, but she encouraged her daughter to keep going since there were more school interviews to come.[1]

In China, competition in education starts at a young age, just as Ms. Zhang's daughter had experienced. In the United States, academic pressure can start to build up in junior high, perhaps if a student wants to eventually be accepted into an Ivy League college, but otherwise the competition is not typically high-pressure until high school. Even then, there is little comparison to the commonplace tension in Chinese education.[2]

In China, competition pressures "trickle down" from high school to middle school, from middle school to elementary school, from elementary school to kindergarten, and from kindergarten to preschool. Jackie is a PhD student at the University of Minnesota who visited my house during summer break in 2011. One of Jackie's friends has a little brother who is two years old, and he has already been to many interviews for day-care programs. And these aren't just ordinary interviews—the interviewers literally test what the kids know at age two. These things aren't rare in China. Good day-care programs cost about RMB 10,000 to 20,000 per month, according to Jackie.

In Beijing we spoke to Li Hongling, a parent who wanted to send

1 Peng Wei. "Applying for Middle Schools Is like College Students Applying for Jobs in Shanghai" *Liberation Daily,* May 8, 2011. http://edu.sina.com.cn/zxx/2011-05-08/1139294807.shtml.

2 There are exceptions of course. There is increasing pressure on the part of some parents in the U.S. to get their kids into the "right" preschool or daycare program to give them the best advantage moving forward, and those with money or celebrity have a decided advantage. The issue is receiving more press and some ridicule. See http://mommypoppins.com/ny-kids/an-overview-of-the-preschool-admissions-game/ for an overview of the similar types of competition.

his five-year-old son to an Olympic Mathematics Class. Both he and his son came to the class. The teacher advised Li that his son was too young to be in this type of class, that he couldn't understand the content in the lectures, and he couldn't sit there for hours to drill on mathematics.

Li responded, "That doesn't matter. I paid the full tuition to the school. As long as my son can sit in the classroom, he will benefit."

Parents who will do anything for their children's education, whatever the cost, have generated a huge business opportunity for education services.

"Today, China is experiencing its own gold rush: in education. In his book, *The Rise and Decline of the Great Powers*, Paul Kennedy pointed out that, historically, the Chinese have spent their capital either on land or on education. And, as a Beijing public school official, I can confirm from experience that Chinese parents will sacrifice everything for their child's education," observed Jiang Xueqin,[3] a deputy principal at Beijing University High School and the director of its International Division, who himself is a graduate of Yale.

In Shanghai, we had several occasions with parents, teachers, principals, and students to discuss parents' support for their children's study. As an educational psychologist, Dr. Zhang Yanping, mother of Wang Jiayi, a rising freshman in the Affiliated High School of Shanghai Jiaotong University in Shanghai asked my brother and me, "What have your parents done uniquely to help you?"

My brother answered, "When my parents came home from work, even if they were exhausted, they always helped me immediately if I said I needed help in my studies. I deeply appreciate my parents' involvement and help in my studies."

Dr. Zhang said, "This is nothing unique or special. Every Chinese parent does that."

---

3 "China's Education Golden Rush" by Jiang Xueqin, *The Diplomat*, November 3, 2010. http://the-diplomat.com/china-power/2010/11/03/china%e2%80%99s-education-gold-rush/.

She was not discounting my parents' efforts. She meant that it was a fundamental Chinese tradition to support a child's learning. Supporting children's education was internalized into Chinese blood from Confucius to the current generation.

Once, while Dr. Zhang attended a national education conference, she used her break time to correct her son's English essays. At that moment, a friend attending the conference came over to greet her. When this friend asked Dr. Zhang what she was doing, Dr. Zhang said she was correcting Wang Jiayi's English essays. This friend said, "That is important, I can't bother you," and left right away.

Dr. Zhang was born in Tangshan in 1976. That was exactly the year China's Cultural Revolution ended, and that city was exactly the time and place where one of history's most devastating earthquakes occurred. She was a survivor. She grew up in the rubble. She witnessed the construction of the New Tangshan. Thirteen years later, in 1989, she was in middle school. Student demonstrations occurred in Beijing first, then spread to other cities in China. Fearing the return to chaos in China and potentially losing the opportunity for future study, she called her classmates and collectively wrote a very emotional letter to the "big sisters and brothers" (referring to the college students participating in demonstrations and hunger strikes), to express her strong desire to have a peaceful environment for study.

She asked her father, "Will this lead to my losing the opportunity to study?"

Her father answered, "When only you are lost among a generation, you need to worry. When a whole generation is affected, there is not much you can do."

For her "lost" generation, the strong desire to study was predominant. She expressed this to her son, Wang Jiayi.

That desire is pandemic among parents. They pour their passion for learning into their sons and daughters. They expect their efforts to pay off. In Shanghai, in Beijing, in Jinan, everywhere in China.

Parents planning their children's future or designing their life course remains common practice in China. They simply don't trust their children when they are young. Parents believe their children need guidance and that they can provide that guidance. Parents treat their children as extensions of themselves. Many Chinese parents are so excessively involved in their children's studies and extracurricular activities that they even select their friends. A Chinese blogger posted this list of parents' "rules" for children, named Eighteen Military Rules[4]:

> Be smart, but don't think that you are super smart.
>
> Find different ways to solve the problem; don't get into a dead end.
>
> Don't say anything you shouldn't say.
>
> Work hard on things that could change your life.
>
> Don't make trouble with others.
>
> Be responsible for yourself.
>
> Be honest, but be able to discern whom to be honest with.
>
> Bear the consequences of being arrogant.
>
> Be alert for potential risks.
>
> Give up those goals that are not obtainable.
>
> Be good at observing. Make choices cautiously, and take timely action.
>
> Don't have a temper.
>
> Take steps humbly.
>
> Convert big problems into small problems, and small problems into no problems.
>
> Challenge yourself; don't challenge others.
>
> The first step is more important than the last step.

4 "Eighteen Military Rules for Children to Behave." http://blog.sina.com.cn/s/blog_6d6622840102dsss.html.

Master the details.

Don't let others distract you.

My visit to Mr. Lu Jun in Beijing was one of my most eye-opening experiences in China. His methods for "home schooling" his five-year-old twin sons was remarkably unique. Mr. Lu lives in a gated community with five apartment buildings, a large courtyard between each of the buildings, and a playground for the children who reside in the buildings. We entered the first apartment building and went to the top floor. There were only two apartments on the twenty-sixth level, rather than the standard six on each of the other floors. Mr. Lu lived in the one on the right, and a famous singer lived in the one on the left. In addition to his apartment, Mr. Lu owned the entire top two stories.

Mr. Lu's sons' "school" was in another apartment building across from the one where they live. Their classrooms were on the twenty-fifth floor.

The boys began school at age two. They started by memorizing Tang poems, China's prime educational materials.

The twins have three full-time teachers and two assistants. They go to school for ten hours each day. Their uniforms are white Oxford shirts, navy shorts, and black shoes with black socks. When I walked into their classroom, the two boys were sitting in the center of what would usually be the living room of an apartment. Their table was a beautiful marbled and polished tree trunk from the 1900s. Hanging on the wall facing the boys was a calligraphy script, and surrounding it, a small white board, and probably a hundred sheets of paper neatly overlapping each other, with complicated Chinese characters on them.

After we spent a few minutes greeting the two boys and the teachers, the twins seemed to become comfortable with our presence. One of them pulled on my hand and brought me to a room with bookshelves, a bulletin board, and a large chalkboard on the wall. The bookshelf had some toys on the top level, and the rest all held books, neatly stacked. As he drew my attention to the chalkboard, he wrote a word that had sixty-four strokes. He looked up at me and asked me if I knew what the word was. I had absolutely no idea. He then explained to me what it meant.

Both boys wrote their English names on the chalkboard, already adjusting to an international society, it seemed. They wrote big and slowly, but with accuracy. Their lines were jagged, but they were being careful. Just watching them work with such concentration brought a smile to my face.

Like most five-year-olds, they were full of enthusiasm. They laughed without any reservation and jumped around and pretended to be robots. They readily showed us words on the board and read scrolls on the walls to us as if they were scholars.

We talked to their father during most of our visit. I found his teaching methods interesting in that he teaches the children traditional Chinese language, and not simplified Chinese. This was hard for me to believe. Simplified Chinese is already hard enough; traditional Chinese is absurdly difficult. Characters in traditional Chinese can involve indescribable complexity that even I could not envision.

"Why do you teach your sons only traditional Chinese—is that not hard for them?" I asked.

"Nothing is easy. I know that. Especially writing Chinese words, neither traditional nor simplified is easy. But at a young age, they do not know what is hard yet. So that is why they have to learn the hard things first! That is why I make the teachers teach them traditional Chinese. Yes, it is hard on them both, but it is for their future."

Mr. Lu's answer was extremely logical from my point of view. We Americans tend to think that many things in our daily lives are "too difficult." But then, who is to blame for this? Why is it that our parents and teachers do not start off by teaching us geometry and trigonometry when we are much younger? How hard can it be when students in the third grade in China are able to learn these things? China outperformed the United States in the PISA[5] by thirty rankings. Students in China can readily list every single dynasty in chronological order—yet how many American students retain key facts about US history? Are American students less inclined to achieve more academically because less is expected of us?

"Are there ever any situations where learning traditional Chinese has been a problem for your sons?" I asked Mr. Lu.

"When they go out to the playground to play with the kids who live nearby, they know that they obviously do not learn the same type of Chinese the other kids learn. Those children can read traditional Chinese, but they cannot write any of it, and sometimes the other children judge my sons a bit for that. Yet, they do not really know the difference at such a young age."

"Do you think that learning traditional Chinese will ever be a problem for your sons in the future?"

"China still offers many written materials in traditional Chinese. Some students learn only traditional Chinese. It should not be a problem with communication, since the two written words share similarities."

Still certain aspects of Mr. Lu's teaching manner with his sons seemed extraordinarily strict to me. I was curious. I asked him what kinds of rewards he gave his sons.

"Like any person, they love toys. They do not like candy, though; they are quite concerned about junk food. The other day our maid brought home some type of sweet drink that had a lot of coloring in it. The two took the box of drinks and threw it outside onto the porch. They will not even have chips or soft drinks in the house. We do not really mind, though. It assures us that they have quite a bit of common sense—mainly from their mother. But in order to get toys, they have to earn fifty stickers.

5 The Program for International Student Assessment (PISA) is a worldwide evaluation that measures the scholastic performance of fifteen-year-olds' scholastic performance in math, science, and reading (coordinated by the Organization for Economic Co-operation and Development (OECD).

In order to get a sticker, they have to fulfill certain standards. For example, after class, if one of them knows how to beautifully read and write all eight characters they learned today, they will receive a sticker."

Even something like this seemed impossible to me. I saw what the two boys were learning. I saw the complexity of the words, and the time they took just to write a single character. To earn a sticker would be nearly impossible for me if I were trying to do what they were doing. But I also saw that, on a bulletin board in one of the rooms, a notebook was tacked up for each boy. These notebooks were full of hundreds of stickers with lines between every fifty or so stickers.

Mr. Lu continued, "Too many kids are spoiled nowadays. I do this so that they learn to earn what they deserve. Is that not how our world works? You get what you give. You put in a certain amount of effort, and whatever is bestowed back upon you is your reward. Something I learned recently is that despite the two's near fluency with simple English phrases, they do not like to speak English to anyone outside of the classroom. So I thought of a solution that would help them become more comfortable speaking English in a different environment. The two have golf lessons every Wednesday, and their coach is an American PGA-ranked player who does not speak Chinese. I told them that for every ten sentences they speak to him, they would earn one sticker. Just yesterday, one son pestered the coach a lot, and by the end of the day the boy earned two stickers. Another reward is ice cream. After their workouts, if they do extremely well, I take them out for ice cream. Both of them are in good shape. They can hit about 500 golf balls in an afternoon while I can hit about 300, and I will be pretty tired by then."

"By home schooling the two, what do you hope to accomplish in the future? What do you want from them?"

"I plan to have them finish their high school education around age twelve to fifteen. I want them both to master about 6,000 Chinese characters and 6,000 English words."

Mr. Lu explained, "There is a big difference between learning Chinese and learning English. One of the hardest things for them is that they do not encounter as much English as they do Chinese. But Chinese is definitely harder than English because between verbal and written there is not as big a difference in English since you spell out what you hear. But in Chinese there's not only pin yin (the form of Romanization) but also characters that don't resemble the sounds spoken."

"What about after high school? How will they be able to adapt to that big difference between being home schooled and going to college? Not to mention the age difference of at least three or so years between them and other students in college."

"College is not a consideration for them. I hope that they will use what they have learned and start something for their future."

This was definitely shocking to me. Mr. Lu hoped to home school his sons to a point where they would not even need to go to college! This was also confusing. Mr. Lu added that he did not even want the twins to take the gaokao.

What did he expect of them? At age fifteen his sons would already be done with all their studies and off to find jobs? I found his thinking astounding.

Keeping to the subject of rewards, I asked, "What method do you use for punishment?"

"To better help the two, if they do something wrong or make a big mistake, their punishment is associated with the class. If one of them talks too much, they have to learn a traditional Chinese word and write it on the chalkboard a certain number of times. This way, not only do they learn, but they also learn it in a rewarding way. I do not prefer punishing them physically like many other Chinese parents, because they do not learn from that. I do not like to see them in pain, and neither do they. With the current method, everyone wins, including them."

Learning from mistakes. I wondered, *Why couldn't my parents have done that?* I would have learned and at the same time found out how to correct my mistakes. I decided that his method was probably the best punishment I had ever heard of in my entire life. There may be some doubts about its effectiveness compared to other possibilities, but there seemed to be proof that his punishment worked: the twins were well-behaved children.

"You have talked a lot about English and Chinese classes, what about math class?" I asked.

"Throughout the day, math class is considered their resting class. If they begin to show restlessness or tiredness from learning English or Chinese, they can switch to math to relax for a bit."

This unexpected perspective left me with mixed feelings. Math is a subject in which many American students do poorly, but many Chinese students excel at it. I thought of Chinese third graders learning geometry and trigonometry. Does the Chinese approach to teaching mathematics to small children explain this difference? Recent research suggests that this is also because in China, young children learn about numbers using two different methods for reading numerals: "the Chinese-based system of number words and the simplicity of Chinese mathematical terms."[6] The Chinese system focuses not only on the numeric terms seen and how to spell out the words coordinating to each numeric term (as does the English system), but also uses Chinese characters to write out the numbers.

While I was visiting the twins, I walked into a large room with two beds. I asked one of the boys if this was their bedroom. The answer was no, this was where the teachers sleep.

I asked Mr. Lu more about the arrangement he has with the teachers. "Do they work for you part time?"

"They live in the apartment right next door." He gestured to the room I had seen. "They eat there, they live there, they work there, twenty-four hours a day."

Being twenty-four-hour teachers requires a lot of devotion. The

6 "Chinese Number Words, Culture, and Mathematics Learning" Sharon Sui Ngan Ng and Nirmala Rao, *Review of Educational Research*, June 2010, vol. 80, no2. 180–206.

teachers had the same requirement as the boys for attire. They wore white blouses or shirts, and black pants and shoes. The assistants did not live within the building.

I asked why Mr. Lu decided to home school the two boys, other than the fact that he wanted them to finish school early.

He elaborated, "I do not appreciate the Chinese teaching system as much as some do. A big problem with education now is with the way we read books. We should not read books for the sake of reading books, but we need to *understand* the content. As you can see, I do not appreciate the slow pace at which students are learning these days. By the time most finish their formal education, they are already done with a third of their life. By the time they finish school, they have already lost interest in learning. You have to go through hardship when you are young, but after the hardship you can pursue more enjoyable work (though still tedious). In China's history, numerous scholars achieved so much at a young age. In our current system, this is not possible."

Mr. Lu believes in four points when it comes to children's education:

One, classics-based traditional education is a time-tested approach that has existed in China for the past 2,000 years. Modern education only came to China in the last 100 years. Traditional education generates masters in almost any field you can imagine. How do we know that the modern approach is superior to the traditional approach?

Two, before anyone is thirteen years old, they are like blank sheets of paper upon which they can draw beautiful pictures; so why not feed them with the classics, both Chinese classics and Western classics, instead of polluting them with modern media and technology?

Three, because children don't differentiate difficult or traditional Chinese characters from easy or simplified Chinese characters, and all Chinese characters are like pictures to them, why not teach them the more sophisticated picture? Traditional education emphasizes morality, including moral responsibilities and obligations. Character is the fundamental root of any person who wants to excel in a complicated world.

This is the Chinese version of liberal arts and education. The techniques and analytical tools are *xiao xue*, or "small learning." From traditional education, we learn how to view the world, how to build relationships with other people, and how to deal with society. As progress makes life easier physically, we risk losing touch with important character-building values, such as honesty, integrity, and perseverance, which are embedded in traditional education.

Four, children are being corrupted with technology. All kinds of information can be found on the Internet in an instant. "This is marvelous and convenient, but it also makes us stupid. With so much information instantly accessible, there is no longer the need to pour through books, memorize significant works, do research, open a curious mind, and spend hours and hours analyzing one topic. This is not the norm anymore," exclaimed Mr. Lu.

Standing in the teachers' bedroom and looking through the windows, Mr. Lu pointed out two structures that represent China's aspirations in science and sports. To the left was China's National Stadium, the magnificent "Bird's Nest" that was built for the 2008 Beijing Summer Olympics. To the right was the Beijing Science and Technology Museum, which is one of the best science museums in China. Mr. Lu's two sons regularly visit both the Beijing Science and Technology Museum and the National Sports Stadium. I concluded that Mr. Lu is putting much "heart and blood" (Chinese translation of a phrase for the deepest dedication) into these two young souls.

Xin wan li lu, du wan juan shu is a saying that means, "Travel a thousand miles, read a thousand books." This proverb reflects one of the important ways my family approaches my education. My father taught me to read "by foot." My father explained to me why my parents drove me around the country on so many educational trips during summer breaks from school. He referred to the parents' mantra mentioned earlier: "Don't lose on the starting line," and explained in his funny way, "We are in the

United States, so we must catch up by foot."

Our 2009 summer trip was an intensive one. It was a long trip from Atlanta, Georgia, to Indianapolis, Indiana, with many zigzags along the way. In Atlanta, we visited the Martin Luther King, Jr. National Historic Site.

Resistant to the road trip in the first place, I trudged alongside my parents down the stone-paved walkway, noticing quotes engraved in the marble on the ground—famous lines from Mohandas Karamchand Gandhi, Abraham Lincoln, and Rosa Parks. My parents made me stop and read every single one, until we realized that we were only halfway done and the buildings were about to close soon. Stepping into the museum, scenes from the civil rights movement were presented like movies.

An outdoor path led to the glorious stone-carved tomb that appeared to be floating upon a large reflecting pool centered in the courtyard. The water was perfectly calm, and the surroundings were silent. Off to the side of the pool in front of the gravesite is an eternal flame that remains lit.

As I stood there wondering how the eternal flame stayed lit when it rained, my dad suddenly said, "Yanna, remember when I made you memorize Martin Luther King, Jr.'s speech a few years ago? Recite it to me."

The last thing I felt like doing was to try to remember something I memorized long ago. Clearly, the purpose of our trip wasn't really to spend some "quality family time" or "to have fun" (though my parents beg to differ on that one), like I'd seen in those movies where families go on carefree road-trip vacations. Our trip was truly an educational experience.

My dad whipped out his cell phone and told me to look up the speech, and then recite it to him in the next few minutes.

I felt a little overwhelmed by the task. I knew my dad would not be satisfied if I couldn't recite the speech to him. Not only did my parents require me to recite the speech, they expected me to read every sign in the park. I was not very thrilled about that. Sometimes I pretended to read them, but then my parents quizzed me. If I didn't have the right answer, they made me to go back to reread the sign in question.

When we arrived at the Jimmy Carter Library, the library was just about to close for the day. But coming all the way from Minnesota, we (my parents) couldn't let that stop us. By speaking with the lady at the front desk, we were able to meet the Public Affairs representative of the museum, Mr. Tony Clark. After showing us around the new renovation, he led us into the storage house for the archives—basically a freezer building for the precious documents and letters of Jimmy Carter, each preserved on microfilm and carefully stored. Mr. Clark gave me a summary of the momentous aspects of Jimmy Carter's four years as president, from the US energy crisis to the establishing of a diplomatic relationship with China, from the boycott of the Moscow Summer Olympics to Jimmy Carter's debate with Ronald Reagan. What a vivid history class! I knew my dad and mom were very happy.

From Atlanta we journeyed north to the border of Georgia and Tennessee to visit the Chickamauga and Chattanooga National Military Park. This was probably one of the most worthwhile stops during the entire road trip. Inside the museum were colorful displays that illustrated aspects of the Civil War. Both sides were portrayed visually, with pictures of the soldiers and generals on two opposite walls. My dad wanted me to read one display board after another, and put all the new or unfamiliar words into my phone to study later.

Coming out of the Chickamauga and Chattanooga National Military Park, it was almost five o'clock. I hoped we would look for a hotel and rest. But my father never stopped. On his travel itinerary, our next stop was Russell Cave National Monument in Alabama, located on the Alabama/Tennessee border, an hour on the highway from the Chickamauga and Chattanooga National Military Park. But it was five o'clock! My mother and I both asked my dad to wait until tomorrow.

"Tomorrow we will tour the Great Smoky Mountains National Park, as we planned," my dad responded, gripping the steering wheel.

"But it is too late. We don't have time today," I said.

"Time can be created," my dad said, focusing his attention on driving westward.

"What?" I said.

He let me punch in the park phone number and hand the phone to him. He planned to request that we arrive after hours. My dad told the park ranger where we were and that we were driving toward the park already.

"You have time," the parker ranger responded. To our surprise, we learned that, even though the two parks are only fifty-five miles apart, they are located in different time zones. When we drove from Chickamauga and Chattanooga National Military Park to Russell Cave National Monument, we crossed from the Eastern time zone into Central time zone, and gained one hour.

My dad's magical absurdity became scientific reality. We arrived in the park just before they closed. This place really was where the excitement was. Fifteen to thirty visitors per day descended along a creaky wooden bridge, while being surrounded and eaten by millions of mosquitoes, to the cave monument. Inside the cave were model figures of natives who once lived there during prehistoric times, some 9,000 years ago. We saw depictions of the Archaic Period, the Woodland Periods, and the Mississippian Period. The inhabitants built their fires in the cave, slept in the cave, did their daily work in the cave, and everything else. Experiencing the cave and comparing the environment to our air-conditioned car, I realized that the advancement of life on our planet has been drastic over these thousands of years. I had never known that such places existed.

In history class, I had not learned about the way everyday life was thousands of years in the past. My assumption was that people just lived in caves and did whatever they had to do to survive. But it wasn't just "whatever," it was the way our human ancestors lived from about 6550 BC until about AD 1600.

Of course, for my dad and mom, this was a perfect anthropology class for me. We haven't gone to Luxor in Egypt; we haven't gone to the Dead

Sea. But we found ancient history right here in the U.S.; we have our own archaeology and anthropology.

By the time we drove into the Great Smoky Mountains National Park, it was about 1 o'clock in the morning, and my mom was the first to rebel against the hour, considering we'd have to drive back a hundred miles to find a motel. But my dad pushed forward.

At the park, it was absolutely pitch dark. Ours was the only car on the road. We could see the stars.

After about an hour driving aimlessly through the park, I broke down in the backseat of the car, crying and whimpering, "I want to go home. I want to go home. I hate it here. It's dark, it's two in the morning, and I want to go home!"

Within minutes, the most dramatic thing happened. We suddenly emerged from the absolute darkness of the woods to be just about blinded from the lights and billboards that appeared in front of us. We had arrived in Gatlinburg, Tennessee. And there, at 2:30 a.m., all the stores and shops, along with numerous hotels along the parkway, were still open, and hundreds of people were bustling about on the streets. It was quite a rush of activity. The contrast was surreal.

We found a hotel to rest for the next few hours before we drove onto the Appalachian Trail in the Great Smoky Mountains National Park. The formation, the geology, and the natural features of the Great Smoky Mountains National Park were the subjects of the tests my father and mother gave me at the park.

Heading north, we arrived at the intersection among the three states of Kentucky, Tennessee, and Virginia: the Cumberland Gap National Historic Park. Looking at a sign, I was trying to convince my parents to skip the hike and keep driving. Without any more specific distance measurement, there was only one sign to warn people: DEEP AND DANGEROUS HILL AHEAD. My parents decided that we would hike up the mountain.

Within five minutes, I was baked by the sun and drenched in sweat.

My head was pounding. I began to cry, protesting that I couldn't do it. Both my parents became frustrated with me, and my mother began asking why I was having a "nervous breakdown."

The phrase, "Go take a hike" would have probably been the best (or the worst) comeback, considering how I felt; but after a few minutes rest, I started out with my parents, back on the trail.

After half an hour, we saw a young man walking down the hill, with a backpack, two canteens, a sleeping bag, and other accessories attached around his belt and backpack. We asked him how much further it was to the top of the hill. He replied that he didn't know. He admitted that he was actually a resident of the area, and he had never gone up the hill before. So today he had tried, but he gave up before he had reached the top.

We parted ways, going in the opposite direction. But it turned out to be only a little further along until we made it to the top. The view was absolutely glorious, with a slight foggy mist covering the forest below us. My mom remarked, "Aren't you glad you came up the whole way? It wasn't that hard, now was it?"

I agreed.

We arrived at Mammoth Cave National Park at about eleven o'clock that night. This place welcomes two million-plus visitors each year. After arriving at the gate, we found that it was still quite a distance before we would reach the main area and park, so we asked the park rangers if there were any hotels with rooms available. He told us that everything was booked up three months ago.

Knowing my dad, who was in charge of the steering wheel, I was not surprised that once again we ventured forward into the darkness. Arriving at the cabin-grounds office, the area was still bustling, and all the lights were on in the building. We heard again that there were no available rooms or cabins. It would be a two-hour trip back to find a motel, and it was already midnight. My dad spoke with the lady at the front desk for about fifteen minutes while my mom and I sat down on the couches, thinking about what we should do. At one point we heard a phone ring, some talking and laughter; and my dad happily walked back toward us. One of the reserved cabins had just been canceled due to illness of the family who reserved it, and we had a place to stay for the night.

It was a miracle, and I give my dad all the credit. He still reminds me to this day of the occurrence. Perseverance is in his blood. He always uses his extraordinary experience, even sometimes just by luck, to educate my brother and me. "If you are persistent, you always achieve something," he explained to me. He quoted those ancient wisdoms whenever he got a chance. "The progress of studies comes from hard work, and is retarded by frivolities. The excellence of conduct is derived from independent thinking, and is destroyed by following blindly," he reminds me. The statement comes from Han Yu, a Tang dynasty Confucian scholar and poet.

Mammoth Cave was definitely worth seeing. My favorite part of the tour was the region called Fat Man's Misery, within which was the smallest tunnel ever. (If you are over 200 pounds, do not go there.) As we made our way toward the main hall of the cave, the tour guide turned off all the lights inside, showing us the darkness and the reality of what this place was like long ago, before the park was constructed. The fish and shrimp found in the cave had no eyes. They did not need vision because there was no light in the cave. My thoughts went to Darwin's theory of evolution.

I had never even known such places existed. Just imagining the possibility that things could be so cold and so dark, I would not have even pondered the possibility that this was a place to be, or even a place to explore before technology gave us easier access.

Though it's just a small example of part of our history, it's a spectacular site, something that, before my dad mentioned it, I had never heard of or imagined. Without the push from my dad, such places would have continued to be unknown to me. The places I see and the things I experience allow me to gain profound understanding in certain fields, viewing situations and places differently than that of my peers. The ability to view situations through a different lens allows me to qualify for the race to the finish line.

CHAPTER 5
Caged Birds

When my brother got into college, my dad wrote to him:

Tian gao ren niao fei,
Hai kuo ping yu yue.

This is one of the most frequently quoted proverbs sent to college students after they enter college in China. Literally, it means, "Sky is high, birds fly freely. Ocean is broad, fish jump freely."

All the schools I visited in China were gated environments with high brick walls or metal fences surrounding the entire campus. I was reminded of a Chinese soap opera I watched as a kid. Juvenile delinquents in the movie were sent to a high school where they had to wear orange jumpsuits to class every day, just as if they were in jail. All the students were troublemakers who were placed on this campus for the duration of high school. One student decided he was going to climb over the wall and escape "the place of hell." Although he attempted to escape several times, he was never successful. There was a weird connection in my mind between this fictional place for juvenile delinquents and the Chinese schools I visited.

I was sure that most of the students in these Chinese schools had never even considered committing a crime. I met numerous smart students, dedicated teachers, and responsible principals in those gated compounds. I am sure that the gates, walls, and fences were most likely for the students' protection. But I had never seen a large school that was gated or walled in the United States, public or private, although most schools have campus security during school hours.

On our trip to Beijing, I visited Fu Xue Elementary School. The courtyard was quite unique. This school facility was expanded from a traditional Confucian learning academy. The classical construction was still there. The Confucius Hall and Temple with red painted wood and marble floors still stand regally and play a symbolic role in discipline, admonition, dedicated learning, and ambition.

In the new facility, the offices for teachers and the principal are one-story buildings constructed with red-tinted wood; it was the type of building I'd expect to see in the olden, imperial days. But then again, I realized, that period only ended a little more than a hundred years ago.

The school looked like a huge rectangle with white granite walls, and big pieces of cloth covered rectangular holes designed as windows.. There was a small jungle gym in the courtyard, and in front of that was a large, green, mat-like floor where the students did their morning exercises and had their recess each day.

It was a bright and sunny afternoon. Summer was in the courtyard; the temperature was above ninety degrees. To the left of the courtyard was a glass plaque with a saying inscribed in gold. As I looked closer, my dad told me that it was the Di Zi Gui: "Rules for Students."

But this plaque was especially spectacular. Standing in front of it, I saw my own reflection. This was obviously intentional planning on the part of the designers. The student reads the words written on the glass while seeing his or her own reflection, which serves as a personal reminder to follow these rules.

My father, brother, and I walked into the school building to find one hallway with five classrooms on each side. Each classroom had a plate over the door with gold lettering that identified the type of classroom—specifically, what grade. Inside a classroom, which was slightly smaller than typical classrooms in the U.S., the room was uncomfortably hot. The pieces of cloth shielded those who sat right next to the window from the blazing sunlight. There were six perfectly lined rows of students. Eight students in each row sat upright and straight as we entered. There were forty-eight students total.

After brief introductions, the teacher asked if any of the students could help carry a few chairs to the back of the classroom so we could be seated. Almost all the students rushed to help; it was a wonderful sight.

Sitting at the back of an actual Chinese classroom was quite an experience. As I observed, the "rumors" about well-behaved Chinese students were true. Students always raised their hands to answer questions or ask questions—never did one just blurt out an answer. If they were called upon, they quickly rose and stood next to the desk, poised and straight, and answered the question. All of their pencil cases sat perfectly in a horizontal position on the front of the desks. The students' feet were flat on the ground. Everyone sat upright; no one slouched or propped their head against their arm. All the students were eager to answer questions or tell stories. When it was time to read from the board, the students read in perfect sync, and with enthusiasm. When it was journal time, every student took out his or her workbook quickly and without question. The journal topic was written on the board, and the word count was 300 Chinese characters.

The teacher was energetic. PowerPoint slides were displayed. This was the most interactive class I'd ever attended. Students responded swiftly.

Ms. Tang posed this topic for the students: An earthquake is occurring. Buildings have started to crumble. The earth is trembling. "Use a proverb to describe this situation," she directed.

"*Tian xuan di zhuan* (Sky and earth are swirling)," the students uniformly answered.

At the earthquake site, a gentleman was standing in the debris without any panic. "Use a proverb to describe this situation," Ms. Tang told her students.

"*Lin wei bu ju* (Being in a dangerous situation without fear)," the students uniformly answered.

After the earthquake, a group of people were working together on the site to rebuild their homes. "Use a proverb to describe this situation," Ms. Tang continued.

"*Qi xin xie li* (working together cooperatively)," the students answered, again uniformly.

"Now we start the essay using 300 Chinese characters. The title is 'A Memorable Activity.' Incorporate these Chinese proverbs. You have half an hour," said Ms. Tang.

As the students in the class began to write the essay, we walked out of the classroom. Ms. Tang said goodbye to us at the door. I felt I had again met a teacher who poured her energy into her students.

The remarkable thing to me was that the students were so polite; their behavior was so courteous and respectful. Each student showed great respect for the teacher and did what they were supposed to do immediately when asked. No one was doodling on their desk; no one was staring out the window; no one was playing games under their desk or goofing around with the person sitting nearby. They acted in unison and their prompt responses created a warm atmosphere in the classroom environment. The discomfort of the warm temperature was overcome by the refreshing exuberance of the students and the teacher.

This was a contrast from the American classroom atmospheres I have experienced. In the United States, it is not uncommon to walk into a classroom where students are slouching in their seats, shoes off, resting their feet on the back of the chair in front of them—the possibilities for casual, and even deviant, behaviors are endless. The atmosphere is quite different. Teachers frequently have to remind us to raise our hands, whether we are in kindergarten or in our last year of high school. How many times do our teachers have to tell us to sit up straight in our chairs, or otherwise, leave the classroom?

But in the Chinese classroom, manners are taken seriously, and intelligence and talent are the only parts of students that are allowed to run wild.

The contrast I observed firsthand between students in the U.S. and China brought me back to the conversations I've had with friends about the whole concept of the contrast of the two cultures.

My parents are involved in my school life. I tell them about my classes, and what happens daily, but whenever I tell them what I got on a test, whether I got a good grade or bad grade, their reply is always, "How did the other students in the class do?"

Being compared to other students is something I've always dreaded, but Chinese parents seem to dwell on it as much as they can. My parents don't care about my absolute points or grade. They only care about my relative level of achievement compared with other students—my position in the class. Implicitly, they put pressure on me to be competitive in school.

When I asked my friend Annie about her parents and the pressure they place on her, she said she feels much less pressure now that she is here in the United States. In China, her parents would knock on her door, ask her about her homework, and remind her to follow her study plans, but that changed when she came to America.

"In China, all parents knew their child's academic performance and their relative position in their class. Even if we didn't tell them, the school had already informed them. Both of my parents are extremely busy; they both have jobs. As a doctor, my mom is on call, yet she always has time for me," said Annie. "But when my parents bother me, I know that they're doing it for my own good—to help me."

Annie said she became very frustrated at times when her mother kept "bothering" her about her school work. But after coming to the United States and living with an American family, she began to realize that there were certain aspects of her parents' attention that she actually missed. She missed her mother's pestering, her indirect affection toward her, and the reminders of everything that they'd given up for her benefit.

The resemblance between Annie and me is quite noticeable to me. We live the way Chinese students live, with parents constantly asking us about our homework, asking us how we did on tests, and being compared to our peers in every test. But we also understand that our parents have given up so much for us; they take out time from their day to make sure we're doing fine. They give up what they could be doing for themselves, for what they can do for us. They sacrifice.

We (students like Annie and me) sometimes think that we are the ones sacrificing. We are prevented from being with our friends. Instead we stay home, cramming for a project or finishing up a research paper. Yet Chinese parents readily give up their leisure time in pursuit of their hopes and dreams for their children. Annie's parents did that, just as my parents have. The parents of my Chinese classmates are the same way.

When I was visiting China, one of things I wanted to figure out was what motivated these students I met everywhere I went. Why are students in China so driven? They seem to express a sentiment I have not generally seen in students in the U.S. Again and again Chinese students talked about being number one—being the best student. Why is it that everyone wants to be number one?

In Fu Xue Elementary School, the Di Zi Gui was inscribed on the wall, right outside the school building. The length of the wall was just like the large screens in Times Square in New York City, extending from one end of the courtyard to the other. Golden calligraphy was carefully inscribed on the wall, each word seeming to symbolize the richness of the "gold" in the design.

A Chinese proverb says that gold is hidden inside every book. Everyone in China seems to agree that knowledge is power. Certainly there is plenty of evidence that income variations depend on workers' education levels. Though some families may convey their philosophy differently, the absolute necessity of education—and a good education for that matter—is the key in life.

The literacy rate in China is greater than 95 percent, and quickly approaching the level of the United States (99 percent). Parents want their children to be the best they can be, and if possible, better than everyone else. But money and books can't always make that happen; success is also dependent upon the student's drive to be the best. This is all about willpower, the willingness to read, the willingness to study, the willingness to work hard, and the willingness to learn. But I still wanted to know why it seems like students in China have so much more willpower than students in the United States.

We visited Huantai Second High School, a boarding school for students in Huantai, China. As we approached the school, we saw three security officers guarding the electronic metal entrance gate. Once inside the school, we met Gao Daquan, the principal of the school; Bi Junhua, a Chinese teacher; Song Lifeng, a geography teacher; and four students, Su Rui, Wang Jinghan, Wang Mengxiao, and Geng Liping.

Our meeting started at 4:00 p.m. and students joined us at about 7:00 p.m. They had been excused from their evening class (which ran from 6:40 p.m. to 10:00 p.m. every night) in order to meet with us.

"What motivates you to do well in school? What drives you to do well in classes?" I asked Wang Mengxiao.

"My parents," she answered. "My parents invested a lot of time in my education, and they sacrifice a lot for my education. Much of what I do is for them. A lot of what we all do is dedicated to our parents. Honestly, we express a lot of thanks toward our parents. It may seem like we do not express it in a physical way, but everyone here knows that it is all thanks to our parents that we are here."

I was quite touched whenever students mentioned their gratitude toward their parents. I am truly thankful for what my parents do for me, but I was not used to hearing other students express this type of sentiment. These students were aware of how much their parents sacrificed for them, and they knew they were very fortunate. In my experience, it seems as though so many children, especially teenagers in the U.S., do not have a full understanding of all that their parents do for them.

In Huantai, I met Li Hui, an English teacher and the vice principal of academic affairs at Century Middle School. We met on a Sunday, but not at her home. She greeted us at the school campus where she was working.

She worked on Sunday to help students make up the English classes they'd missed over the previous weekend because senior high school students had utilized their classrooms for the gaokao.

"Those three days were a legitimate break," I observed. "Why do they need to make up the classes?"

"Without studying for three consecutive days, they will become idiots," Vice Principal Li told me.

Students in the United States would be thrilled to have three days off when there is a teachers' conference or parents' conference. But in China, students and teachers count every day and every hour. They don't want to lose even a few minutes from their academic work.

Presuming that procrastination is probably a weakness that everyone suffers from, I wondered whether this was true for students in China. Back at Huantai Second High School I asked Geng Liping, "Do you guys ever get distracted from studying?"

"Of course we get distracted. There are usually a few students that run around and create a ruckus, create a commotion, but we try to stay focused. There are of course students who are in dating relationships with each other at our school, and everyone knows who they are, including the teachers. But the teachers do not get into their personal lives. Most people, including the students, discourage such things, though, because we are here to study, and not to waste time in a relationship that everyone knows will not last."

The American journalist Nicholas Kristof interviewed students on one of his many trips to China, and his experience was similar to my own. When he asked about romance, a tenth-grade girl remarked that it was "a waste of time," and she did not plan to have a boyfriend in high school.

The students I interviewed in both Shandong and Shanghai thought the same way, and believed that dating was stupid for students their age. Their parents or their teachers did not permit them distracted from their studies. Kristof encountered a third-grade student who, if she had extra time in the evening after her school work, did not watch TV or hang out with her friends. Instead, she reviewed her work and did extra exercises for her classes. Her classmate's father allowed his child to watch TV during the summer breaks—for ten minutes only at a time. Kristof's conclusion: "These days, the tables are turned, and now we need to learn from China."

Han chuang shi nian, meaning "cold window for ten years," is a phrase that describes this educational phase of life experience. If a student wants to achieve, the student must sit on the cold bench for ten years, with no distractions. Students in China are so focused because they have to be. Memorization, long hours of classes in school, review sessions after class, zhongkao, gaokao—all these keep students in a "cage": they must drill, drill, and drill. Most high school students in China get out of their cage only after they are accepted into college.

In Huantai Second High School, when I asked the students for some long-lasting memories of their experience at the school, every single one recalled something that was academically related. Wang Jinghan talked about being challenged by the complexity of science in his first year, and how his physics teacher helped him to get out of the maze. He talked about the necessity for a foundation built through hardship and challenges, and how he knew it would all pay off in the end when he really began to learn the hardcore material of physics, biology, and chemistry.

"The important thing about learning is the idea of independence," Su Rui emphasized. "In school, the teacher introduces you to all the subjects in a classroom, but then you have to probe further to truly learn. You cannot depend upon the teacher to always direct your life; the teacher is only there for assistance. Students cannot grab onto the teachers, or even their parents, hoping they will be there with them forever. We all know that people come and go, and we are in a life cycle."

"How do you guys, as students, describe your school and its relationship to education?" I asked.

"I feel that everyone in our school is hungry for education. Everyone wants to be the best, and everyone is willing to do anything to get there. When the teachers are walking in the courtyard, you rarely see them walking alone. When teachers are standing in the courtyard, they are not standing alone. There will almost always be a student beside the teacher, asking questions," said Su Rui.

This reminded me of an image from a lesson I studied in the Chinese-language textbook in my Chinese-language school in St. Paul. The textbook lesson described how every morning on the campus of Princeton University an old man was seen explaining mathematics problems to a twelve-year-old girl. The girl was a student in hope of finding someone who could help her with her mathematics problems. People who didn't know the pair thought it was a grandfather and his granddaughter. The old man was in fact Albert Einstein. Though in class the moral we learned focused on the idea that even geniuses are humble at heart and willing to help, Su Rui's comment made me realize that anywhere you go it is important to ask questions to anyone at anytime.

"What do you consider the basic skills you need in life?" I asked the students.

"Definitely social skills—the ability to communicate with friends, classmates, teachers, the principal. Those things will eventually prepare us for going out into society in the future. Another important concept is to become involved, take the steps to be truly involved in something. Having the ability and motivation to do something is the key. Without that, it is almost impossible to accomplish anything," Geng Liping answered.

This is a dramatic difference from my father's generation. When he was a student, the popular slogan on college education was *Xue hao shu li hua, zou bian tian xia dou bu pa* (If you obtain the skills of mathematics, physics, and chemistry, you will be fearless anywhere).

In the late 1970s and 1980s Chinese students rushed into mathematics, physics, chemistry, and other hard-science majors. These majors provided opportunities for good colleges and safe jobs for their future.

Though every student hopes to get into a good college, the students in the villages and countryside in China are finding it more difficult to get accepted. Former Chinese Premier Wen Jiabao recalled, "When we were in college, students from the countryside accounted for 80 percent; now it's different."[1] Though 50 percent of China's students live in the countryside (China's population was split fifty/fifty between urban areas and rural areas at the end of 2011), the elite colleges and universities in China accept more students from the cities and metropolitan areas. Those in the countryside can only get into community colleges and technical colleges.

Traditionally in China, the smartest students came from families which exercised strict discipline and could come from anywhere in China. But students in the metropolitan and urban areas now have greater resources in terms of review classes, materials, and high-caliber teachers. They attend review sessions after class, are able to pay for expensive individual tutoring services, and other educational luxuries such as the newest technology and labs. The questions on the national exam tend to favor metropolitan students as well, using references to Internet languages and topics such as fashion trends, which are far more familiar to city students. This dynamic creates imbalances that make education more available to the powerful and wealthy families—the elite class.

In the entire nation, 72.3 percent of the students who took the gaokao were accepted into college. In Shanghai, 89.3 percent of students who took the national exam were accepted into college. In the top colleges, the percentage of students from the countryside kept declining after 1990. In Beijing University, students from the countryside accounted for more than 30 percent in 1990, but only 10 percent in 2010. In Qinghua University, that percentage was down to 17 percent.

Lei Lei, a college student from China Central Science and Technology University in Wuhan, Hebei Province, came from a small village in Piling County, Shanxi Province. He took the national exam in 2006 and was accepted by a four-year college. But he wanted to attend a better college,

1 "Even with Gaokao, Can You Compete with the Second Generation of the Rich?" *Jinan Daily*, February 24, 2012. http://edu.sina.com.cn/gaokao/2012-02-24/1630328680.shtml.

so he gave up this opportunity. He decided to study for another year and take the national exam again. He took the gaokao for the second time in 2007 and was ranked number five in Piling County. He was then accepted into China Central Science and Technology University.

The differences between cities and the countryside are vast. When Lei Lei was young, he needed to get up early every morning and walk four kilometers to his school. By the time students in his area got to school, some of them were already exhausted from the morning walk. Lei Lei was the first student in his village to go to college, and his college, China Central, was the best college any student in his village had ever gone to.

When Lei Lei entered the college, a classmate who had come from the Affiliated School of the Northwest Industrial University told him, "My performance in the national exam was poor, that's why I came to this university." In her school, 97 percent of the students passed the level for the top colleges. This encounter hurt Lei Lei so much.

This kind of pressure becomes a strong source of self-discipline. A study comparing high school students in the United States, China, Japan, and South Korea was jointly conducted by the China Youth Research Center, the Japan Youth Research Institute, the Korea Youth Development Institute, and the Eddy Resource System Corporation in the U.S.[2] The survey shows Chinese high school students are at the top in self-motivated learning, independent problem solving, voluntary review of classes, and voluntary extension of study time.

Among the four countries, Chinese students appeared to face the most pressure from three primary sources. The first source is parents: 24.5 percent of parents expect their children to be ranked in the first ten places in the class. (This number is the highest among the four countries.) The second type of pressure comes from the students themselves. The third pressure comes from peers. Traditionally, classmates helped each other. Now, students view their classmates and peers as competitors. They

2 "Chinese Students Face the Highest Pressure Among Japan, United States and Korea" *Education Development Research*, July 2010.

don't even let their classmates know if they are working additional hours, reading more books, practicing extra problems, and/or participating in after-school review classes.

From 2000-2005 in the same locations, using the same survey techniques, the survey found that the amount of pressure on the students escalated as they got older. They slept less, and spent more time on homework and after-school review classes. Their leisure time was reduced.

The China Youth Research Center conducted a survey called China's Youth Demographics and Health Report[3] that covered the first-tier cities of Beijing and Guangzhou; the second-tier cities of Jinan in Shandong Province and Xian in Shanxi Province; and the third-tier cities of Tongling in Anhui Province and Kaifeng in Henan Province. The subjects were high school students and technical college students. Students in Beijing reported feeling the highest amount of pressure to do well academically.

The five pressures affecting high school students were all related to studying. Number one, satisfaction of test scores; number two, outcome of the test scores; number three, low learning efficiency; number four, peers' learning pressure; and number five, high expectations from parents.

A survey conducted by the Shandong Province Social Science Association and Shandong Province Polls Center[4] showed that high school students in Shandong had strong motivation and will to do well on "The Test" (the gaokao); 97.3 percent of the high school students that were interviewed were prepared to take the 2010 test. If they failed, 80 percent said they would take the test again. Only 20 percent said that they would start looking for employment.

Although China's educators and the Ministry of Education attempted to reduce the burden of pressure on the students, this effort was unsuccessful. Why? Primarily because of the pressure students put on themselves. The director of the China Youth Research Center and

3 *Beijing Youth Daily*, August 18, 2010.

4 "Investigation in Shandong," 2009.

Chinese coordinator of the survey, Sun Hongyan, commented, "Students take the expectations of others, especially their parents and their teachers, and place them as their own expectations. This means they internalize the outside pressure."

The survey found that the satisfaction level toward their own academic performance is the lowest among the students in China: 84.1 percent are not satisfied with their academic performance. This insatiable desire for academic satisfaction drove them to the top position in PISA rankings. American students are the opposite: 82.1 percent are satisfied with their academic performance. In the survey, the Chinese students preferred the subjects covered in the gaokao, such as Chinese, mathematics, and foreign languages. American, Japanese, and Korean students reported that they liked music and art the most. Though the survey showed that the negative emotions of Chinese students were the highest, skipping class and fighting among students was the lowest in China compared to the other three countries.

Chinese students have very little time to be with their parents, because they spend most of their time in school or in an academic environment outside of the home. The only time spent with parents is usually lunchtime and dinnertime. And when students do spend time with parents, all Chinese parents ask the same question: "How was your test?" Either good or bad, the next question is: "How are the other students doing?"

In the United States, a more common question among parents and their children at the dinner table is, "How was your day?" We may tell our parents about certain upcoming tests, but probably not every single one. And when we do, they may care, but typically they don't do anything other than wish us luck or remind us to do our homework. They may remind us that we shouldn't be fooling around when we're supposed to be studying for the upcoming test, but they don't sit next to us or guard us as we study. If we do poorly on the test, we are more likely to receive a disappointed look, or possibly lose phone, TV, or Internet privileges. But our parents don't have as much influence on the way we perform the next time we take a test as parents in China do.

One of our neighbors came to my mom, complaining of insomnia and stress associated with a problem her daughter was having in math class. The teacher required students to stand at the board and solve math problems in front of the other students. The girl's mother said this caused her daughter to experience a form of performance anxiety. She kept worrying and asking, "What if I don't know the answer?"

As the woman saw her daughter becoming more and more upset about this situation; she decided to take the girl to a therapist to help her deal with her stress. The mother also went to the school principal to complain about this situation. She told him that this was an improper teaching method, and that the school should stop it immediately. She felt that the situation creates too much pressure on kids, causing anxiety and even pain for some. Seeing that her daughter was so stressed, she had herself become stressed, and then developed insomnia. The severity to which parents worry over their children varies, but a worried mindset is second nature. But looking at this case I question whether or not the minute task of doing a problem on the board balances out with the effects of the anxiety on both the student and the parent.

It's not unusual for me to sit in math class and suddenly be called upon by the teacher or even volunteer to do a problem on the board. It certainly isn't rare in China, either. I can't help wondering if a better idea to try before seeing a therapist would be to use that time to help the child study.

We have a family friend with two kids in a private school where most of the kids come from very wealthy families. The mother talks about her children often. She says they are not very good students, usually getting C grades. The parents are perfectly satisfied with that level of achievement. They bring their children on golfing trips and vacations, and make those family events a major part of their life. Every few months the kids miss school so that they can vacation in places such as Europe. When the kids turned sixteen, the boy was given a golf membership and the girl was given a new car.

But when the time came for the daughter to prepare for taking the SAT, the parents took her to a doctor, claiming she had attention deficit hyperactivity disorder (ADHD). This woman found out that she wasn't the only one making this claim. The parents of half the class at the school brought their children to the doctor's office for a written confirmation of a diagnosis of ADHD. It turns out that if a doctor diagnoses a student with ADHD, the student is allowed extra time to take the SAT.

These parents were willing to elicit the help of a doctor to bail out an underperforming student in an attempt to procure a better chance to do well on the SAT. When family vacations take precedence over the value of school and studying, it seems to me that the parents may have lost sight of their primary responsibilities in favor of viewing the teachers, or the school, or doctors, as responsible for their children.

Whether in China or in the United States, students like to use the Internet. More than 70 percent of American, Japanese, and Korean students can go online without restrictions. But only 39.3 percent of Chinese students are allowed to freely go online. Most students have parental restrictions on what sites they can visit and for how long. Chinese parents are very nervous about the Internet. They fear that students will become addicted to the Internet. When they leave the house, many parents take the computer keyboard with them.

I was curious about extracurricular activities in China. I had not heard much about China's gym classes unless students were training for school teams or gold medals.

One student replied, "Yes, of course! Just last week we had a students-versus-teachers basketball tournament. It was a lot of fun and everyone enjoyed it. We have school teams for basketball, table tennis, badminton, etc., just like any other school. Most schools, including ours, are pretty big on student bondings. We are like a family. The teachers are like our parents, and we depend on each other for support."

However, after continuous meetings at different schools, I concluded that, in China, classes like gym and sports do not matter. Unless you are going to be an Olympic gold medalist, or obtain some additional points for gaokao, such activities are a waste of time from an academic perspective.

A security guard in Huantai Second School remarked, "Bad teachers can always be made gym teachers; they receive the lowest honor from students."

In the U.S., many students love gym class because it is an escape from the walls of a classroom, and you have the freedom to run around and forget about learning for an hour. Many schools religiously follow the concept of an hour of physical fitness a day. There have been studies done with schools that show a significant increase in the efficiency of a student after a physical workout. Having a break, like a gym class (or even an art class), is also important because it will give your brain a break. Reporters and representatives from China admit that their students are mentally developed, but not necessarily physically fit.

After the freshman year of high school, students are separated into two groups. The first group is focused on math and science; the second group is focused on humanities, history, and social studies. Fifty percent of Chinese high school students supported this division. Seventy percent of the high school students chose a college based on their preferred profession. Among the top choices of professions were: science, education, health, and medicine. Less than 1 percent of the students wanted to be farmers.

In the Shandong Province High School Students Survey, the average number of hours students spent studying each day was 11.13 (including school). The average amount of sleep the students had was 7.54 hours. More than 50 percent of the students felt strong pressure related to performance on The Test and in finding the right employment opportunity. A majority of the students were influenced by their parents when choosing a college and a profession. 66.5 percent of the students said they communicated with their classmates and their friends when dealing with pressure while only 20 percent said they communicated with their parents and interestingly only 1.3 percent reported communicating with their teachers. Why are so few students communicating with their teachers on issues relating to stress? Because teachers expect that their students will achieve academically; everything else is secondary.

At my school in Eden Prairie, Minnesota, students are often told that if we are being bullied, or if we feel overwhelmed with stress, we should not be afraid to talk to our teachers or our parents. Keeping feelings inside can cause stress to build up to the point of crisis. This can be prevented. At the start of the school year, students are assured that if we ever need help with anything, the adults of the school will support us. We are also assured of a 100 percent confidentiality policy (unless a death or serious abuse is occurring). We are made to feel safe talking about issues at home. We talk to our friends as well, but sometimes we know that even our best friends can't help. That's one of the reasons we have counselors. Students are allowed to talk about their parents, their teachers, and their life without anyone else knowing about this. We know that we can talk to the teachers, too, though some are more approachable than others. During my freshman year of high school I was able to talk to a few of my teachers due to some stress issues I had in class. I told my parents about this, too, and they didn't mind me telling them or talking to my teacher about it. Many students stay more stress-free because we know we have someone to talk to. We don't have to hide the pressures we are experiencing from anyone.

A 2010 survey conducted by Shanghai Social Science Academy's Youth Institute polled Chinese, Korean, and Japanese high school students on sources of stress. Three main sources were identified: tests, employment, and relationships with friends. The results showed that Chinese high school students received the most family support compared to Japanese and Korean students. Chinese high school students (62.2 percent) felt their pressure was related to tests and tests scores; only 35.4 percent were concerned about employment.

Jao Hong Mei is director of Zhengzhou Psychology Consulting Association in Zhengzhou, the capital city of Henan Province (the largest province in China with over 100 million people). Jao Hong Mei said, "High school students in Henan are facing huge pressures. The pressure mainly comes from the gaokao. During the time before the National Entrance Examination, the frequency of visits for psychological consulting among high schools students increases dramatically. The results for their performance on the National Entrance Exam determine their future. This pressure causes anxiety, depression, fear, and compulsions."

China's gaokao-centered education system forces both students and their parents to be far too focused "inside the box" resulting in many becoming ignorant of, and indifferent to, how to best prepare their children for success overseas. Jiang Xueqin was invited to Affiliated School to Beijing University to build an international program for students to study abroad. When parents call the program for inquiry, "they don't ask what makes our program special, tell us why their child is suitable for our program, and often don't even know why they're sending their child abroad. They ask three simple questions: Do you have SAT cram courses? Do you have an Advanced Placement curriculum? Do you offer an American high school diploma? These questions tell us how short-sighted and single-minded parents are: All that matters is that their child gets into an American university, and they ignore their child's welfare, happiness, and development as a human being,"[5] wrote Jiang Xueqin.

5 Jiang Xueqin, *The Diplomat*, Australian National University. August 11, 2010. http://thediplomat.com/china-power/beijing%e2%80%99s-study-abroad-market/#more-902.

CHAPTER 6
Drills and Drills

During summer break when I was in middle school, my dad made me memorize a few famous speeches, such as Martin Luther King, Jr.'s "I Have a Dream" speech and Abraham Lincoln's Gettysburg Address. The assignment was definitely hard—harder than I expected. I had never been asked to do anything like that in school. My teachers never required me to do that kind of learning. Even for essential information that we use frequently, teachers often advised students not to bother memorizing the material.

Though my dad didn't major in literature or anything of the sort, he can fluidly recite many of the Tang poems. In Huantai Second High School, we met a group of students who had just finished a rehearsal of Di Zi Gui (Rules for Students). My dad asked if any of them still remembered Han Yu's essay *On Teachers*. Han Yu is a Tang dynasty essayist. The students had studied this essay four months before. In the meantime, they had not "used" any of their knowledge of that material. Over time, people tend to forget newly learned information if they don't review or use it in some way. But every single student harmonized perfectly and recited the essay without missing a beat. The teachers had a twinkle in their eyes, and we could not have been more impressed.

On Teachers

Gu zhi xue zhe bi you shi, shi zhe. Shuo yi xuo yi chuan dao shou ye jie huo ye, ren fei sheng er zhi zhi zhe, shu neng wu huo? Huo er bu cong shi, qi wei huo ye, zhong bu jie yi. Sheng hu wu qian, qi wen dao ye, gu xian hu wu, wo cong er shi zhi. Sheng hu wu hou, qi wen dao ye, yi xian hu wu, wo cong er shi zhi. Wu shi dao ye, fu yong zhi qi nian zhi xian hou sheng yu we hou hu? Shi gu wu gui wu jian, wu zhang wu shao, dao zhi shuo cun, shi zhi shuo cun ye.

Here is a translation, with help provided by my father:

> For anybody who wants to learn, he first must need a teacher. A teacher's responsibility is to explain theories, lecture principles, and answer confusing questions. Nobody was born with knowledge and the understanding of the world. Who does not have questions? If you have questions that you don't ask the teachers, your question will never be solved. Whoever was born before me, he understands the world before me; I should learn from him. Whoever was born after me, he understands more than me, I also need to learn from him. I'm searching for teachers; I don't care if he is younger than me or older than me. Whether noble or humble, young or old, where is knowledge, where is my teacher?

I was totally amazed by the students' perfect unison. This was not a planned recital. It was merely a literature piece my dad picked up randomly during our conversation that I also found in the students' textbook.

My dad said, "Look, Yanna, they are real Chinese students."

After this experience, I fully understood why my dad had me memorize those famous speeches and essays. In American schools, we don't typically emphasize memorization; we more often dismiss memorization as though it has no value. My history teachers never asked us to memorize the dates on which major events occurred. My chemistry teachers didn't ask us to memorize the chemical elements in the Periodic Table. This always confused my dad. He once asked me, "We think of American students as creative. But without a strong base of knowledge, how can you be creative?" He applied his economics terms to learning and studying: "Without sufficient stocks, how can flows be generated?"

Learning new information and reviewing the old through practice is the first rule in the Confucian tradition. Study in Chinese, called *xue xi*, is composed of two parts: *xue* means learning, and *xi* means practice. The opening sentence of Confucius' *Analects* is "Learning and practicing, shouldn't one be happy?"

In Fu Xue Elementary School, the principal said that a student's ability to memorize is best before age twelve. "Memorization and learning by heart is the best method. This is the best time to lay the foundation for a student's future learning. Understanding analytical abilities is not the priority."

"What they should memorize?" I asked.

The principal responded, "Confucius' *Analects*, collections of ancient essays, and the English edition of the Bible. If they can memorize these three whole books, they have a solid foundation, combining the Eastern and Western cultures."

"Why do students need to memorize so many classics?" I asked.

"There are four reasons: the first one, when students are young, their brains are just like blank paper. They have a huge capacity to store information. Second, memorizing classics loudly by heart helps train them to be inspirational. Third, memorizing, but not fully understanding, follows children's nature, it does not destroy their nature. When they grow up, they can select and modify to create from these classics. I don't recommend students read a lot of 'fast food' books. These books are not time tested; they preoccupy a lot of space in the brain, even destroying their nature. Fourth, before the age of thirteen, the essence of education should offer students a moral standard, and only these time-tested classics can serve this purpose. We don't require them to fully understand these classics; for as they grow up, they gain life experience, and will gradually understand more. And they may need guidance from teachers. But these classics will accompany them throughout their whole lives and help them in the different stages of their lives. They benefit from these classics. From these classics, they can broaden, deepen, and extend their knowledge. This is just like a tree with a deep root—an abundance of leaves and fruits grow."

Ren zhi chu, xing ben shan.
Xing xiang jin, xi xiang yuan.
Gou bu jiao, xing nai qian.
Jiao zhi dao, gui yi zhuan.

Xi meng mu, ze lin chu.
Zi bu xue, duan ji zhu.
Dou yan shan, you yi fang.
Jiao wu zi, ming ju yang.

Yang bu jiao, fu zhi guo.
Jiao bu yan, shi zhi duo.
Zi bu xue, fei suo yi.
You bi xue, lao he wei.

Everybody was born with a kind heart.

They share the same nature and temperament,

they grow in different environments,

and their differences of habits appear.

If one receives no strict education, the kind nature will be diverted.

The Dao of teaching and education is to focus, and keep

your attention on learning.

In the old times, Mencius's mother moved three times and finally settled in a neighborhood with a school.

In ancient times, Mencius escaped school. Mencius's mother cut the fabric she made to admonish her son.

In the old times, a person called Dou Yujun knew how to teach children.

He had five sons, and they all became prodigies.

If you give birth to a child, and you don't teach them, that's the parents' mistake.

If you teach them not strictly, that's the teacher's fault.

If you don't learn, that's the student's onus.

If you don't study hard when you are young, what can you achieve when you grow up?

These few sentences are the beginning of *San Zi Jing* ("Three Character Classic")—a household name in China. It is a classical primer of home education for preschool kids and was written in the thirteenth century. *San Zi Jing* distills and expresses the essentials of Confucianism in a way suitable for teaching young children. *San Zi Jing*, as a Confucian catechism, was written in couplets of three Chinese characters for easy memorization.

In the Chengdu Shuangliu International Airport, we came across a best seller in a small kiosk, *50 Memorization Techniques*. In this book, targeted for parents, the author claims that the source of wisdom comes from memorization. It says that the ability of memorization is of wisdom, but without the capability of memorization what wisdom do you have?

The author lists fifty techniques on memorization. A few examples are listed below:

Number 4: Build confidence for memorization.
Number 14: Read loudly for memorization.
Number 21: Have parents set up memorization goals for their children to guide them in a direction.
Number 27: Draw outlines for memorization.
Number 32: Transform texts into rhyme forms and stories for memorization.
Number 33: Make comparisons for memorization.
Number 43: Make a code for memorization.

Memorization is a quintessential technique for student learning. The following is a translation my father helped me with from my cousin's middle school Chinese textbook. This book is the mandatory text for all schools in Shandong Province. It presents "tips for memorization."

> Memorizing classics and important articles is a tradition in China's education. Before memorizing, one should read the article loudly, pronounce every word correctly, pause appropriately, and emphasize on the tones to create fluidity. At this point, one should roughly understand the article, not completely, but partially—understanding the subject of the article, the structure, the theme, and the critical phrases, words, and sentences. Based on this, one should read quickly, quietly, and repeatedly, resulting in the ability to read the article fluently. And now one is ready to memorize.
>
> Memorize paragraph by paragraph. In one paragraph, memorize layer by layer. In one layer, memorize sentence

> by sentence. Memorize one sentence, and continue with the next sentence, connecting the sentence into layers. Memorize one layer, and continue with the next layer, connecting the layers into paragraphs. Memorize one paragraph, and continue with the next paragraph, connecting the paragraphs into the article. One should progress steadily, and retain the paragraphs firmly. After one has memorized the whole article without referring to the book, focus on those critical sentences and phrases in which it is easy to make errors, until you have memorized to the point that the article can flow out of your mouth without any pause.
>
> Memorizing is not simply rote learning. When you attempt to remember the sentences, the layers, and the paragraphs, ponder them, understand them, and combine your mouth with your mind; memorization is a natural process, like water flowing out from a spring. Memorization is learned by the heart. One should make the paragraphs and sentences come from one's own mouth; the meaning comes from your heart. This is the essence of memorization. Translate the nutrients of the book into the blood and flesh of your body.

Memorization doesn't come easy. The practice faces criticism both in China and in the United States. But Bill Gates provided some justification for memorization when *New York Times* columnist Thomas Friedman met him. "When I asked Bill Gates about the supposed American education advantage—an education that stressed creativity, not rote learning—he was utterly dismissive. In his view, the people who think that the more rote-oriented learning systems of China and Japan can't turn out innovators who can compete with Americans are sadly mistaken. Said Gates, 'I never have met the guy who doesn't know how to multiply who created software . . . Who has the most creative video games in the world? Japan! I never met these 'rote people' . . . Some of my best software developers are Japanese. You need to understand things in order to invent beyond them."[1]

The concept of rote learning is a focus on memorization, learning things by constant repetition; as you repeat again and again, your ability to remember the information will become easier. Rote learning is also included in the method of "cramming." If there's a test tomorrow, it's not rare for students (myself included) to use the method of rote learning, but without the usage of repetition.

Rote learning is used to memorize the Periodic Table, multiplication tables, statutes in law, etc. This method has been heavily embedded into the culture of many countries across the world, including China, where rote learning has become the culture in every school. But in China, rote learning has also been translated to suggest the idea of "pushing" knowledge into a student. Memorizing facts creates a foundation of basic knowledge. From a solid foundation of basic knowledge, creativity is able to emerge.

My friend Annie admitted that she hated memorizing the Chinese way. "I'm majoring in an area with a heavy emphasis on math and science. I feel like if I don't major in something using those subjects, everything I will have learned will be wasted. Memorizing literature and history wasn't really my thing. But like everyone, I memorized hundreds of poems, literature pieces, short essays, facts, quotes, etc. After coming to the United States, none of it seemed like it was put to any use. In class we're not really required to memorize anything, aside from the things that we are going to be tested on. As for those famous speeches or the wording of historical documents, after we read it in class, we put it away. We aren't expected to know it inside and out. It almost surprises me. This is unheard of in China!

"The teachers here in the United States are so different," Annie added.

1 Thomas Friedman, *The World is Flat*, 352.

"In China, students basically learned the material by reading the textbooks and doing exercises. The teachers cleared the confusion and assigned homework questions to fill in the gaps, and then the students took the test covering the material. Teachers always found practice questions pertaining exactly to the holes that needed to be filled in. Class discussion was limited. Students didn't want to waste their own or the teachers' time in class discussion. But in the U.S., it seems as though teachers just teach and give out homework, then students take the test. But class discussions also take a lot of time."

Annie's perception about the two education systems highlighted the contrast in the classroom. Teachers in China carry a responsibility requiring them to produce students entirely devoid of any uncertainty when it comes to answering questions. But since the system in the United States focused on many other aspects, class time was often focused on helping students with the broad spectrum of the course.

Class discussions in China are kept to a minimum mostly because the teachers are presumed to know everything and the students are there just to listen and learn, not participate. In the United States we often have class discussions on various topics. These discussions are intended to provoke some insight in the students by allowing them to share their thoughts.

After a few weeks at Breck School, a private high school in Minnesota, some students asked Annie if she would like to join their study group. This is common in the United States, but not for students in China. Annie said, "I don't like study groups. There are so many distractions, and it's just an excuse for students to hang out together. The only way I can study is if I am in my room by myself, with the door closed, and everything else is silent. That's just what students in China are used to. Reflection, comprehension, and logical analysis need a quiet environment. Definitely, memorization requires no distractions at all."

I am part of a Google generation. With ever-advancing search technology, memorization seems outdated. Facts and figures are at my fingertips. With Google Map, geography seems redundant. We face a catch-22. Advancements in technology upgrade some of our learning skills, and also degenerate some of our learning techniques.

Du Runze, a University of Minnesota student from China, commented when he visited my house in the summer of 2011, "Google is great because you can Google a question from your homework, or a test, or a book, and you can find an answer or solution that is similar enough to yours. There are now tons of websites that list hundreds of textbooks with the solutions to questions in them. Things like these are absolutely restricted in China." Having access to answers in the Internet allows many students to continue their learning process outside of school with the certainty that they are doing their problems correctly. There are many other positive attributes associated with access to homework answers via Google, but Mr. Du's tone changed when looking at the negative side effects

Mr. Du said that finding the answers to test or homework questions online, as is common practice for some students in the U.S., corrupts the learning process. Relying on online answers reduces a student's efforts at hard work and problem solving, and will not help students in China to achieve high scores on the gaokao. Learning well entails hard work.

My parents had different learning experiences. My dad had a classmate when he was in college who bit into the hottest peppers to keep awake to study. To study English, he just used a dictionary. He memorized everything from the first to the last page. My mom had a classmate during medical school who ate the most pungent garlic to keep awake to study. He wanted to amass a huge amount of knowledge in traditional medicine by memorizing classical texts and prescriptions.

There are famous Chinese stories about ancient scholars studying in innovative ways, such as *Tou Xuan Liang* (Pulling the Head up by a Rope to the Log Supporting the Roof) and *Zhui Ci Gu* (Drill Oneself with an Auger). These are household stories in China.

The story of *Tou Xuan Liang* takes place in the Han dynasty (205 BC–AD 220), during the time that the scholar Sun Jin lived. When Sun Jin was young, he was very good at studying. He had a remarkable memory.

He read classics and said his books were his life. He always took notes as he read. Frequently he read and studied until late at night. But late at night, he often began to doze off on his desk. When he woke up, he always regretted the time he lost while sleeping. One day he looked up and noticed the horizontal logs that supported the roof. He had an epiphany. He found a rope and looped one end around the log, and the other end to his ponytail (Chinese men in ancient times wore their hair in a braided ponytail, never cutting their hair). From then on, when he dozed off, his head was pulled up by the rope, awakening him. This way, he stayed awake and alert, gaining additional time for studying. Year after year, Sun Jin obtained wide knowledge in classics, poetry, and history. He became a renowned scholar. In northern China, he became a tutor, and attracted many, many students who followed him to study.

The other story is about Su Qin, a politician and strategist during the Warring States Period. When he was young, people showed no respect toward him because of his low social status and lack of scholarship, which his family also despised him for. This hurt Su Qin a lot. He was determined to study. Like Sun Jin, he studied late into the night. When he felt sleepy, he would drill himself in the leg with an auger. The pain woke him up, and he would then go back to reading. He later became the prime minister for six countries.

Both *Tou Xuan Liang* and *Zhui Ci Gu* are oft-repeated stories in China. As a Chinese American, I don't have any particular sympathy for Sun Jin or Su Qin. But they are my dad's favorite tales. It seems he never saw them as boring—these stories are deeply implanted in my dad's cerebral cortex. I don't know how many times my dad has repeated them at our dining table.

In 1978 when my dad was preparing for his national entrance exam, China held its first National Science Conference. At that conference, the Chinese poet and scholar, Guo Moruo, delivered an inspirational speech. He encouraged the youth and students to make up for the time lost during the Cultural Revolution by referring to the spirit of *Tou Xuan Liang* and

Zhui Ci Gu. My father's generation heard that call. "Time is life. Time is speed. Time is strength." (*Guo Moruo*) and later "Time is money." (*Deng Xiaoping*) Both Guo Moruo and Deng Xiaoping encouraged the younger generation to make up the lost time due to the Cultural Revolution. That was the era and the spirit of my dad's generation. And those from that generation extended that call to their children. My parents' hunger for education, for reading material, and for knowledge has been placed on my shoulders.

While my dad was in college, China began to print more and more books. Whenever my dad had spare money, he went to bookstores to buy those books. His longing for books and knowledge carried him all the way to the United States.

My mom confirms that my dad has an obsession with books. With more than 20,000 books (including the collection of 10,000 books at the college he founded) in our household and in his office, my dad still continues to collect more. He collects classic Chinese essays. He collects contemporary Chinese writers' works. As for the William Faulkner, Ernest Hemingway, F. Scott Fitzgerald, and John Steinbeck series, my dad has them all, neatly stacked from the ground up. He has Plato's philosophies, William Shakespeare's plays, Lewis and Clark's journals, not to mention the stacks and stacks of every issue of the *Wall Street Journal*, *Time*, *National Geographic*, and the list continues. When anybody visiting China asks him what he wants them to bring him back from China, it is always books. His actions represent what people from his generation wanted the most, because for them inside every piece of paper is knowledge and power.

My dad collected many of those books for my brother and me. From his childhood, my father was deprived of the knowledge and wonder of books, and he doesn't want my brother or me to experience the same thing. Sitting at the dinner table, I often asked him if we had a certain book that I needed for a class in school. If we didn't already have a copy, I found it sitting on top of my desk the very next day, newly purchased from Barnes & Noble.

"Wang Qing was accepted by Stanford University!" This announcement thundered through my house early one morning when a phone call came from Jinan, the capital city of Shandong Province in China. The call was from Wang Qing's dad, my mom's high school classmate.

Six years ago, Nanyang Technology University started recruiting students from mainland China, and Wang Qing was a rising senior student in the elite Jinan Foreign Language School. In a very competitive selection, Wang Qing was chosen by Nanyang Technology University and offered a scholarship that included a tuition waiver and room and board. In return for this generous offer, every student in the program was required to work in Singapore for five years after graduation, otherwise a large sum of money (about $200,000) would have to be compensated back to Singapore. Wang Qing stayed at the top of the class.

Two years ago, Wang Qing was about to take his Graduate Record Examination (GRE) to advance his studies. He was a remarkable student, but he would have done poorly if he did not practice, because his English skills were very limited. He devoted all his available time to writing more than 200 essays so that he would be prepared for the writing section of the test. In order to receive feedback, he then translated the essays into Chinese and sent them to his father, who could only read Chinese. His father edited the Chinese versions of the essays after his busy days at work, and sent them back to Wang Qing with notes and comments. Wang Qing then translated his father's Chinese versions back into English. Both he and his father showed remarkably strong devotion to the betterment of his learning. They both sacrificed time and effort in the hope that it would make a difference in his performance on the test.

Wang Qing visited the United States in 2011. He liked the American universities very much. Although he was already accepted by Singapore Science and Technology University to continue his PhD studies, he also applied to ten American universities. He was accepted into the doctoral program at the University of Illinois at Urbana-Champaign and offered a scholarship. He was excited, but that was not the end of the story. Like other smart Chinese kids, Wang Qing had a lofty dream of studying at a top American school. So he applied to MIT and Stanford University.

Even before Stanford offered him an interview, Wang Qing's father sold one of the three houses the family owned in case Wang Qing was accepted, in order to pay the compensation for leaving Singapore without fulfilling the contracted services. As they anxiously awaited the acceptance of Stanford University or MIT, Wang Qing's parents invited two fortunetellers to their house. They rearranged their furniture in keeping with feng shui principles to balance the energies in their home to boost their son's chances of acceptance. When Wang Qing was in Jinan, his grandparents also helped, even though acceptance into an American university meant their only grandson would live thousands of miles away from them.

That Wang Qing was officially accepted by Stanford University was what prompted his father to call my mom with the big news. He told her, "We will support Wang Qing to go to Stanford University, no matter what it takes." He was prepared to put another house on the market to pay the compensation if necessary. He was ready to fly to Singapore to make the payment and explain to the professors and the university about his son's American dream.

Selling two houses to support their son to go to Stanford meant a sacrifice of their family's entire life savings. But Wang Qing's father was not sad about this; he was filled with pride and joy.

My mother has a colleague with a six-year-old son in a top elementary school in Beijing. When we had dinner together in Beijing, he held up his smart phone and said, "Look at this, Yanna, the homework is coming in through email."

Before we finished dinner, another message arrived, saying, "A quiz for mathematics will be in the first class tomorrow morning."

Every day after school the boy practices English for an hour, listens to tapes, and does some reciting. Though it may not be as effective as having an actual teacher with him, the child's mother watches over him every day for that hour. And the grandma helps, too.

A 2009 issue of *Time* magazine, was an article called, "5 Things We Can Learn from China." The second "thing" listed was that education matters. Referring to the urban Chinese students in particular who learn reading, math, and science, William McCahill, a former deputy chief of mission in the US embassy in Beijing, said, "Fundamentally, they are getting the basics right, particularly in math and science. We need to do the same. Their kids are often ahead of ours . . . The Chinese understand that there is no substitute for putting in the hours and doing the work. And more than anything else, the kids in China do lots of work."

The article cited a 2007 survey by the Department of Education, where 37 percent of tenth graders in the U.S. in 2002 spent more than ten hours on homework each week. According to a 2006 report by the Asia Society, Chinese students spent twice as many hours doing homework as their peers in the U.S. This article did not mention the fact that school hours in China are longer, they have classes on Saturdays, and many have half days on Sundays, in addition to their after-school review sessions and evening studies. The article talked about a seven-year-old student who, when he came home each day, was greeted by his grandparents who put him through his after-school paces. His mother said simply, "This is normal. All his classmates work like this after school." If it's not the grandparents watching over the child, it's usually the parents.

China's one-child family planning policy produced extra difficulties for the education of this generation. In 2008 China Central Television Station (CCTV) aired a Chinese soap opera (TV series) called *Elite School*. The TV series was about the education of students under the single-child policy in China in a very competitive environment. All students in the show were single children. A company called Yingkai Corporation wanted to invest in Beijing's Yuhui School to create a talented youth class. They selected top students from the ninth grade.

The first episode began on the day of the last interview. The parents and students were coming in to be interviewed for a class when a student was hit by a car and fell down on the roadside. Yingkai's human resources director was on his way to the school when he saw the accident. Though many parents and students witnessed this accident, none of them stopped to help or call for help. John Josh Wallen, who was a sponsor of the talented youth class, became upset to see that, when these parents and other students saw a threatened life, they all ignored it. For their children to get into the class, these people were willing to participate in any method to win, even if it meant disregarding someone's death.

If this dynamic were truly representative of China's 150 million students in this single-child generation, then China will have entered a time of complete darkness. The students in the TV show had become so competitive that they were willing to do anything to secure a position in a prestigious school or classroom. I find it impossible to imagine something similar happening in the U.S., say for instance if someone was going to an interview at Phillips Exeter Academy, or about to go take the SAT. Someone would at least call the police or an ambulance. How could China still hold its head up high, proud of its students when incidents like these dramatized events are occurring? Are students so desperate to achieve academic success that they're willing to risk everything and anyone?

The fictional youth talent class revealed a number of disturbing trends. Students skipped classes related to patriotic education. Students bullied other students who had strong social backgrounds. At thirteen years old, students still had their housemaids give them baths and showers, simply because they didn't even know how to bathe themselves. Once John Josh Wallen learned about these problems, he nullified the contract and pulled out his funding. But Zhang Yibai, the talented youth class supervisor, did not want to give up.

If the top colleges were to accept 98 percent of Yuhui School's graduates, who apparently don't know anything about their moral responsibilities to society, how could these people be expected to shoulder the future of China? These students were super intelligent, but without a moral compass of ethics and values, how could they succeed in a global economy?

Facing that challenge, Zhang Yibai then implemented the traditional education approach to the students. When the students came late to class, they were disciplined. When students bullied other students, they were disciplined. And every morning Zhang Yibai led the students to do morning exercises, and to run a few miles in the stadium. If students fell behind, they were disciplined. The disciplinary action was in the spirit of Mencius who said, "If Heaven (God) places responsibility on your shoulder, you must suffer from internal trauma, labor your bones and tendons, causing hunger, thin your flesh, inflict the pain of poverty, disorient your mind, and creating a will inside yourself, such that you are alert, strengthening your character and expanding your abilities."

This television show was fiction, but close to reality in China and mirrors numerous news reports in the last decade, according to my parents.

Many Chinese parents and Chinese teachers want to turn the "spoiled generation" into international competitors and global citizens. In Beijing, I heard one parent say, "Steel and iron are smelted this way." It means achievements come from hardship, suffering, discomfort, persistence, and perseverance.

CHAPTER 7
Devoted Gardeners

Chinese teachers enjoy a graceful name: "gardeners." This name was bestowed upon them by parents and students. Teachers talk not only of teaching students, but also nourishing them. Students are like delicate plants and flowers whom teachers must water, trim, and nuture.

"*Shi nian zhong shu, bai nian yu ren*" (It takes ten years to grow trees, it takes one hundred years to nurture students) stands at the entrance of Yali School in Changsha, Hunan Province. This is a widely embraced philosophy in Chinese education.

"Only two professions are absolutely and uniquely bound with strong moral obligations to their clients. One is the teaching profession; the other is medicine," said Dai Qun, the principal of Shanghai Jian Qing Experimental School.

The day we met Principal Dai Qun at his school, it was raining. The sky was dark and gloomy, but it seemed the students on the campus liked that even more. We entered the school during break time. The students were running wild among the inner area of the schools, occasionally splashing outside in the puddles of water collected on the sidewalk. The gate security man led us to Principal Dai Qun's office.

Principal Dai's office was typical of a high school principal's office, with two side walls of bookshelves filled with textbooks, government regulations and policies, and school documents. A teacher for over thirty years, he placed great emphasis on moral education.

"The students are very aware of moral education," Principal Dai said. "Our school builds on four moral concepts. The first includes high motivation, ambition, knowledge. When we talk to our students, we often ask them about their future goals. Hundreds of times I have heard students reply that they want to get into the top schools, not just nationally, but internationally. We don't enforce any set goals on students, but somehow they are driven to do well, and we want to help them keep their momentum."

Principal Dai described the second moral concept as strictness, discipline, and educational wisdom. "We want the students to understand the seriousness of education, thus we enforce simple rules: absolutely no tardiness to class, no harassment among the students and teachers, improper behavior is prohibited, etc."

The third moral concept is preciseness. "We have a very concise outline in class every day, and we want to make sure that the students are able to understand every single, small detail about a certain area."

Principal Dai said that the fourth and last moral idea is flexibility. "Students have to be flexible in their own minds. They must practice being flexible in order to handle complicated questions. Like my student mentioned, there is more than one way to solve a problem, and if you are stubborn about one way, then there will only be one solution, or maybe no solution. You have to exercise your mind and allow ideas to run free. If a student sees a problem, usually their mind is already glistening with ideas on how to solve it before they're even finished reading the problem. But this isn't just in our school; it's practiced among all students. We want our students to always excel in this concept, which can be practiced through flexibility."

Teachers understand their lifetime influence on their students. They pour their knowledge into their students at every opportunity. They know they must be their students' role models. Teachers influence their students in many different ways.

Deng Yan, a junior student from Loudi First School, had a Chinese teacher by the name of Xie Benma. Mr. Xie was a diligent and dedicated teacher. He believed that local air and water best nourished a student. Students were most impressed by his approach using stories of the People's Republic of China's founding father, Mao Zedong, to motivate students to study hard.

Mao Zedong was born in Shaoshan, Hunan Province. Shaoshan is just a two-hour drive from Loudi First School. During a lecture on "Snow," a famous poem written by Mao Zedong in 1936, Mr. Xie poured out his passion to his beloved students, describing the beauty of the content within the lines—the description of the swirling snow. Mr. Xie then connected the poem with China's history: the extravagant dynasties, the first emperor's Qin dynasty (221–205 BC), Han Wudi's Han dynasty (202 BC–AD 220), Tang Taizong's Tang dynasty (AD 618–907), and Song Taizu's Song dynasty (AD 960–1276).

He continued Mao Zedong's story: In 1918 Mao Zedong came to Beijing University as a library assistant. With volumes of books surrounding him, Mao Zedong began reading about the American Revolution, the French Revolution, Western philosophy—including Karl Marx and Friedrich Engels—and the history of Russia. He was absorbed by the ocean of knowledge. His appetite for reading books never decreased from that time forth. From 1949 to 1966, Mao Zedong checked out 5,000 books from the Beijing Library. His essays and speeches on the Chinese Revolution were filled with inspiration for the generations to come. Mao Zedong said, "I can live a day without eating, I can live a day without sleeping, but I cannot live a day without reading."

Deng Yan said, "Mr. Xie repeats this to us very often. We know that Mr. Xie is using Mao Zedong's words to motivate us to study hard allow us to realize the true importance of learning. Though sometimes his constantly repeating can be excessive, it does show us the true meaning of learning."

Another of Mr. Xie's lectures was on "Changsha," which was written by Mao Zedong in 1925 and expresses his high ideals. He asks the boundless universe, "Who will master the rise and fall of nature?" (*Wen cang mang da di, shui zhu chen fu.*) "This is a moment for our youth, abundant energy and unlimited motivation" (*Qia tong xue shao nian, feng hua zheng mao*).

My dad told me, "Although many people don't agree with Mao Zedong's theory, practices, and revolutionary ideas in China, most people agree that 'Snow' and 'Changsha' are some of the most beautiful and inspirational poems ever written."

In one of Mr. Xie's lectures he directed his students' attention to Ju Zi Zhou in the Xiang River, which is located across Changsha city on a resort island in the river. He specifically pointed out the years of 1915–18, when Mao Zedong studied in Changsha during one of the most turbulent times in China's history. During this period, Mao Zedong amassed a huge amount of knowledge about Chinese history and literature. In Changsha Normal College, Mao spent all his evenings and breaks just reading. This prepared him to be a revolutionary with effective writing skills.

Mr. Xie continued, "During the most difficult time of Japan's invasion of China, Mao Zedong spent his nights writing 'On Protracted Wars,' a document that guided China to win the war with Japan. Also during that time, working in Yan'an's caves with only an oil lantern, Mao Zedong completed his two famous essays of philosophy, 'On Contradiction' and 'On Practice.'"

Deng Yan explained, "Mr. Xie tries in every way to drive us toward learning whether it's motivating us with inspiring quotes or expressing anecdotes centered around the theme of knowledge."

When we visited Beijing Fifth High School, we met with a graduate of the school, Lin Lin, who was now a college student at the arts school neighboring her old high school. She was able to connect us with her English teacher, Ms. Chen Haiyan. Apparently the senior classes had just got out, a week after the gaokao. When we entered the gates I noticed a different feel to the school. The building was like any other—white brick walls that stood four stories high. But as we entered the building, there was a large glass board with a large chart drawn on it. There were columns with items like "bathroom, classroom, trash," etc., labeled, and rows with class numbers and grades. Inside each intersection of the row and column was a box. Most boxes had red star or flag stickers, while a few did not. At the bottom was a tallied score up to 10. Only one of the groups had a 10, while all the others had grades in the 9 range, and none below.

Lin Lin explained that all classes had a week in which they were assigned cleaning duty along with an area in which they are always in charge of cleaning up, including the bathrooms and hallways. The scoreboard shows how well the classes are doing. "In a way it is a small, fun competition, but it also makes the students take responsibility for their own actions by seeing on the chart whether their chores have been done."

As we went up the first flight of stairs along an outside wall, I could see outside the glassless windows a group of boys were playing basketball in the courtyard. Seeing the students enjoy their afternoon in the free outdoors offered a dynamic contrast between the students in the school and the students outside through my viewpoint.

As we progressed to the third level, we met Ms. Chen, the English teacher. After introductions and greetings, she took us on a small tour around the school building, including the fourth level. She remarked that the rest of the building was pretty much the same. There is just one hallway per level, and each hallway had a few classrooms on each side. Between classrooms were poems, duplets (two lines), and literature written by the students in the most beautiful calligraphy. As I walked with them in the hallway, some of the writings were explained to me.

> *Happiness cannot be ranked, but success can. (Calligraphy by Long Guo)*
>
> *The moment you feel too late is the right time to start. (Calligraphy by Li Huangrui)*
>
> *If you complain for missing the twilight in the morning,*

then you will miss the starlight all over the sky. (Calligraphy by Zhao Zhongyi)

If you nap this moment, then you make dreams; if you study this moment, then you fulfill dreams. (Calligraphy by Li Jing)

A thousand miles cannot be reached without the first step; an ocean cannot be made without the first drop. (Calligraphy by Zhang Shen)

The meaning becomes obvious by reading a hundred times. (Calligraphy by Kong Lingwan)

After a brief description of the school's history, we decided to take a seat in one of the classrooms to continue our discussion.

In the U.S., many schools have a good system of helping students who fall behind the rest of the class, whether it is with the help of the teachers, the principal, or counselors. But some schools do not. I wondered how Chinese schools handled such students.

I asked, "Do you pay more attention to students who are at the top or at the bottom of the rankings?"

Ms. Chen answered, "Both. Our school has a system where there are about nine or ten classes per grade, and the classrooms are split by rankings. We try to get the lower classes to be better, and the higher classes to be even better. There will not ever be a point where everyone in the school will be on the same intelligence scale, but we try to do the best we can to help every student be better."

"Do you love your job, Ms. Chen?"

"More than anything."

"And why is that? Why are teachers in China so enthusiastic about their teaching?"

"Because being a teacher is the most rewarding job of all. It is as though you raise kids for three years and watch them grow day by day. It is both thrilling and exciting—who could ask for a better job?"

I asked, "How you can make your students more effective in learning English?"

"We have foreign teachers for improving their conversational English. I require and motivate my students to recite every text in *New Concept English* to train their hard skills in reading and writing. After they memorize those 100 pieces of text in the second volume of *New Concept English*, their English level is improved significantly. There are no shortcuts for learning a foreign language," said Ms. Chen.

From what I can tell, something that teachers in the United States seem to lack compared to China is performance pressure among peers. Teachers in China are expected to perform the best. Being humble is their character, a Confucian tradition, but no one wants to admit that the teacher in the next classroom might threaten to beat them at the next midterm test. The tension for Chinese teachers is not just the hope that they will do well, but also that their students will do well. If a teacher wants to look good in front of parents and students, they have to do well in their class, and their students will have to do well academically.

In China, the tension between teachers and parents can sometimes be intense. Teachers are sometimes blamed for bad performance by parents who see that their children are slipping in class especially if they know how hard their children have been working. But in reality, most agree that poor performance is the student's fault. Teachers will do all that they can to help a poorly performing student. Teachers that teach the top classes have more pressure compared to the teachers in the lower classes, not necessarily from each other, but often from parents and principals.

"How are the teachers affected by their students' performance?" I asked Ms. Chen.

"There is one teacher per two classes for each subject. The pressure between the teachers is not enormous, but it is still present. We have rankings for all classes in school. If a class is ranked number one, but then drops to number two, the principal calls the teacher to his office and tells the teacher that he or she has to do better next time. The principal has a big job in the school, not just keeping order in the school, but also making sure that the teachers do not slack off. If the teachers slack off, then the students will slack off, and the worst thing is to bring in the parents when there is trouble."

At the end of the hallway on the third floor of the building, I saw multiple panels and display boards with student names listed by their academic performance in recent tests. One display board was for the junior-high-school class. The top twenty students in the humanities focus were listed and congratulated on the upper portion of the red board (red indicates lucky or happy things in Chinese culture). On the lower portion of this display board were the highest achievers for individual courses, such as Chinese, mathematics, English, history, geography, and politics. Following the students' names were their total points and the points for individual classes. At the bottom of the display board was this advice for students: *The only failure in the world is to give up easily and lack motivation. Nothing is more important in the world than perseverance.* In China, listing how each student performs is quite public—whether the performance is good or bad. In the U.S., we might view this same practice as a violation of personal privacy.

"What types of help do teachers offer students?" I asked Ms. Chen.

"We as teachers are obligated to help students the best way we can. For example, for each paper the student writes, we will call the student in for a one-on-one conference to discuss it. We do this to help the student and also for the reputation of our school. The student's future relies much on how well the teacher takes the students' academics seriously. A poor teacher leads to a poor student. We don't have poor students. We only have poor teachers," Ms. Chen asserted.

Ms. Chen continued to remark, teachers admitted that being judgmental is not the best way to view the students, and they try to refrain from that. But being judged does not mean treating the students differently; they want to help the students the best they can. Nor did they do this for the sake of the school's reputation; they did this because when the students grow up to be adults and look back on their life, the teachers want them to remember where they built their childhood, the place that brought them to wherever they ended up in the future. Teachers want to make an imprint in each student's mind so that they have a positive association with of the school.

Teachers in China do not appear to be relaxed. An English teacher at the Affiliated School to Shanxi Normal University, He Li Na, said, "The new education system which emphasizes creativity and independent thinking always creates new problems and questions for students. Students have to work hard on these new problems, making learning harder than just memorizing facts and accumulating knowledge . This transformation is not easy for everybody. It actually appears to be harder for students to adapt to the new educational system, versus using the old one. The traditional system was a top down system. Teachers had the authority. Everything the teacher said was considered true, and they spread their knowledge among the students. Teachers and students were clearly on two different levels, and teachers could not be challenged. The students who accumulated the most knowledge were the best of the best. But in the new system, the situation is reversed. For students' creativity to prevail, they must challenge authority. They must doubt their authorities in their search for the truth."

In both the traditional system and this new exploration, teachers' role in transforming students is extraordinarily significant. Zhang Yong was a student in Beijing University who came from a small town in Shandong Province. The sky is gray for most high-school seniors in China due to the pressure of the gaokao. But Zhang Yong thought that the sky was black for him. He lived in a town with an average income of RMB 260 per month (US $40) in 2005. For him and his classmates, a good college was the only choice for them to get out of the poverty trap. His dream was to be accepted into Beijing University. After being accepted into Beijing

University his dream became a reality. He expressed deep gratitude to his high school teacher, Yang Xiaofeng, thanking him for bringing him the success assured in his future.

Looking back at his experience, he recalled a memory that sculpted the kind of person he had become. During his senior year in high school, the school was still conducting review classes during winter break. Several of his older friends were coming back from their colleges for winter break.

"They invited me to a party," he said. "I was reluctant to go. If didn't go, I would disappoint my friends, but if I did go, I would miss the review class."

At that point, one of his friends told him, "You're number one in your class! It doesn't matter if you miss one review session!"

So he went to the party, and later expressed that it was a joyful night.

"On the following day, I carried my schoolbag back to school. When I stepped into the classroom, I found that my desk and my chair had disappeared. I asked a classmate what had happened. He said that Mr. Yang had removed the chair. I was confused. I asked Mr. Yang why he removed my chair. He replied, 'Why did you skip class?' I told him I went to a student's party. Mr. Yang then asked me, 'Is this your excuse?' I told him that I was always number one in the class for the past three years; didn't he forgive me for missing that one class? He replied, 'Number one in your class? What does that mean? Does that give you the privilege to skip class? Being number one is your responsibility. You must be a role model for other students.' Mr. Yang's words really shocked me. It shook me on the inside, and made me realize my arrogance. For the first time, I felt heaviness on my shoulders for being number one."

Zhang Yong explained his realization. "Number one was not an honor. It wasn't a privilege. It was a responsibility. That revelation led me to my dream school, Beijing University. When I received the acceptance letter, my burden was relieved. Mr. Yang's moral guidance changed me. It transformed me."

As Mr. Yang said, being number one comes with responsibility. Being number one also entails a moral obligation. This case isn't rare in China. The teachers care about their students; they consider every aspect of their students' lives and apply their own devotion to their achievement and success.

When students are absent from class in the U.S., teachers may wonder why, but they don't appear to care nearly as much as Chinese teachers do, or confront their students as often when they are absent. The implication is: "This is your life and your decision either way, whether you succeed or fail."

But Mr. Yang is more typical of teachers in China, who express to their students the importance of living up to their potential, and the importance of knowing what their priorities are.

A University of Minnesota student attending a party hosted by my family told me, "It's so different in the United States. Once I had to read a work by some poet, and I read every single sentence like they were all true. Then in class, the teacher and students began critiquing the writing. At one point my professor took the piece of literature, threw it on the ground, and stomped on it. You'd never see that in China. Seeing that caused almost a feeling of angst in me—mixed with relief, too."

The student remembered a professor who was recruited from China a few years ago. Professor Zhang upheld his Chinese culture and ways of teaching, including these rules: be on time, no talking in class, no cell phone use, no leaving early (if anyone did, he embarrassed the person in class). Once when a student got up to leave a few minutes early, Professor Zhang stopped teaching and asked the student where he was going. Everyone in the lecture hall turned to look at the student.

When the student replied, "None of your business," Professor Zhang ranted for several minutes, questioning the student. At last the student sat back down, his face bright red, and fully embarrassed.

In the U.S., teachers and professors rarely interrupt when a student is talking, even if the remarks are irrelevant and not in the spirit of inquiry. We students can feel as though the entire class is a waste of time if we are forced to listen to someone ramble on about nothing, rather than trying to learn something. In China, when trying to learn certain subjects, students really hang on to their inquiry, listening to their teacher and asking further questions until they fully understand the topic inside and out.

My friend Annie spent the first year of high school in Ren Da Fu Zhong in Beijing, and then two years at Breck School in Minneapolis. She was a top student in both schools. I asked her to compare teachers in China and the United States.

As we discussed the differences, she seemed particularly frustrated with certain methods of teaching in the United States. "The problem is that teachers never ask their students to repeat! Repeat! Repeat! Repeat! They are going in one direction—forward. They don't intentionally let students stop and reflect on how new information connects with previous learning. That is the only way the students retain knowledge! After students learn material in China, the teachers will go back to the old material to make connections with the new material. This way, the students will not only be learning their new material, but they will also review the old material and be able to make the connection between things."

Her comment sounded so familiar to me. *Wen gu er zhi xin* (Review the old, understand the new) is a phrase from Confucius that my dad always quotes to me at our dining table.

Annie thought the problems assigned for homework are much harder in China than in the United States. "For example, in high school geometry, my mathematics teacher in Ren Da Fu Zhong always constructed a few complicated problems. Sometimes we would be asked questions such as, connect the points where the pyramid plane is tangent to the ball located at the center of the pyramid. Then the teacher would ask us to prove some properties of a right triangle or rectangle, or other geometrical shapes. This kind of problem attempts to disorient you at first. You must have a clear strategy to prove it. There are many steps from the assumptions to the conclusion. The proof process might need a number of basic theorems as tools. For these problems, sometimes you feel very deceived, and sometimes you are stuck for hours or days."

Annie felt that the problems assigned for homework in the United States were very simple and straightforward. "I never see problems needing more than two basic theorems to prove them."

Bi Junhua was one of the Chinese teachers at Huantai Second High School. She had an extremely warm personality, and she seemed very close and caring toward the students. She said her role in the school was like that of every other faculty member. "We teach the students. That's our job. But one other important job for a teacher is to help raise students into young adulthood. Students' high school years are the most important part of their lives for learning. Their minds are developing, and they need an environment that will support that development."

"The teachers here are like our own parents," Su Rui chimed in. He was a pudgy young lad who smiled as he told a story. "I remember one winter, it was a Sunday night, and it was quite late at night when a blizzard hit. The courtyards were packed with snow. We students watched as all the teachers went outside and began shoveling the courtyard. They were making sure we could get to class safely in the morning. Just looking at them, it sort of touched our hearts, thinking about what they were doing for us."

Wang Jinghan, another student, continued Su Rui's thought. "The teachers really encourage us to perform better. Since we reside here, our parents cannot see us often, so the teachers feel as if they need to be our secondary parents."

Ms. Bi remarked, "We teachers live on campus. We want to be accessible to the students twenty-four hours a day, seven days a week, and we act also as part-time security guards for them. We try to be role models. In the morning, when we wake up, we meet the students in the courtyard, and do our daily exercise routine together, *guang bo ti cao*.[1] We're part of the school, we're part of the students' families, and we're expected to participate in everything the students participate in."

Continuing some small talk, Su Rui accidentally knocked over his

---

1 Radio Exercise, so called because the moves are directed to students over large speakers. This practice is common all across China, consisting of stretches and warm-up exercises, usually completed in the mornings, during class breaks, or at school assemblies. It includes things from eye massages to high kicks and air punches.

books, and out floated a packet of formulas (similar to what one might see in an SAT math section, except more complicated), which landed in front of my feet. I picked up the packet, and asked Su Rui if this was his test-reference sheet. He laughed and said, "If we were allowed to use this packet on the test, then everyone would get a 100 percent on the test!"

I asked, "How do you use the formulas? Every day in class?"

He replied, "Before class we have warm-up exercises, and we have to use the formulas we memorized to compute the answers."

These so-called warm-up questions weren't your normal, "plug it into the formula" problems. In order to compute the answers, students were expected to use not just one formula, but from five to ten formulas in order to compute the answer. And the teacher expected the students to always find the answer no matter how many turns and detours there were.

"But why would the teacher require students to do this? Couldn't you just look up the formula later?"

Su Rui corrected me, "When we use the formulas in real world applications, the answers won't be derived from one formula, but from many. Our teachers want us to train to the point where we will have the formulas continuously rolling in our minds, so that when we see a problem, we'll immediately know how to execute the problem."

This corresponded to Annie's observation about Chinese teaching. I thought of my own science class, when we learned the formula to compute kinetic energy. We had two short pages of homework that night, consisting of plugging in the mass and the velocity to find the kinetic energy. When it came to the second page of homework, it was the same problem with a twist: we were given the kinetic energy and mass, and we had to find the velocity. As for our science final exam, the extra credit problem consisted of using a formula we had learned earlier in the year, and then using the kinetic energy formula (that's two formulas). Only four students of my class of thirty-one had answered it correctly.

Su Rui continued, "The teachers build much of their curriculum around the students. They assign their homework from not just textbooks, but also from their own notebooks. They look at the level, progress, and difficulty the students are at and work with that." They do not have class rankings. Everyone lives so close together, it is easy to know who is on the top and who is at the bottom. "You can tell by the type of questions students ask, or how they answer the questions, how much they have studied the previous night."

The fact that parents in China have high expectations is partially what drives their children to excel. But expectations don't only come from parents. Teacher Bi Junhua tells students to remember the school motto, "Always be *your* number one!"

She went on to explain that it is not possible for everyone to be number one, but it is 100 percent possible to be "your" number one. "Every student has his/her potential to be number one. Teachers need to tap that potential." Her approach makes students feel more hopeful and motivated.

The teachers repeat this motto in class and it is also written on the side of their math building. "It is just there to remind us that we should never give up being the best that we can be—and sometimes, it is that which matters," said Su Rui.

Just as we were turning a corner, Ms. Bi saw one of her students walking toward us and called her over. She had just finished her math class, and we asked her what they were studying. She described proving a trigonometry proposition in class, and the teacher showed three ways to prove each problem. Then the teacher explained five very common mistakes that students often make, and then talked about the concept of the necessity of assumptions for which the theorem holds true (if you dropped an assumption, then the proposition wouldn't be provable). The student was in a rush to go to her history class and pardoned herself.

I was quite astounded by her explanation of the curriculum in her class. Usually, in my classes, when we can find one proof to a theorem, that's good enough. The idea of pointing out students' common mistakes was something I'd not seen in an American classroom. One reason may be because teachers don't actually grade the students' homework very often anymore. It's more often a "if you did it, you get credit" situation. And if students have questions about a specific problem, they can ask the teacher later. That's how it usually works in the public schools where I live.

A *Time* magazine 2010 Annual National Service Issue topic addressed "How to Recruit Better Teachers." The article referred to hundreds of programs that have appeared around the U.S. to encourage people to leave jobs practicing law, brokering real estate, or selling furniture to start teaching. "In Memphis, for example, you can be sitting at a bank desk, poring over quarterly reports in May and be teaching algebra by August."[2] The article pointed out that in the next decade, our nation will need 2.2 million teachers due to the retiring of current teachers and increasing enrollment of students. Currently programs such as Teach for America (TFA) and the New Teacher Project (TNTP) are providing training. But the programs educate adults for only a few weeks and then send them to schools to teach. This hardly seems adequate. "According to a forthcoming McKinsey & Co. study, just 23 percent of new teachers in the U.S. come from the top third of their college classes; 47 percent come from the bottom third. In other words, we hire lots of our lowest performers to teach, and then we scream when our kids don't excel," reads the article.

We complain that students across the nation are falling beneath the minimum standards, yet we are apparently willing to accept people who are not qualified as teachers. This certainly suggests that we Americans are setting ourselves up for continuing failure.

There is a Chinese phrase that refers to teachers who are not adequate in their role. That is, *Wu ren zi ti*, which means, "Those who are not qualified are corrupting the students' future." Teachers matter. Chinese parents understand this and respect teachers. Many Chinese proverbs are in praise of teachers, addressing them with adulating tones and remarks.

While flipping through the pages of a 2008 issue of *National Geographic* called "China, Inside the Dragon," I wasn't shocked to see

2 "How to Recruit Better Teachers" by John Cloud, *Time*. Sept. 23, 2010.

the phrase, "A bad grade brought a clampdown at home." A story about a student in China described a school day that ended with the teacher expressing the moral: "Don't feel bad if you lost this time . . . It just means you must work even harder. You shouldn't let yourself relax just because you lost." Chinese parents and teachers believe that if you lost this time, you better get back up on your feet as soon as you can and win the next time. No parent or teacher wants his or her child to lose, even when there can only be one winner. Though it might seem similar to the moralemany American parents hold, the point is that every Chinese parent wants their child to be in the number one position.

A study conducted by Harvard professors Raj Chetty and John N. Friedman and Columbia professor Jonah E. Rockoff[3] showed that the average effect of one teacher on a single student may be modest. However, all else being equal, a student with one excellent teacher for one year between fourth and eighth grade will earn an additional $4,600 during their career, as opposed to a student of similar demographics who had an average teacher. The same student with the excellent teacher for that one year would be 0.5 percent more likely to attend college. The authors of the article assert that having better teachers has an exponential increase in the potential overall income of the students in class over their lifetimes. The difference can be enormous. Although this study only addresses economic returns, it firmly demonstrates that teachers make a huge difference to a student's life. The role of a teacher is indeed like that of a gardener, but in China, these gardeners are truly devoted.

3 "The Long Term Impact of Teachers: Teacher Value-Added and Student Outcomes in Adulthood" by Raj Chetty, John N. Friedman, and Jonah E. Rockoff, *National Economic Bureau,* Working Paper 17699, January 2012.

CHAPTER 8
Role Models

"In China today, Bill Gates is Britney Spears. In America today, Britney Spears is Britney Spears—and that is our problem," observed Thomas Friedman in 2005, in his book, *The World Is Flat*. Friedman refers to China as a "model culture." They follow models. They live with models. These models are not just symbols; they are calls for followers.

For the female students from my parents' generation who grew up in the 1970s and 1980s, Marie Curie was a role model. Her dedication to science encouraged millions of Chinese students. Her stories was written into textbooks again and again. Both textbooks for Chinese Language School and Chinese Class at my school contain biographies of Madame Marie Curie. Her biographies were some of the most widely read books in China in the 1980s. Reading about Curie made people want to be scientists; they made people want to achieve something.

For the aspiring male students of my parents' generation in China, an article called "Goldbach Conjecture" that appeared in early 1978 provided a role model. Chen Jingrun, the Chinese mathematician who advanced the proof of the Goldbach Conjecture[1] became a role model for Chinese students who embraced a new passion. They actively pursued mathematics as a profession. My father has often commented how "unbelievable" it seemed that a news report influenced the choices of a whole generation of students.

---

1 One of the oldest unsolved problems in number theory, which states that every even integer greater than 2 can be expressed as the sum of two primes.

Marie Curie and Chen Jingrun provided Chinese students with new role models for pursuing their dreams. In the new century, those lucky students who are accepted by Beijing University, Qinghua University, or those top schools in the United States and England become idols for China's high school juniors and seniors.

In 2000 a book called *Harvard Girl: Liu Yiting* became a best seller in China, selling millions of copies. Even after more than a decade, it remains on the best-seller list. This book made Harvard University a household name and Liu Yiting a role model for many high school students who were inspired to pursue an Ivy League education in the United States. The book tells the story about a girl from Sichuan Province who was accepted by Harvard in 1999. The book documents her studies in elementary school, middle school, and high school, but starts with the sacrifice of her mother.

Liu Yiting's mother, Liu Weihua, was an editor for a local magazine, and her values and choices are representative of millions of mothers in China. In July 1984, in her early thirties, she was accepted into Shanghai Opera University. Among all the applicants who participated in taking the entrance examination, she was ranked first place in the class, as well as being the only female student among the forty students accepted into the class. When she received the acceptance letter, she was very excited. She had experienced the trauma of the Cultural Revolution, lost the opportunity of advanced training, studies, and colleges, and finally was accepted by one of the most famous colleges in the country, in her beloved profession, the study of opera theory. More than that, she was thrilled to be a student of Yu Qiuyu, a famous professor of opera theories.

Liu Weihua had the opportunity to revive the pursuit of her passion. However, she decided to give up this glorious opportunity. Liu Weihua was a single mother. Her daughter, Liu Yiting, was four years old and in kindergarten. If she went to Shanghai to study, who would take care of Liu Yiting? And who would be responsible for Liu Yi Ting's education? Liu Weihua considered the option of bringing Liu Yiting to Shanghai for kindergarten so she could still attend Shanghai Opera University, but the cost was too exorbitant. Liu Weihua's monthly income was RMB 70. Kindergarten in Shanghai would cost her RMB 60 per month. So she sacrificed her own dream for the sake of her daughter.

With her mother's support, Liu Yiting did well academically and graduated from Shang Ye Chang Elementary School in 1993. During her six years of elementary school, she was able to sustain a position among the top three students. On all of her assignments and tests in mathematics, she always got perfect scores. She was guaranteed to get into Chengdu Seventh School, one of the most famous schools in Sichuan Province. But there was a policy change that year; acceptance into the Chengdu Seventh School was no longer determined just by academic performance but by a computerized randomization system. She would still have an opportunity to get into a top school, but she would have to pay RMB 25,000. For Liu Weihua, an editor who received a modest income—or for anyone in southwest China in the 1990s—it was an astronomical number.

Once Liu Yiting was guaranteed placement into one of the best middle schools, now she was on the fence. With the random placement technique, students had to wait for their assigned school, which could be a mediocre school even if he or she deserved much better. Liu Yiting and her mother didn't want to wait for what could be terrible news.

During this time, Chengdu Foreign Language School, one of the fourteen schools established by China's Ministry of Education, had become a hot and competitive school. In light of the randomization process, many of the best students chose to participate in a test for the chance of getting into that school. Six thousand students registered to take the test. The school only took 120 students, at an acceptance rate of 1.8 percent.

Liu Yiting decided to give it a try, following her mother's desires. After an intensive written test and many interviews, Liu Yiting was selected. Holding the acceptance letter, Liu Yiting's teacher said to Liu Weihua, "You know, this piece of paper is worth RMB 25,000." Liu Yiting's continuing academic achievements ultimately led to her admission to Harvard.

"Ivy League" became a buzzword in China as a result of the popularity of the story of Liu Yiting. Even her name became a household name. Harvard girl, Yale boy, Cambridge student, and Oxford student all became inspirational symbols and role models for Chinese students in the first decade of the twenty-first century. Now, Chinese students not only have goals and dreams to attend Beijing University or Qinghua University, but they also have dreams of these global brands. Chinese parents now expect their children to achieve what Liu Yiting achieved.

A casual review of news media revealed the names of students, including those zhuangyuan who became the darlings of China in recent years, trailed by acceptance into either Harvard University, Yale University or Princeton University.

I had a direct experience with this Chinese phenomenon the day my brother received his early-action acceptance letter to Harvard University. My parents were having a board meeting for the college they run that same night, and the business meeting turned into more of a celebration. That was a very happy moment for my parents.

Dr. Li Gu, a senior doctor working at my parents' college and affiliated clinics, said, "We hear about Harvard and Yale students all the time, but now I feel like there's one in my family! It's absolutely unbelievable!"

The celebration even extended across the sea. When my brother visited the village where my father was born, the whole town came to see him, gathering together to see the student from Harvard and later Yale University (for medical school). They looked at him as if he were a demigod. When my brother was introduced to family friends and classmates of my dad's in Beijing, he was praised with joy and excitement. Anywhere we went in China, England's Oxford University and Cambridge University, China's Beijing University and Qinghua University, and the Ivy League schools of the United States held a very prestigious position. In Shanghai, Beijing, Chengdu, Changsha, and Jinan, when I visited schools and interviewed students, my brother's Harvard and Yale credentials were my "green pass."

My friend Annie's mother told her she should apply to Harvard and

Princeton, but she warned her, "Don't just be in the denominator."

Annie explained the comment to me: When applying to colleges or schools, there is always some fraction out of a hundred—the nominator being the number of people accepted and the denominator being the number of people who applied. This fraction is the acceptance rate of the school. She had to be in the "nominator."

This type of strong ambition and expectation on behalf of a parent can happen in the U.S. or in China; but the reality is, in China it's more common. A large portion of China's population is still made up of farmers and industry workers whose income is not substantial. But even parents with a low income try to do everything they can for their children, not only to raise them, feed them, and nurture them, but also to focus intently on their education.

In the United States, parents are driven and care for their children like no other, but they don't all expect their children to be straight-A students or only get into Ivy League colleges.

At O'Hare International Airport in Chicago, as my father went to retrieve our tickets for our flight to Beijing, my brother and I sat at our gate. Devouring what would be my first of many McDonald's meals, I watched the groups of people who approached and sat in the empty chairs near us. Chubby little Chinese kids ran around the suitcases while their grandparents told them to stop, glancing over at the parents who sat reading Chinese magazines. A man lay down on the benches, stretched across four chairs with a newspaper draped over his face, while his shirt barely covered his large belly. After about a forty-five-minute wait, I looked up to see my dad walking toward us with an Asian woman who was talking to him. Knowing my dad, unless she was a friend of his, I figured he probably found someone in some unusual situation, and he was probably going to educate us about how we should learn from her remarkable story.

Her name was Ouyang Ruirui and she was on her way to Macao, China. She was thirty-one years old and planning to create a Macao conservatory with the help of financial aid from sponsors she hoped to find along the way. She had graduated from Oklahoma City University with a major in music. Since then, she'd been teaching piano to students in her area for a few years, and had decided to do something different with her life.

When Ouyang Ruirui mentioned that she gave piano lessons and majored in music, I thought about Lang Lang, the well-known Chinese pianist. Lang Lang's story is truly astounding. Lang Lang is not only a role model, but also a hero in China. My dad had the same thought and mentioned Lang Lang to her.

Ouyang responded, "Since I was little, I've been very familiar with famous musicians, especially Lang Lang. I dreamed to be like him. He grew up to be perhaps the most amazing pianist of our time. His childhood story was extremely touching, and the hardship he endured is heartbreaking. But the thing is, Lang Lang is a miracle. You cannot recreate a miracle—that is what makes it a miracle. There is only one Lang Lang, and there will only ever be one Lang Lang. He was beaten as a child, beaten into a prodigy. Many Asian parents believe that this is the way to raise a child, but it does not work. Lang Lang was an exception from what many presume is the way to create a prodigy child. The violent methods of his father may have worked on Lang Lang, but that does not mean it will work on anyone else.

"Piano is a livelihood," Ouyang Ruirui continued, "but for many Chinese students, piano is not their choice. It is their parents' choice. Parents choose, force, and coerce their children to study and practice piano." (Piano is the most popular instrument for Chinese students to practice, for kindergarteners, elementary schoolers, middle school students, and high school students.)

Pressures from parents can be absolutely terrifying. Lang Lang grew up subjected to his father's "extreme parenting." At one point when his father was angry with nine-year-old Lang Lang, he told the boy to kill himself, shoving a handful of pills in his face. The boy ran to the ledge of a building, and his father demanded that Lang Lang jump to his death. Lang Lang escaped the situation but refused to touch the piano for three months.

"Suicide rates of children and young adults in China have increased in the past few years, and it is often due to the pressure exerted from parents or teachers to have the child succeed," said Ouyang Ruirui, and she was right. China is the only country in which the suicide rate for women is greater than that of men,[2] a reverse ratio from the rest of the world. Approximately 13.9 people out of 100,000 commit suicide. Compared to other countries, China has a medium suicide rate but is still in the top few countries. The main reason for suicide, in general, is that the victims feel as if there is no escape from their bad situation or no other choice. Could it be possible that Chinese students feel pressured to an extent where they feel as if there is no escape?

Ouyang Ruirui went on, "As a miracle, Lang Lang can't be imitated, although many parents see him as the role model for their children. Many students play well in China. They receive all kinds of awards. But they are not Lang Lang. China's model culture hurts many parents."

During my interviews with high school students, I kept hearing that their top dreams were to go to the best college, such as Qinghua University or Beijing University, or to study abroad at an Ivy League School. They referred to alumni or somebody they knew and wanted to emulate. A role model is somewhere around them, supporting their dreams to succeed in this way. An elite education is a predominant priority. The top school graduates have the perception that they are entering the "noble class," the "elite class." The perception includes the unsubstantiated suggestion that there are plenty of openings in top government-service posts, in Fortune 500 companies, in top multinationals waiting for these students, and they are the luckiest of the lucky.

Seven American presidents come from Harvard University. Five

---

2 "Women and Suicide in Rural China," World Health Organization. http://nitawriter.wordpress.com/2007/05/11/suicide-rates-of-the-world/.

presidents come from Yale. Four of the nine Standing Committee members of Politico Bureau of China's Communist Party are from Qinghua University. Seventy-nine alumni of Beijing University were billionaires in 2011. "This is an era of meritocracy," a parent I met in Beijing told me.

"Beijing University tops the university list of billionaires in three consecutive years," exclaimed Beijing University's president Zhou Qiren, who gave a speech to the Beijing University Entrepreneur club on June 27, 2011.[3] ""Students and their parents express a hope and expectation that once they have been accepted into this elite club, opportunities will be sliding into the palms of their hands by the hundreds, maybe even the thousands. Gold will be the equivalent of water, running from the faucets, collecting in their bathtubs, and amounting to millions and billions of dollars. The promise of wealth and prosperity is foremost in their minds," a Beijing parent commented. Wealth, power, and fame have become the new magnetism of China's elite schools: even the president of the top university in China couldn't resist this illusion. Celebrities and moguls are crowned in these top universities. They have become the new role modles in China's transformative time where "getting rich is glorious".

3 *Beijing University Entrepreneur Clubs*, June 27 2011. http://finance.gucheng.com/201106/1247568.shtml.

CHAPTER 9
A Scholarly Icon

Upon landing at Beijing Capital International Airport in June 2011 I saw a billboard that quoted Confucius: "That friends should come to one from afar, is this not after all delightful?" This is the first encounter with China that greets international arrivals in the new terminal. As we waited in line for customs clearing, I saw ten huge banners hanging from the airport ceiling, proclaiming a welcome to international travelers:

> *You peng zi yuan fang lai, bu yi le hu! (Chinese)*
> *Welcome my friends! (English)*
> *Herzlich willkommen bei Freunden! (German)*
> *Soyez les bienvenus! (French)*
> *Calurosos Bienvenidos! (Italian)*

This phrase is the opening sentence in Confucius' *Analects*. At the airport, it is translated in the above languages, and also in Russian, Korean, and Japanese.

On August 8, 2008, China chose the day with the luckiest numbers to open the 28th Olympics Opening Ceremony. Huge scrolls larger than football fields were unraveled on the grounds of the stadium to greet the 90,000 attendees from 205 countries, 16,000 athletes, eighty countries' heads of state, and a television audience of four billion people around the globe watching the ceremony. A huge Chinese character appeared, *he*, which means harmony, the central concept in Confucian philosophy. The arena was filled with the beats of 2,008 percussive instruments and the same welcoming chant in Chinese: *You peng zi yuan fang lai, bu yi le hu!* The theme of Confucianism was deeply embedded throughout the entire opening ceremony.

During his life, Confucius traveled around the different kingdoms in China, expecting those kingdoms to implement his philosophies, but none did. So instead, he directed his teachings to his disciples and students. Some 2,500 years later, his dream is finally coming true. The Confucius Institute is an organization affiliated with the Ministry of Education of the People's Republic of China, which aims to promote Chinese culture and language, and supports Chinese teaching internationally.

China is moving toward another era of Confucius: that of global influence. A movement was founded in 2004 in Tashkent, Uzbekistan. The first Confucius Institute opened later that year in Seoul, South Korea. There are now 322 Confucius institutes plus 369 Confucius classrooms all around the world.

For other cultures to understand China, the first step may be to learn about Confucius. Roughly 2,500 years of Chinese civilization were built on his philosophies. His thinking and philosophy became the fundamental base for Chinese culture and education. The Confucius Institute feeds the strong, escalating appetite of the world's desire to understand this ancient civilization, along with learning about the Chinese language. The Confucius Institute has become a tool for China to demonstrate its "soft" power. Confucius is an icon, and plays a more significant role than powerful and wealthy corporations in society.

At Huantai Second High School Principal Gao cordially agreed with this idea, telling me, "The whole of Chinese education is based on the Confucian philosophy. If you want to understand China's education system, you must study Confucius."

From the time I was little, my dad recited Confucius' phrases and proverbs to my brother and me all the time; but, honestly, I never understood the meanings. He quoted sayings by Confucius naturally and frequently; it was natural and fluent for him. He had to explain the deeper truth about each proverb with a story, and he told me I would understand it eventually. He repeated this to me again and again!

According to Confucius, the goal of education is to cultivate oneself into a "gentleman." This means students must have proper and suitable behavior and cultivation, and the cultivation of character is accomplished through observation, learning, and reflection. Confucius encourages his students to search for knowledge and truth, and to be humble. In *Analects* Confucius said, "Among three men who are walking together (myself being one of them), there is always something I can learn. I can emulate the good in them and correct the flaws."

To be a good learner, study and reflection must interact. "Study without reflection is labor lost; reflection without study is dangerous." Learning is a process of observing subjects whether they are books, objects, or people, followed by reflection (serious thought and contemplation) that leads to revelation or self-change. Learning is a highly personal and individual activity. Real learning can awaken a person. Such learning can be achieved through teachers who have developed their own characters. As a teacher, Confucius tailored his methods to different students. Instead of structured classes or examinations, he suggested to each student what they should study, and then discussed it with them, and listened to them. He is said to have evaluated each student and encouraged their strengths and improved their weaknesses. Because of this individual attention, he sometimes answered the same question quite differently to two different students.

The curriculum of Confucius' teachings included music, ritual, the *poems,* literature, and history. Books did not hold a particularly prominent role in his teaching. His teaching style laid the foundation of traditional teaching in China. In Confucius' world, society starts with the individual, and one must first develop oneself to later develop one's family. The family serves as a model for the community, the community as a model for the state, the state as a model for the country, and the country as a model for the world. The educational process is first and foremost the responsibility of the individual, followed by the family, then the community, then the state, and then the country. Regarding relationships with others, the golden rule is, "Don't force another to do what you are not willing to do."

In order to learn more about Confucius, my uncle drove my brother, my dad, and me to Qufu, the hometown of Confucius, 100 miles away from my grandpa's home. My dad and my brother had visited Qufu several times. But this was my first pilgrimage to this culturally important and historical city that includes the Confucius temple, Confucius cemetery, and Confucius mansion.

When we arrived at the Confucius temple that summer of 2011, it was a whole different world for me. First off, it was probably ninety-some degrees. For twenty minutes or so, a young girl, Liu Junlan, pursued us, asking us to let her be our tour guide. She would not take no for an answer. When my dad finally agreed to allow her to guide us, she immediately noticed we were from the United States. When she heard me speak in English to my brother, she assumed that I might not learnChinese, especially the classical Chinese characters. She directed me to the signs with both Chinese and English so I could follow along.

Standing in front of Da Cheng Dian (The Hall of Great Accomplishment), we saw the highest honors awarded to Confucius by emperors throughout the various dynasties. All types of honors were bestowed upon Confucius and his descendants. Emperor Kangxi, one of the greatest emperors in China's history, awarded Confucius the title of *Wan Shi Shi Biao* (Role Model of a Thousand Generations). Emperor Guangxu named him *Si Wen Zai Zi* (Scholarship Is Right Here). Emperor Qianlong referred to Confucius as *Yu Tian Di Can* (Penetrating the Heaven and Earth).

Ms. Liu told us, "These statements put Confucius into the position of highest scholarship and greatest learning."

Confucius taught his son, Kong Li, *Bu xue shi, wu yi yan* (if you have not studied poems, you will have nothing to say) and *Bu xue li, Wu yi li* (a man cannot stand without practicing rituals). The descendants of Confucius were educated, and rituals were practiced in *Shi Li Tang* (Poem and Ritual Hall). Poems and rituals became defining characters of celebrated families in China's long history. A scholarly tradition in a family linage is a long-lasting legacy for Chinese families.

All the regal constructions in the Confucius Mansion and Confucius Temple were extraordinary. I found them only comparable to the Forbidden City in Beijing, where the Ming and Qing dynasty emperors resided. This area is the epicenter of Confucianism, and it radiates to Beijing, Shanghai, Changsha, and to schools and families everywhere in China, and to Korea, Japan, Singapore, Taiwan, and the United States.

Ms. Liu told us, "In 1985 a group of scientists from around the world including seventy-five Nobel Prize winners gathered in Paris, issuing a statement that, if we wanted to survive in the twenty-first century, we must look for wisdom in Confucius—one of the three greatest teachers in the world, along with Socrates and Jesus, who have ever lived. He is really a Chinese scholarly icon."

While visiting schools, I was able to witness students of any age memorizing and speaking Confucius' famous quotes, lines, stories, philosophical remarks, you name it. In my home, if my father did not quotie a line from Confucius at our dining table at least once a week, I would be surprised.

My father told me, "When I was in China, people in the village quoted a few lines from Confucius even if they didn't have any education. They were not showcasing their knowledge. It is just that Confucius' teachings are flowing in their blood. It is a miracle that we modern people still use his words in our daily communications, though the sayings were written 2,500 years ago."

I wonder why it is that in US classrooms, students barely even read things written by great writers such as Thoreau or Emerson. It seems to me that a superficial culture permeates our classrooms. If I were to ask a student in the U.S. to recite on the spot a philosophical quotation or piece of literature, could they do so? Do students in the U.S. think that would even matter in the Google age? What about the Declaration of Independence? Or Martin Luther King, Jr.'s "I Have a Dream" speech? These remarkable writings not only shaped our nation's history, but who we are as people, yet few students can recite a line from any of them.

Students in China don't necessarily first learn about Confucius' philosophies in classrooms. His sayings are an integrated part of culture that is passed down by their parents and family members over generations.

Until the early twentieth century, most people in the U.S. could readily quote passages and verses from the Bible. This may be the closest thing to a common culture in many Western countries. A more common shared culture now is promoted by the media, and includes areas of commercialism, show business, and the entertainment industry. American young people are more likely to be able to recite all the words to advertisement jingles or sitcom theme songs than the words from an important literary source or historical speech.

The widespread popularity of Confucius can also be attributed in part to modern news media and movies. During the Chinese national holiday in 2007 a series of lectures were aired by the China Central Television Station (CCTV). A lecture about Confucius' *Analects* was delivered by Yu Dan, an associate professor from Beijing Normal University. Yu Dan turned the Chinese Confucian classics into popular culture, and so doing, became a celebrity. The revival of simple stories, principles, and arguments brought new inspiration and meaning to many souls. In the lecture, Yu Dan brought to life a godlike personality and spirit that mesmerized every family and household.

China has been undergoing a dramatic transformation from a traditional society to a modern society, from an agricultural economy to an industrial economy, from a primitive economy to an information economy. This vehement transformation has affected every corner, crevice, and soul in China. The pursuit of wealth has prevailed in this transformational stage. When Yu Dan presented these ancient wisdoms, it was like a time warp, from the past to the future, which filled the empty souls with nurturing wisdom.

Yu Dan's seven lectures talked about the art of the gentleman, the principles of making friends, the morality of souls, the ethics of dealing with society, the methods of ideals, the path of life, and the truth of the Dao of the universe. On November 26, after Yu Dan's lecture notes were compiled and published, four million copies were immediately sold out. Grandmothers rode the train in from Shijiazhuang to Beijing, office clerks rode the train from Nanjiang to Beijing, and businessmen flew in from Lanzhou to Beijing, all to see Ms. Yu Dan at her book signing at the Beijing Zhongguancun Bookstore. Yu Dan signed 12,600 copies of her book that single day.

Yu Dan's lecture inspired China's reflection on its morality, its relationship among people, and its past ideals. With so much competition in society now, reading a few lines from Confucius' *Analects* feels like a breeze blowing on us in the hot, humid weather. Twenty-six-hundred years ago, Confucius knew what we feel now! The series ignited a passion for reading the classics. The old classics had instilled some guidance into our contemporary lives.

At the Confucius Temple, the guide said to my father, "Young people like to watch the movie *Confucius*. You should get a movie for your daughter and son." My father bought the DVD and I watched it while we were in China, and learned more about that period in history. Chow Yun-Fat, a popular movie star, starred in the title role of the 2010 movie.

Twenty-six hundred years ago, the Zhou dynasty was on the verge of collapse. Kingdoms competed to dominate. This special time in China's history was called the Spring and Autumn Period, and a legendary period it proved to be. Warriors, heroes, thinkers, great literature and epics arose during this period.

Confucius was born to a declining noble family in the kingdom of Lu. He worried about the social disorder in China. He wanted to influence the course of history through his philosophy and ideas, which were based on *ren* (kindheartedness), *he* (harmony), and *li* (rituals). Just like the sages in every civilization, he was ahead of his time. He was appointed as a justice minister in the kingdom of Lu and was looked upon with respect and hope for his incisiveness and wisdom. But sadly, his political ideals collapsed as he faced the harsh realities of the time. Confucius led his disciples to travel and lecture in different kingdoms for fourteen years. But no state adopted his ideas. Power and bullying were still the dominant political "philosophies" among the kingdoms. He was trapped in the midst of political military turmoil and was often misunderstood.

In the later part of his life, Confucius traveled back to his home state, Lu, and pursued teaching while compiling his writings. Although he was no longer involved in politics, he was still very ambitious and expected that one day his political ideas would be fully implemented.

China intentionally arranged the release of *Confucius* to be on January 22, 2010, close to the Spring Festival holiday, the longest holiday period, when more families and students go to movie theaters. China only comes out with a "big" movie every few years, and the hope was that *Confucius* would beat the blockbuster, *Avatar,* at the box office.

Avatar had been released on December 18, 2009, in the U.S., and on January 2, 2010, in China. *Confucius* showcased one of China's most famous actors, China's history, and the ideals and philosophy of Confucianism. On the other hand, *Avatar* brought to the screen a 3-D experience, a decade's worth of new cinematic technology, and sophisticated animation.

Avatar had as its goal, both inside and outside of the movie, to dominate the nation. It wanted to conquer the land of Pandora and the box office sales. In the movie, modern technology had been what was pushing society forward. But in *Confucius,* through a warring era, Confucius wanted peace across the land and to introduce the concept of a harmonious society. He believed that managing a country did not require the use of weapons—or even violence for that matter—and governing should be done through peace and finding balance among the two nations or kingdoms. *Avatar* was the opposite. *Avatar* portrayed in film what is actuality happening to the world today: we are exhausting our human resources, slowly destroying the homeland, and more often, looking beyond the earth. *Confucius* looked inward and asked how we can lead our own souls to settle in peace. As it turned out, *Avatar* beat *Confucius* in the box office by about 2.5 times per day during its release in theaters.

On July 16, 2011, I was leaving Chengdu for Beijing and sitting in the Chengdu Shuangliu Airport and saw again how Confucius' teachings permeate every aspect of Chinese life. The newly expanded airport was a world-class creation and is centrally located in the Sichuan basin. Inside the airport there were many flashing signs standing high, one of which was extremely impressive. It showcased one of Confucius' sayings, "The summit is high, but your ambition is higher."

After boarding a newly-acquired A321 airplane, the captain announced a welcome over the intercom, in Chinese and in fluent English. Pulling out an in-flight magazine, I was intrigued with a few pages I flipped to. I found an article, the left side in Chinese, and the right side in perfectly lucid English, translating the Chinese. The article was entitled, "Revelation of *The Great Learning*."[1]

The Great Learning is a classic book of Confucianism. The book consists of short texts explaining the teachings of Confucius. The article talked about certain principles of teaching and learning, such as the idea that everyone is capable of learning. It doesn't matter what the person's social status, economic status, or political status is; everyone can become a learned person. Thus success is the result of one's effort to learn and isn't based on anything else. Learning is the process of connecting our knowledge together. We can't learn if we isolate ourselves from other perspectives; if we do so, we will fail. In order to learn, we must set priorities and goals. We have to know what the most important thing is, and we have to follow that vision.

A famous line in a section of *The Great Learning* can be translated

1 *Sichuan Airlines Inflight Magazine*, June 2011, Sichuan Airlines, Sichuan.

as, "Wishing to be sincere in their thoughts, they are first extended to the utmost of their knowledge. Such extension of knowledge lies in the investigation of things." This "investigation of things" requires one to look around the environment, reflect on it, and learn from it. By doing so, we are able to harmonize, balance, and understand the important things of life such as family and friendship.

The article said that *Great Learning* shows the "rectification and improvement plans, including the scheme and path of life orientation, life accomplishment, life planning, and life welfare, and also the theoretical approach and operational scheme for state administration and world harmonization based on moral character cultivation."

The article entailed a nearly philosophical plan dedicated as a guide for people to understand the importance of life and the things that life brings. The book has influenced China in cultivating certain skills, such as working hard, honing abilities, accumulating knowledge, respect, and the ability to work together. China is now succeeding more in many of these ideas, following the path that was drawn out by Confucius. By doing so, China has become a great learner.

When I was in Shanghai, Dai Qun, the principal of the Shanghai Jian Qing Experimental School explained to me that he believed school was a place to acquire the basic knowledge and abilities of the main subjects, but that wasn't the whole purpose.

He said, "Anyone can acquire knowledge of basic principles. The real goal is to acquire the idea of finding your own self through learning. It's a confusing concept, but I'm talking about the fact that we want to teach our students to 'be a better self' than they were when they walked into the school. We want them to leave every day feeling a wave of accomplishment; we want to make it so that students can be the best people they can possibly be. That is what school is about." Following the footsteps of Confucius, Principal Dai continues to emphasize moral education in the process of acquiring knowledge.

CHAPTER 10
Family Affairs

With two older sisters and an older brother, my mother is the youngest in her family. Her parents had a plan for their children: the oldest son would be an engineer; the oldest daughter, a teacher; the middle daughter, a teacher; and the youngest, a doctor. But due to the Cultural Revolution, only one of those dreams came true. None of my mother's siblings went to college. The end of the Cultural Revolution left the son in a factory, the oldest daughter in a state farm, and the middle daughter in a large state-owned enterprise. The sudden transition was a shock. The family was unprepared for what was to come, and it was a struggle for them, along with the rest of China. The world they knew was a strange place. The Cultural Revolution had left them nearly brainwashed. They were left with nothing. But my mother was the lucky one. She was young enough to avoid being sent to a manufacturing workshop, or to the state farm.

The Cultural Revolution seemed to have created an advantage for the next generation. A few years ago, I visited my uncle and his family in Beijing. They had a daughter who was only six years old at the time. Upon entering their apartment, math workbooks, English cassette tapes, and Chinese practice exercises were scattered on the floor, the couch, the kitchen table, and in all of the bedrooms. The workbooks were almost torn, looking as if they had been reviewed hundreds of times. The cassette tapes were nearly worn out, and the exercises were cluttered with notes and comments in the margins. I learned that after my young cousin came home from school, she did more hours of practice and exercises until bedtime.

My cousin wasn't allowed to watch any television except the news, and only during dinnertime. Their portable television was no bigger than a textbook, and had only five channels. She wasn't allowed to use the computer, and she wasn't allowed to play any electronic games. Despite my uncle not having gone to college and receiving the least amount of education compared to his other siblings as a child, his intention for his daughter was the same as every other parent of China: to giver her a good education.

I've heard it said that good ideas lead to great expeditions. Whoever said that was wrong. It is not rare that while at the dinner table, my dad suddenly looks at me and says, with a big smile, the five words that will torment me for the next few weeks: "I have a good idea!"

At a summer camp I attended during my sophomore year, I learned about six-word memoirs. In six words, and six words only, we had to summarize our life (one of my favorites was, "Mom Mom Mom Mom Mom, Food" written by a classmate).

If one were to be written by my dad, I'd suggest it to be: "I have a great idea! *Not!*" Every time he elaborated on his great idea, it was always about my studying or my brother's studying.

During the winter of 2011 I truly began to write. At first it was a hobby, in hopes to improve my writing ability in school and outside of school. But soon the hobby became a passion, and the passion grew.

I wrote an essay for a Second Amendment essay contest. I wrote an essay for a Women Mathematicians essay contest. I wrote an essay for an Environment essay contest. I wrote an essay for a John F. Kennedy essay contest. When I reflect on my accomplishments, I can see that my parents made plans for my education. They simply don't want me to waste any time in my life.

During previous summer breaks, my parents piled huge stacks of classics on my study table, which include Benjamin Franklin's *Autobiography*, Miguel de Cervantes' *Don Quixote*, Leo Tolstoy's *War and*

Peace, Harriet Beecher Stowe's *Uncle Tom's Cabin*, Walt Whitman's *Leaves of Grass*, and many more. They knew I couldn't understand everything in these classic books. But they required me to take notes, and highlight sentences and paragraphs that are critical to the development of the stories in the books. In the evening, when they came home from work, I had to tell them the stories from the books. This is one more example of how my parents' lifelong hunger for books was impressed upon me.

The day after my school year ended in the spring of 2011 I went with my brother and my dad to the Minneapolis/St. Paul airport at four o'clock in the morning. We flew to China to obtain more of the stories and interviews shared in this book. During the course of a week, all my meetings in China were with teachers, students, principals, and parents. We visited schools, colleges, academies, and after-school programs. We got back on a Saturday night, and on the following day I left again at four in the morning for the airport, this time to Washington, DC. After winning the State Award for the National Peace Essay Contest, I was more than excited to attend the one-week program that would further improve my understanding of foreign affairs.

The trip was unforgettable. On the last night, my parents and brother joined me in Washington, DC, for the awards ceremony. After the program, I packed my bags and we started to drive toward Amherst, Massachusetts, where I would be attending the Great Books Summer Reading Program. It was the 24th of June, and it was a nice morning. I had to be at Amherst College, on campus, checking in by 3:00 p.m. on the 26th of June. The trip was only an eight-hour drive; but with my dad on this expedition, there were bound to be some detours.

Sure enough, we made pit stops in Maryland, West Virginia, Pennsylvania, New Jersey, Delaware, New York, and Vermont. This was tiring, yet thrilling.

The point of this trip wasn't to torture me before I was sent off to a party-filled camp. We knew it was probably one of the few trips we would take as a family perhaps for long time. Now that I'm in high school, with grades to maintain and activities to attend, my parents and I don't take trips together as much as we'd like to. My parents are more active in their work as well. With my brother in medical school and already engaged, two days together as a family brought us back to a time when we were all younger and had more freedom. This was an amazing experience that my parents wanted us to share as a family, once again.

Leaving Washington, DC, and crossing the Potomac River, we drove to Harper's Ferry National Historical Park, the spot where Virginia, Maryland, and West Virginia meet at the confluence of the Potomac and Shenandoah rivers. At Harpers Ferry, hundreds of acres were devoted to John Brown's historic attempts to end slavery. What surprised me the most there was how much I was able to learn outside of a classroom. I had learned about John Brown's raid on Harpers Ferry in my freshman year in high school, and we spent a good amount of time on the event, yet it amazed me how the teacher didn't cover much of the significant material, and neither did our textbook. Of course we can't learn everything we need to know about one specific moment of history in a class that covers the whole of our country's history, but as I stood there reading the signs, I felt like I had learned nothing in the classroom compared to the few hours I spent at that park.

From there, we drove north along the Hudson River. My brother and I knew my dad would put me in the Franklin Roosevelt Presidential Library to soak up more American history. Once there, we read nonstop until the very last minute, when the library closed. Rather than enjoy the panoramic Hudson River views, we fed on the Great Depression, the New Deal, and World War II.

My father's plan was to pass Albany, drive through upstate New York, then cross into Vermont before stopping for the night. My parents had created a goal for me to set foot in all fifty states before I graduate from high school. I had already traveled in forty-five states; Vermont was to be the forty-sixth. But this time, after an intense argument, my dad surrendered to my mom, my brother, and me. Majority rules in my family. Dad compromised, and we stayed that night in Albany.

The next morning, getting up early, we continued on. Dad was still upset because we didn't travel as much as he had planned. I had to be in Amherst at 3:00 p.m., and my parents' airplane departed at 5:00 p.m., so we could only have a short drive through southern Vermont. On County Road 9, surrounded by dense trees and bushes, a high tower emerged. We stopped. The tower was the Bennington Battle Monument located in the small town of Bennington. I learned that the Bennington battle paved the way for the "red coat" general, John Burgoyne, who eventually surrendered at Saratoga, considered the most crucial battle in the War of Independence. My dad was very happy for me to learn this, because neither he nor I had ever heard of the Bennington campaign. This gain for him was actually a gain for me, too. Even more exciting for him was what he found in the small gift shop in the shadow of Bennington tower. A parchment map detailed each battle and campaign during the eight-year War of Independence.

My dad's face brightened as he told me, "I am happy with this short-cut route because of this map. By the time you and your brother have kids, I will be retired, and I will drive a van and bring your kids to all these spots. History can be learned by feet!"

My brother said, "I need to consider your offer."

(I said nothing.)

My dad, mom, and brother dropped me at Amherst where I became immersed in the Great Books program. Every day, I had to report to my family at home about what I learned, and send them twenty vocabulary words learned from class.

Among the best public learning places in my home state, the Minnesota Science Museum is the most often visited by my family. Going to the science museum isn't just for fun; it is a time for me to learn some things I might not learn in the classroom, and experience education from a different perspective—my own experience. With any exhibit at the science museum, my routine is to read every single sign and make a list of new vocabulary words. My mom, dad, and brother have each asked me to do that. When the King Tut exhibition was at the science museum, reading the article published in *National Geographic* was an assignment from my dad. Reading a small book on King Tut was an assignment from my mom. When the Scrolls of the Dead Sea were exhibited at the science museum, I had to write down new words from every panel, including those referring to ancient Egyptian rituals, and present a review of every section from the exhibition to my parents. This has been something my parents have told me to do since I was little.

The Guthrie Theater, located on the south bank of the Mississippi River in Minneapolis, presents two Shakespeare plays every year. From Guthrie Theater's high windows, you can oversee Saint Anthony Falls, the only natural waterfall on the upper Mississippi River. Shakespeare plays are must-go events for me and my family. This is one of my parents' requirements for my extracurricular activities. When I was in middle school, before we went to the Guthrie to see *Macbeth*, my brother recommended that I read at least the *SparkNote Study Guide* version and the Wikipedia description of the play. When we went to the theater to see *Julius Caesar*, my parents asked me to narrate the story to them. When we went to see *Winter's Tale*, my father asked me to read the major critiques from the leading authorities in the program catalog. When we went to see *Much Ado About Nothing*, my parents asked me to read aloud Act II, which was a selection in my Great Books program at Amherst.

Reading is an important part of my family's life. I'm in high school, and my career is being earned through education. My brother is in medical school, and reading is his main business. My mother is a doctor; she squeezes out time for reading each day. My dad works in a college where reading and even writing a book is part of his work. My parents and my brother have supported me from an early age in reading books. They have tried to help me develop reading as a good habit as well as a hobby. The older I get, the more books I read.

By reading books they recommended, I found that my brother, my mom, and my dad each have their own unique reading habits and skills. Therefore, I want to discover as well as develop my own reading skills and habits. By reading, we can ignite passionate interests, and learn and understand other people's thoughts and ideas.

My father's reading habits are very interesting. When picking up a book, he first flips to the index in the back. By skimming the index he is able to quickly understand the theme of the book. He especially appreciates books with long indexes; he finds that those books have a lot to offer in the text. My father's favorite books and readings revolve around the topics of current affairs and history. He pays special attention to books and sections of books that relate to countries such as the U.S., India, Russia, etc. My dad has quite an interesting collection of nearly all the books published in the last two decades that relate to the rise of China, or the changes in China. After a long day at work, my father picks up a book after dinner, positions himself on our living room sofa, a quilt covering his legs, and sits motionless while reading. Towering on the coffee table in front of our sofa is a pile of books, magazines, newspapers, and novels. My father rarely reads a book page by page. Often he flips the pages of the books he reads, skimming, before selecting a single chapter, which he reads before he tosses it aside. He says that in this way, he can still understand the main context of the book in the most efficient way possible.

Recently I introduced my dad to the iPad. He finds it utterly amazing that if there's a word you don't know, you can simply highlight the word and the dictionary definition will appear. Sometimes I think that he uses the iPad just so he can use that convenient feature.

My dad likes to keep my brother on top of things. When my brother left home for college, my dad gave him ten books to take with him. Some were chosen by my dad, and some were my brother's favorites. These books included the *Analects of Confucius*, Sun Zi's the *Art of War*, Stephen Hawking's *A Brief History of Time*, and Paul Kennedy's *The Rise and Fall of Great Powers*.

My brother's reading habits are perhaps the most standard. He will carefully read every book he has chosen. He reads with intensity, making sure he understands everything that goes on within the book. He mainly enjoys political commentary, best-selling novels, and classic literature. During his first year at Harvard, he read Thomas Friedman's *The World Is Flat*, Jeffery Sachs' *The End of Poverty*, and Barack Obama's *The Audacity of Hope*. He often enjoys rereading books. He's read the Harry Potter series quite a few times. Even in medical school, despite the fact that he's in the clinical stage of his schooling, he took some of the Harry Potter books with him, reading a few chapters every so often.

My mother's reading habits are the most interesting. My mother doesn't like to read from the front to the back, she doesn't like to look at the index, and she doesn't read very intensely, either. She reads from the back to the front. She finds that the quickest way to seize the main idea of the book is to read the end. Interestingly, my mom loves to share stories about the books she just read; but often, she'll get the story mixed up, stating things that happened first, last, and vice versa. My dad and I find it quite amusing. My mother has a very strong reading habit. Every night before she sleeps, she reads for an hour or two. No matter how late, no matter where we are, she has to read or else she can't fall asleep. My mother strongly prefers reading biographies, travel essays, and nutritional books. She enjoyed the biographies of Soong Mei-ling as well as Yu Qiuyu's prose. She also enjoys flipping through *National Geographic* as well as *Forbes* magazine.

My reading habits are much like my brother's, perhaps because we are both students. I like to read page by page, chapter by chapter. After reading a book, I read another book. I read a lot of American fiction. I like Hemingway's *The Old Man and the Sea*, John Steinbeck's *The Grapes of Wrath*, F. Scott Fitzgerald's *The Great Gatsby*, and Henry David Thoreau's *Walden*. *The Magic Tree House* series written by Mary Pope Osborne for primary school students includes more than forty books, and I still like to read those. Although a book of this series takes less than an hour to read, I am always moved deeply by the story in each book. I frequently browse through other great works, and I pay special attention to the beginnings and endings of those books. Charles Dickens's *A Tale of Two Cities* left me remembering the first line: "It was the best of times, it was the worst of times." Margaret Mitchell's *Gone with the Wind* left behind a concluding remark, "After all, tomorrow is another day." Leo Tolstoy's *Anna Karenina* left me with the opening words, "Happy families are all alike; every unhappy family is unhappy in its own way." F. Scott Fitzgerald's *The Great Gatsby* left behind "So we beat on, boats against the current, borne back ceaselessly into the past." Louisa May Alcott's *Little Women* left me with the first sentence, "Christmas won't be Christmas without any presents."

In our family, we often recommend books to each other. In the past year, my brother recommended Randy Pausch's *The Last Lecture*. My father recommended Amy Chua's *The Battle Hymn of the Tiger Mother*. My mother recommended Laura Hillenbrand's *Unbroken*. I recommended the English version of Lang Lang's autobiography, *Journey of a Thousand Miles: My Story*. We discussed Randy Pausch's courageous battle with cancer and the tiger mother's extreme parenting. We discussed Louie Zamperini's inspirational tale, and Lang Lang's tough road to success. Of course, my mom and dad always use these stories to inspire me.

At the dinner table, our family enjoys discussing the top articles in the most recent issues of our favorite magazines. My dad is always talking about the *Economist*, while my brother likes to discuss columns from the *New York Times*. I like to look at *Time* magazine, and my mother likes *Newsweek*. We always try to discuss the story in the article, as well as our understanding of the author's point of view. We exchange articles written by columnists such as Thomas Friedman, Nicholas Kristof, Fareed Zakaria, and Niall Ferguson. When an interesting new blog entry is posted by my brother's former economics professor, Gregory Mankiw, Dan always forwards it to us.

Reading books takes a lot of time, but somehow our entire family finds ways to squeeze out the time. Even on the toilet, we each have a book in hand. In our bathrooms we have mounds of books on the floor, near the sink, behind the toilet. If any one of us goes into the bathroom and finds out that someone has cleaned out all the books, we run out to find a book before returning to "do our business." Whenever we invite friends or family over, my mom's first duty is to straighten up the bathroom, removing those magazines, books, and newspapers. Then the next cycle begins.

A Chinese family that exemplifies the concept of a hard-won education in China shares common ground with my family. Liu Yaolin is a librarian, working at the college my parents founded. He is also a retired professor from the China Academy of Forestry Science in Beijing. Before Professor Liu came to the United States, he was a leading scientist in his field. His story is a classic example of how education is a family affair in China. Professor Liu lived in a very decent middle-income family before the communists took over China in 1949. His father served as a president for a local agricultural technical college. His mother was a well-educated housewife. They had six children who reached adulthood, He Xiuli, He Zhili, He Jinli, Liu Yaolin (who was adopted by his aunt and took that family name to pass down for future generations), He Zhili (there were two children of this name, one older and one younger), and He Yuli. With her parents' strong support, He Xiuli, the oldest sister, attended Sichuan University, majoring in economics. She graduated in 1947, one of the most turbulent years in China's history. The nationalists and communists fought in their bloody civil war as the nationalist government teetered on the brink of collapse. No jobs were available. However, she studied with Peng Dixian, one of the most famous economists at that time. During her college years, He Xiuli was the assistant to Peng Dixian because of her beautiful calligraphy and her essay-writing skills. Without a job, He Xiuli wanted to go home, but Mr. Peng advised her to pursue a second degree, law. She spent another two years obtaining a law degree in Sichuan University. That year, 1949, the communists had already taken a majority of China, but the communists and nationalists still fought their last battle in Sichuan. However, there was no uncertainty that the communists would win the civil war.

He Xiuli had studied for six years in the nationalist system, earning two degrees, but because the communists were ideologically opposed to the nationalists, it was impossible for her to find a job. Thus she went back to her home county, Gao Xian. The nationalists were gone, and the communists were coming. She began teaching at a middle school in the spring of 1950. At that time, her husband was also an economist, working in Chongqing (the capital city of the nationalist government during the Sino-Japanese War). Although Chongqing and Gao Xian are both on the banks of the Yangtze River, they are separated by mountain ranges. Finally He Xiuli's husband was able to find her a job in Ren Ji nursing school in Chongqing, teaching Chinese and mathematics. In the nursing school, most of the staff members were nuns—at a time when China was experiencing a dramatic transformation from the nationalist regime to a communist regime.

Starting in 1950, China became involved in the Korean War. The political movement focused on re-educating officials and capitalists to work with the new communist government was also in the process of commencing. After 1949 the communist party had taken over all the schools, including the nursing school where He Xiuli worked. The nuns did not know any policies of the new government. He Xiuli, as a talented student from Sichuan University, turned out to be the main communication link between the government and the nuns and staff of the nursing school. She was later promoted to president of the nursing school where she stayed until her retirement.

The second sister, He Jinli, was enthusiastic about the new government and joined the army in 1950 while she was still in high school. She was only fifteen years old. She was assigned to the police department of the Lu Zhou district.

The winter of 1950 was extremely cold in Sichuan province. Liu Yaolin's hands and ears were itchy because they were exposed to the damp cold weather. The same winter, the new communist government had taken over Sichuan completely and the newly established government wanted to clear the area of nationalists. The father of the family, He Chengxi, was a nationalist party member, serving the invalidated nationalist government as the director of education in his town. Furthering his nationalist beliefs, he had once joined the nationalist army as a lieutenant. He Chengxi was put to death. This event was earthshaking for the family. The financial support for the family fell apart. Now the whole family had to depend on the mother, a housewife, for their living. Relatives wrote letters to the oldest sister, He Xiuli, and advised her to bring her sisters and brothers to Chongqing. Otherwise, her siblings would not be able to survive by themselves because of their extreme poverty.

He Xiuli used her savings to bring her older brother, He Zhili, to Chongqing, and allowed him to take the college entrance exam. He was then accepted by Chongqing University. The newly established government desperately needed geologists and provided assistance to students of geology. Accordingly, He Zhili chose geology as his major. He studied with Professor Ding Daoheng, who received his PhD in geology in Germany and was one of the most famous geology professors in China. When He Zhili graduated from college in 1955, he was assigned to teach at Changsha Metallurgy College. He also worked at Changsha Mining College. In 1958 both colleges wanted him to work exclusively for them, but in the end, He Zhili chose to work for Beijing Geology Institute, under the Ministry of Metallurgy. He later became a tenured professor and PhD advisor at Beijing Iron and Steel College, the predecessor of Beijing Science and Technology University.

With the oldest sister working in Chongqing, the second sister joining the army, and the oldest brother studying in Chongqing, the mother and the three brothers and sisters were left at home. Among the three, Liu Yaolin was the oldest. He delivered coal to every household in his community. He was only thirteen years old, and life was very challenging for him. He Zhili and He Xiuli pondered about how they could get the younger brothers and sisters out of this impoverished situation. He Zhili and He Xiuli decided to eat less to save money, and then sent the saved money back home, allowing Liu Yaolin to join them, though he was only in middle school at that time.

To join them, Liu Yaolin had to walk one-and-a-half days from Gao

Xian to Yi Bin, then take a one-day boat ride from Yi Bin to Lu Zhou, then take a bus from Lu Zhou to Long Chang. Long Chang was the closest railroad station between Chengdu and Chongqing. It then took him ten hours from Long Chang to Chongqing by train.

Once in Chongqing, Liu Yaolin led a studious life to prepare for college. With his sister and brother's support, he transferred to the Affiliated School of Southwest Normal College. In 1956 he was accepted into the department of physics at Sichuan University. Luckily, this occurred just before 1957—the year China started the Anti-Rightist Movement. All professors and intellectuals with liberal ideas were sent to labor camps for re-education. The political left surged and a student's social background became a determining factor again. From 1957 until the end of the Cultural Revolution in 1976, there was no chance for Liu Yaolin to get into college with his social background associated with his father's persecution by the communist party. Yet Liu Yaolin graduated from college in 1961 and was assigned to do research at the China Academy of Forestry. He became an esteemed scientist.

During this time, He Zhili wrote a letter to He Jinlin, who was in the army at that time, and asked her to come to Chongqing to continue her education. She resigned from the army and went to Chongqing to take exams. She was accepted by the department of medicine of China Western University. Later she was assigned to Chengdu First Hospital. He Jinli sold her watch and her coat to invite their younger brother, sister, and their mother to join them in Chengdu.

By this time, He Xiuli and He Zhili had families of their own to support. Supporting the youngest brother and the youngest sister became the responsibility of Liu Yaolin and He Jinli. Liu Yaolin supported them until he got married in 1974, at the age of thirty-five. In 1962 He Zhili (the younger one—this *zhi* means "will") was accepted into the engineering school at Sichuan University. He was fortunate, because after 1957, one's social-class background was crucial to being accepted into colleges. He Zhili was definitely not politically qualified to go to Sichuan University.

After the "Great Leap Forward" in 1958, China's extreme approach to a communist society brought disaster to the country. Many people died from this man-made catastrophe. Mao Zedong was asked to retreat from the front. Liu Shaoqi and Deng Xiaoping were more actively involved in governing the country. In 1962 a conference was held in Beijing, in which the Chinese government (Chairman Mao) acknowledged intellectuals in addition to the working class and relaxed the political background examination for students. This momentary shift in politics created the opportunity for He Zhili to be accepted into college. The youngest sister, He Yuli, with support from her brothers and sisters, graduated from high school in 1966.

Then the Cultural Revolution began. All colleges and universities were closed. Students were to be educated by workers, peasants, and soldiers. He Yuli waited for her opportunity. Finally after the Cultural Revolution ended in 1976 and Deng Xiaoping resumed a policy of college education, He Yuli took the national exam and was accepted into Chengdu University in 1978. For this day, she had waited twelve years.

China's last hundred years of history has been extremely turbulent. But for He's family, dedication to education never faded. Liu Yaolin's father was also a graduate of Sichuan University. Liu Yaolin remembers when he was young, every night after work his father would tutor his oldest son in classical Chinese essays. After the tutoring sessions, father and son turned to the rich poetry of the Tang dynasty for pleasure. Liu Yaolin recited one poem every night from memory, especially those of his father's favorite poet, Du Fu. Later, when Liu Yaolin attended college in Chengdu, he walked in the gardens attached to Du Fu's home, and committed three hundred of Du Fu's poems to memory.

Before he fell asleep each night, he watched his mom knitting clothes for his siblings. When he woke up, he saw his mother doing laundry for her children. His mother calligraphed many essays that were used to educate her children, essays such as "On Reading," "On Time," "On Self Independence," "On Friendship," and "On Respecting Parents." All six children acknowledged that the wealth inherited from their parents was not monetary; it was comprised of diligence, honesty, hard work, independence, and the belief that science can save a country—a modern version of Confucian philosophy.

Because of political uncertainties, Liu Yaolin's parents had asked all of his siblings to study science and technology. This became a golden rule for many families in China during the three decades from the 1950s to the 1970s. In that period of time, China was filled with political events such as the "Anti-Rightist Movement," the "Great Leap Forward," and the "Cultural Revolution," some of which were catastrophic. Oftentimes, when these traumatic events hit a family, the family would fall apart. Studying science and technology was one way to avoid the negative impact of these events. All six brothers and sisters were high achievers in their fields, becoming scientists, engineers, professors, and educators. And though they were all scientists or educators, everyone in their family could write beautiful poems, from the calligraphy to the content, including their mother and their father.

In 2000 the six brothers and sisters proposed to the Sichuan government the creation of Yibin University, Today, the university has more than 10,000 students. The older He Zhili is the academician of Uzbekistan and the International Mining Resource Academy. In 2003 the six brothers and sisters proposed to the Yibin city government the making of a documentary movie for one of the four rural culture centers, Lizhuang. Lizhuang was a protective base for Chinese intellectuals and artists during the Sino-Japanese War (1937 to 1945). These accomplished brothers and sisters understand the value of these legacies. They value the land that nourished them. They give back to the community and to their country.

"My six brothers and sisters lived through the rifts of China's history. Every time, when the political campaigns were alleviated, one of us got into college luckily," Liu Yaolin recalled.

"I married Yaolin because of his personality and his scholarship," said Dr. He Xinrong, Liu Yaolin's wife, and my mom's associate.

Dr. He is ten years younger than her husband. From a first impression, it is easy to identify Dr. He as a people person and Liu Yaolin as a scholar. Professor Liu and Dr. He have been guests in our home at least one hundred times since I was born. And some of Professor Liu's brothers and sisters have visited from China. Their story is something I have heard many times over the years.

CHAPTER 11
A Tale of Two Poets

One day, my father gave me an article from the *Wall Street Journal* called "Don't Know Much About History," which contained some startling and disturbing information. How do you respond to hearing that only 12 percent of your country's high school seniors have a "firm grasp of our nation's history," and only 2 percent of those students know the significance of the Brown vs. Board of Education case? As I read that only 0.24 percent of the entire population of high school seniors know the significance of this landmark case that shaped the education structure in place today, I couldn't help hoping that this .24 percent would be the history teachers of the future, and not the 99.76 percent who remain unaware.

"Who influenced you the most besides your parents?" I asked Liu Yaolin, after he told me about his siblings' education.

"Du Fu," Liu Yaolin answered without hesitation. "When you walk into Du Fu Hut, you will be absorbed into an atmosphere of learning and scholarship. You feel the deepest homage to Confucian scholarship there."

Following Liu Yaolin's recommendation, I, with my dad and brother Dan, visited Du Fu Hut when we were on a trip to Chengdu in China. We walked on a trail with bamboo plants shooting into the sky and bridges hovering over the rivers quietly flowing below. This was not only an escape from the hot summer day, but a feast of images and information, with classical poems inscribed on stones, walls, hallways, and scrolls, and duplets written on the doors. We saw a group of students led by a teacher rehearsing a Du Fu poem.

Liang ge huang li ming cui liu,
Yi hang bai lu shang qing tian.
Quan han xi ling qian qiu xue,
Men bo dong wu wan li chuan.

Two yellow orioles sing on the willow tree,
One string of great egrets flies into the sky.
The window frames the western hills' snow of a thousand autumns,
At the door is moored, from eastern Wu, a boat from ten thousand miles away.

They stood in the shade of the tall bamboos and recited another household poem from Du Fu used in primary school education, also taken from an elementary school textbook. Their voices seemed to echo around us, drawing a gust of wind that carried us toward the history of this place.

Hao yu zhi shi jie,
Dang chun nei fa sheng.
Sui feng qian ru ye,
Run wu xi wu sheng.
Ye jing yun ju hei,
Jiang chuan huo du ming.
Xiao kan hong shi chu,
Hua zhong jin guan cheng.

The good rain knows its season,
When spring arrives, it brings life.
It follows the wind secretly into the night,
And moistens all things softly, without sound.

On the country road, the clouds are all black,
On a riverboat, a single fire bright.
At dawn one sees this place now red and wet,
The flowers are heavy in the brocade city.

Du Fu is one of China's most famous poets—he is named the "poem sage." He lived in the Tang dynasty, which is considered the pinnacle of China's poetic literature. He wrote about 1,400 poems. His poetry is the most popular among Chinese students. About two dozen of his poems are found in elementary school, middle school, and high school textbooks. Students of all ages are required to memorize these poems with no exceptions or bargaining allowed. In China, even the mediocre students can recite all of them. Everyone knows them; and once you memorize them, they stay with you, they aren't forgotten.

We walked into the Du Fu Hut, so named because of Du Fu's humble little house when he lived here. Though called a hut, Du Fu Hut is actually like an "imperial garden" that occupies 240 Chinese acres.[1] It was built during the Five Generations Dynasty, after Du Fu died. It was then rebuilt and expanded in the Song dynasty, Ming dynasty, and Qing dynasty. Over the last thirteen hundred years, poets, writers, students, scholars, politicians, and dignitaries have come to pay homage to Du Fu. The "hut" kept expanding, to its current large scale. The garden has every feature of classical Chinese gardens: bamboo, flowers, temples, pavilions, bridges, rivers, stone mountains, and labyrinths.

We walked into the Epic Hall that is the central architectural feature of the Du Fu Hut, where Du Fu's statue is located. Du Fu's poetry reflects the rise and fall of China's most magnificent dynasty, the Tang dynasty. Commentaries claim Du Fu's poems reflect history, and his poems are used to supplement history. Students who come to Du Fu Hut learn poetic

1 Du Fu Hut is located in the city of Chengdu, a metropolitan area in southwest China.

skills and history, but visiting the park also offers moral teaching, that is, "nourishing yourself concerning your country," the park ranger explained to me. In the Epic Hall, many poems praising Du Fu are displayed. Students standing in front of Du Fu ponder the responsibilities of a person who has contributed so much to literature.

When Du Fu lived there, he built the hut by himself. In AD 761 a gust of wind blew off the thatched roof of his cottage. He was emotional, thus he wrote:

An de guang sha qian wan jian,
Da bi tian xia han shi ju huan yan.
Feng yu bu dong an ru shan.

If I can build thousands of mansions,
Let the poor come in, and let us be hilarious.
For despite the wind and the rain, we will be stable like the mountains.

These opening words of a poem by Du Fu were selected for middle school textbooks by China's Ministry of Education—an absolute requirement for memorization. The high moral standard implied in the poem is promoted in the Confucian tradition of education. When students come in, standing under the thatched roof, they begin to feel the connection between themselves and the history and culture of their country.

At Du Fu Monument, we encountered a high school student. I asked her if she had any of Du Fu's poems in her high school textbook.

She answered, "Of course! There's *Shu Xiang* (Shu Prime Minister), *Deng Yue Yang Lou* (On Yueyang Tower) and *Yue Ye* (Moonlit Night)."

"Did the teachers require you to memorize them?" I asked.

"Yes, every single one of them," she replied.

"Do you still remember them?" I asked.

Without hesitating, she began to recite,

Chu shi wei jie shen xian si,
chang shi ying xiong lei wan jing.
Xi wen dong ting shui,
Jing shang yue yang lou.
Wu chu dong nan che,
Qian kun ri ye fu.
Qing peng wu yi zi,
Lao bing you gu zhou.
Rong ma guan shan bei,
Ping xuan di si liu.

Of old I heard of the waters of Dong Ting Lake,
Now I've climbed to the top of Yueyang Tower.
Here Wu and Chu are split to east and south,
Here heaven and earth are floating day and night.
From family and friends comes not a single word,
Old and sick, I have one solitary boat.
War horses are riding north of the mountain pass,
I lean on the railing as tears flow down.

These poems reflect the splendor of Dong Ting Lake and express the poet's loneliness, his homesickness for his relatives and his family, and most importantly, his worries about his country's future. This is a very classical setting with a Confucian tradition, the student told me.

"Why do you memorize these poems?" I asked.

"That's not a question here," she said. "Nobody asks why, we just memorize them. It's been the teaching for thousands of years. Nobody asks why. For the poetic skills, if you memorize three hundred poems, you will be able to recite them as if it was second nature."

"But don't you ever question why you have to memorize the poems?"

"If you question why, then you are questioning your own culture and your own history. From where we stand now, it seems as if we're not at a point where we need to question why. Everyone knows them, and if we don't memorize them, all of our history and culture will be lost. What we know will be carried on to the generation after us, and that will continue. We can't break history."

"What other poems do you learn that you can recite?"

"Quite a few. We have selections from Li Bai, Bai Juyi, Wang Wei, Su Dongpo, Xin Qiji, and many other poets. We memorize all of them."

Du Fu was a Confucian. His works reflect his concerns about social justice. He was concerned about the poor, about history, and about his country.

"He was treated well by his students and his people," the park ranger told me. "Du Fu is honored. Du Fu is not lonely."

Back in 2006, when I was visiting my brother at Harvard with my parents, we all decided to take a trip up to Concord, Massachusetts. We visited the Walden Pond State Reservation, the location of Henry David Thoreau's home for two years, and Ralph Waldo Emerson's mansion. This was also where Thoreau wrote his book, *Walden*. It was late in the fall when we visited, and the area was absolutely beautiful. It was as if nothing had been touched for more than a hundred years. The replica of Thoreau's cabin, the scenery, and the landscape all stood like they stood when Thoreau lived there. The pond was still; the trees on the banks touched the water. The leaves fell like they were dancing around me, and the sunset reflected on the water. It was stunning to think Thoreau had once looked at the same sight I was now looking at. There were only a few other visitors wandering around the area.

"Did you read Thoreau's *Walden* in high school?" a school teacher from Ohio asked my brother.

"Yes, as part of our transcendentalism unit," my brother answered.

"I wish Thoreau's *Walden* and *Civil Disobedience* were in my school's curriculum," he said.

The teacher and I read the inscription on the site where Thoreau had lived: "I went to the woods because I wished to live deliberately, to front only the essential facts of life, and see if I could not learn what it had to teach, and not, when I came to die, discover that I had not lived."

Coming out of Walden Pond, we drove towards Ralph Waldo Emerson's mansion. We stopped at the Minute Man Statue on which Emerson's "Concord Hymn" was inscribed.

By the rude bridge that arched the flood,
Their flag to April's breeze unfurled,
Here once the embattled farmers stood,
And fired the shot heard round the world.

The foe long since in silence slept;
Alike the conqueror silent sleeps;
And Time the ruined bridge has swept
Down the dark stream which seaward creeps.

On this green bank, by this soft stream,
We set to-day a votive stone;
That memory may their deed redeem,
When, like our sires, our sons are gone.

Spirit, that made those heroes dare,
To die, and leave their children free,
Bid Time and Nature gently spare
The shaft we raise to them and thee.

Those guns smoking from the War of Independence were gone. The sky was blue. The autumn breeze caressed our faces. It was very quiet on the streets of Concord. A few visitors strolled around in bookstores, shops, and restaurants. I read the "Concord Hymn" with my brother. But honestly, I can't recite any of Ralph Waldo Emerson's poems. I can't recite any poems by Emily Dickinson, Robert Frost, Edgar Allan Poe, e.e. cummings, Maya Angelou, or Walt Whitman, even though poetry is one of the five literature genres we must study in high school along with fiction, drama, biography, and prose. We were never asked to memorize poetry in school.

My father remains confused about the American approach to education, saying, "I know that the American education emphasizes creativity and independent study. If those famous pieces of literature are not on the lips of your mouth or on the surface of your memory, how can you create some elegant work?"

When we arrived at the Emerson House alongside the Cambridge Turnpike, it was lunchtime and the house was closed. A paper clock on the door pointed to 1:30 p.m. as reopening time. We took a break as well for a light lunch and came back right at 1:30 p.m. My family of four were the only visitors. The tour guide was very nice. After we waited a few minutes, and it seemed nobody was coming to join us, she started the tour.

We walked into the living room. We kept quiet as the guide told us, "This living room was the hub of the Transcendental Club. Ralph Waldo Emerson entertained Amos Bronson Alcott and Louisa May Alcott, Margaret Fuller, Henry David Thoreau, and Orestes Augustus Brownson here. He published his first significant work, *Nature*, anonymously after he moved into this house. This was a central place for America's Renaissance."

In Emerson's study, his chairs and desk remained, although some furnishings were on display across the street in the Concord Museum. A bookshelf of Latin literature stood against the wall. "It was exactly here in this room that Ralph Waldo Emerson wrote 'The American Scholar,' which is a powerful statement of individualism, and 'Self Reliance,' which expresses his philosophy of individualism," the guide explained.

Ralph Waldo Emerson published two volumes of poetry in this house, *Poems* in 1846 and *May-Day* in 1867. However, we didn't see anyone recite Emerson's poetry. There weren't even any inscriptions of lines from his poetry on display. I guessed that his poems rest quietly in libraries.

When Emerson traveled to Europe, Henry David Thoreau took care of the house and helped the family chop wood for the fireplace. The pile of chopped wood near the house emphasizes the realness and antiquity of the house.

Unfortunately, the house was also moldy. My mom can't tolerate that smell for long. After the guide finished the half-hour tour, my mom immediately stepped out of the house. The rest of us lingered for a little while before leaving. The sun was shining on the white house. I thought that Thoreau might have enjoyed the sunshine. Perhaps Emerson might have written more in the sunshine. We left Ralph Waldo Emerson's mansion and the tour guide behind. We were the only visitors during the two hours we were there.

Looking back on the two scenarios involving great figures from history, all with such strong minds and stamina, and all of whom left enormous legacies to their cultures, I wondered why it seemed that Thoreau's and Emerson's pasts were waning while Du Fu's was rising. His home has become a bustling site of homage where the buildings will be kept perfectly intact, while Thoreau and Emerson's former haunts were only given a name plaque and scant attention from a ranger. Are parts of American culture slipping away? Perhaps this fading is not in the legacy itself, but rather, it is in us, in how we honor or neglect our culture in our curriculum, in our education system, and in our schools.

In his book *The World Is Flat*, Thomas Friedman quotes a *New York Times* story reporting that the average American college graduate's literacy in English has declined significantly over the past decade.[2] The National Assessment of Adult Literacy, a widely respected nationwide test

2 Thomas Friedman, *The World Is Flat.*

administered by the Department of Education, is considered the nation's most important measure of how well adult Americans can read. When the test was given in 1992, 40 percent of the nation's college graduates scored at the proficient level, meaning they were able to read "lengthy, complex English texts and draw complicated inferences." But the 2003 test showed that only 31 percent of graduates demonstrated those high-level skills. There were 26.4 million college graduates. The director of an institute within the Department of Education who helped oversee the test, Grover J. Whitehurst, observed that more young Americans spend their free time watching TV and surfing the Internet than reading for pleasure, and "it's showing up in our literacy levels."[3]

As founders of Transcendentalism and America's renaissance, Henry David Thoreau is lonely, and Ralph Waldo Emerson is mildewy. But in China, Du Fu is not lonely.

3 Ibid., 340.

CHAPTER 12
Cultural Genes

On June 12, 2011, ten hours after my delayed arrival via United Airlines from Chicago to Beijing, I was standing in front of the tomb of my great-grandmother, attending a memorial service for my father's grandmother, who died four years before, at the age of ninety-seven. It was astonishing to see so many uncles, aunts, and grandpas coming from Qingdao, from Zibo, and from Jinan, joining us for the service. I only met my great-grandmother once, but I know she was a remarkable woman. She had been widowed for seventy-three years, even before my grandpa was born. For seventy-three years, my grandpa was her only child. Her only hope was to raise her son and let him have a good education, continuing the Gong family. My grandpa went to school for only three years, but by educating himself, he became a secretary of a township, and later a teacher at his local middle school. My great-grandma was highly respected by her neighbors and the community. She gained a great deal of respect for the great deed she accomplished of nurturing a child by herself.

On the gravestone that stands tall, I saw my name carved along with the names of my brother, dad, mom, uncle, and aunts. Even more prominent were the educational degree labels: MD and MPH after my mother's name, PhD after my dad's name, and my uncle and aunts' doctoral degrees. Even my brother's Harvard and Yale credentials were there. I was curious, and asked my father why the degrees were carved in the gravestone.

My dad said, "This is a Chinese tradition emphasizing education. You will see more of these as we travel around China."

Engraved and painted with golden ink, it looked almost like a family tree, with lines connecting one generation to another. It was interesting to read all the names and to see my name there, knowing that it would be there for as long as the stone stands, for my children to see, for their children to see, and for all the future descendants of the Gong family to see.

My father grew up in the Central Lu Plain of Shandong Province, belonging to northern China. Confucius, Mencius, and Sun Tzu have left their legacies on this culturally rich land. They are the towering figures of China's Spring and Autumn period and the following Warring States period, corresponding to the era of Socrates, Plato, and Aristotle in Europe, and the life of Siddhartha Gautama in India. Confucius, Mencius, and Sun Tzu laid the foundation of Chinese civilization, which centered on Confucianism. But Confucianism didn't stop in Shandong, or northern China. It radiated and penetrated everywhere in Han culture and to every developed area in China. It was inculcated in every village, and in every long-lasting institution and tradition. On our trip to China, I followed my dad and brother as we studied and investigated these cultures.

Every village in China has a unique culture. It is based on the organization of China's family traditions, for most villages are composed of one or a few families with many descendants that have grown into a population over time. In traditional Chinese society, the village is the generic social, administrative, and communal structure.

China's traditional society was agricultural. Only a very small portion of the population lived their whole lives without engaging in manual farming work. The only way for anyone to get out of this farming life was to pursue opportunities for taking the imperial test, and becoming a *xiucai*, *juren*, or *jinshi*. The xiucai is the honor and title given for passing the local-level test. Juren is the honor and title for passing the province-level test. Jinshi is the highest degree in China's imperial exam from the Ming dynasty to the Qing dynasty. The juren and the jinshi both carried the hope of the whole family, and that person also had the responsibility of enhancing their family's prosperity. For any family to achieve this success required much support from the parents and family members, as well as the efforts of the villagers and the community. But the road was very long, sometimes only achieved through generations of effort. The typical pattern in China was for a family to live a farming life for a few generations, accumulate some wealth, acquire land, and become a landlord. At that point their children could finally receive a good education. Their children continued the tradition, building family temples, family academies, and family facilities for this purpose.

Jiang Village is located in Jingde County, at the foot of Huang Mountain. In this village, before students get into school to study Confucian classics, they have Jiang family lessons (precepts/teachings). It is a common practice for families in China to have their own precepts, but among all family precepts, the Zhu family precept are the most famous. It has been modified by many, many families in China, for their own family teachings. The Zhu family precept includes the statement, "Children may not be geniuses, but they cannot give up reading Confucius' classics. Reading to follow the sage is not necessarily obtaining the highest honor of the imperial examinations." But moral education is fundamental to a person's life.

Several passages posted on the walls of the family halls cover topics such as respect for teachers, friendship, respecting parents, and rituals. In the section about respecting teachers, it says: "The young must practice their language and behavior; for if one meets a ceremonial occasion, they must dress up and learn to pay their respect to others by bowing with their hands in front of them. When someone of higher class walks in a designated zone, one must pardon oneself to make way. One must call a gentleman 'mister,' and as for any teacher who has taught you to show respect for others, you must treat him with respect, too. From when you are young, you must always understand that the teacher deserves great veneration. When you are ready to start school, you must learn to bow in front of the teacher, and more specifically, you must be serious when you do so, showing your respect. You need to learn from the teacher's speech, behavior, observations, actions, and appearance; for these are the basis of rituals; one must grasp the most appropriateness out of the traits."

The section about recitals in the Zhu Family Precept starts with reading Chinese characters, understanding the Chinese characters, connecting them into phrases, and then sentences. Reading starts from easy to difficult, from one to two, "from humans to the universe." When verbally reciting, one must learn by repetition, simply being diligent at first, and later becoming skillful. Good behavior comes from what you learn, for example, to obey your parents, be kind to your brothers, and bow with your hands in front of you. Confucius believes that etiquette comes from detailed activities such as the manners of eating and sleeping. The children must learn that these are basic skills for the wise.

In the section about rehearsing poems, students above the age of ten are instructed to practice reading at five o'clock in the morning, calligraphy at seven o'clock, and poetry at nine o'clock. There must be five students in a group while they practice reading three chapters and three poems each day. The poems chosen must be elegant and epic. The one who recites must stand up in front of the others. The listeners must sit quietly, and if they don't follow, their behaviors and actions must be corrected. Anyone who does not follow these rules is disciplined. The first time a mistake occurs, the student is corrected. After the second mistake, the child repeats the recitation again. The third time, the child is made to kneel on the floor. Rehearsing poems strengthens the students' wills, enlightens their spirits, exercises their voices, and makes the contents of the poems a subconscious normality. In the Jiang Family Precept, this rehearsal of poems helps students to acquire knowledge. Rehearsing poems and practicing calligraphy also helps students obtain artistic skills, and practicing rituals cultivates moral character.

One of the success stories of the Jiang family lessons was Jiang Zehan, a professor of mathematics at Beijing University in the twentieth century. He was also one of the founders of the China Mathematics

Association. He introduced the concept of topology to China, making an extraordinary contribution to algebraic topology. He went to his family's private academy. When he grew up, he went to Tian Jing for college, and continued his pursuit of a PhD at Harvard University. He recollected the years of his youth in Jiang Village when he wrote, "I sit on the desk to read, opening the windows and I see beautiful mountains. As I am facing the book, the mountains face me. When I grew up, attended college in the United States, and later lived in Beijing, the green mountain still appeared in front of me every so often and was always in my heart. I was determined to study for my country, but that concept started when I was young in that village. I started in my family's school; then I was accepted into a private academy. Despite Jiang Village being a small village, you could always hear the children reciting essays and rehearsing poems from dawn to dusk."[1]

In Principal Dai's office at Shanghai Jian Qing Experimental High School, we talked about Shanghai students' exceptional PISA performance. Principal Dai was proud of their achievement, but he was also very humble. "Some of my students participated in the tests. But this is Shanghai. Shanghai can't represent the whole of China."

I repeated my question to Principal Dai Qun, "What is the motivation for Chinese students to work so hard and do so well?"

"Shanghai is a metropolis of immigrants. We don't have pure, native Shanghaiese. Shanghaiese came from all over the country. Many families came from neighboring provinces, such as Jiangsu, Zhejiang, and Anhui. These families connected with their roots there. The parents or the older generation still frequently visited the places where they were born. They brought their children there. When they stand in their family temples, their ancestral halls, and their family academies, they feel shameful if they don't study hard."

"Why?" I was curious.

---

1 Fang Guanghua: *Jiang Village* in Village Culture Series, Hefei Industrial University Press, 2005.

"Just visiting there, you can understand easily why that is," said Principal Dai. He didn't give me the answer. It seemed that he had instead directed us to a destination.

We traveled to Xiong Village, Shexian, Anhui Province. Xiong Village is located at the foot of Nan Mountain, facing the Xin An River, and across the river is Bamboo Mountain: a geographical landscape that thrives and flourishes from a feng shui[2] perspective. Though only 2,000 residents live in the village now, over the past four hundred years the area was famous for the ambience of culture and education that once thrived in this land. At the entrance of the village was a stone monument. Eight names were carved into the stone, Cao Xiang, Cao Shen, Cao Lou, Cao Xue Shi, Cao Wenzhi, Cao Tan, Cao Cheng, and Cao Zhenyong. All eight of them are jinshi from the Cao family. Cao Wenzhi and Cao Zhenyong were father and son. Cao Wenzhi was a jinshi in 1760. Cao Zhenyong was a jinshi in 1781. Cao Wenzhi served the Emperor Qianlong as his adviser and later as his minister of the interior. His son, Cao Zhenyong, served as Qianlong's historian and later as his minister of appointments. After Emperor Qianlong passed away, Cao Zhenyong served as the prime minister for Emperor Jiaqing. Xiong Village was named the "Home of the Prime Minister" from that time forth. The Cao family was well known as an illustrious family.

Before Cao Wenzhi and Cao Zhenyong became prominent figures at the beginning of the Qing dynasty, the Cao family was in the business of salt trading. Cao Wenzhi's great grandfather, Cao Jinyi, became very rich in this industry, laying a foundation for the family. Cao Wenzhi's father, Cao Yinqing, further enriched the family business.

Cao Yinqing had three sons. He allowed his oldest son to continue running the family business, the second son to manage the properties, and the third son to prepare to take the national imperial examination. On the strength of his family's superior situation, strong support from

2 Feng shui (wind water) is the study of using the laws of heaven and earth to improve the balance of qi (life energy) in one's environment.

his parents, and his own hard work, Cao Wenzhi was able to succeed in the local, provincial, and national exams, becoming a jinshi in 1760. His son, Cao Zhenyong, bolstered by his family's financial support and political connections, obtained his jinshi and served Emperor Qianlong, Emperor Jiaqing, and Emperor Daoguang for a total of seventy-five years, as he was highly trusted among the emperors. At one time, he was even the acting emperor for a few months, the only time in China's history when anything of this sort occurred. The combination of Confucianism and commercialism is what all families wanted in China back then, and today as well. Many families in China keep up this tradition through generations of effort. They succeed financially, then pursue public service to earn a reputation.

In Cao Village, behind the stone monument was the Bamboo Mountain Academy built in 1759 by Cao Wenzhi's brothers. His older brother was in charge of running the family business, and his middle brother was in charge of taking care of the property. This private academy was just for the Cao family members to read classics, rehearse poems, and conduct rituals. This is an example of the institutionalization of a family tradition. The elegant architecture integrated both a school and a garden with many osmanthus flowers (*guihua*). *Gui* is a homonym in the Chinese world for nobility. Once there was a juren in the family, indicating that he had met the highest standards for the provincial test, the family could plant an osmanthus flower in its garden, declaring that the family was flourishing and thriving. I saw sixteen *guihua* in this garden. The roots of five of the plants are connected, being planted by brothers who simultaneously obtained the titles of juren. This kind of high social honor and superior family treatment motivated future descendants to pursue a call for academic achievement, and then public service.

Inside the academy was a bamboo garden. Bamboo, a plant the Chinese enjoy very much, symbolizes humbleness by the tilting of the stalks, which illustrate the concept of being virtuous and standing elegantly. Bamboo grows in segments, indicating to people that one should always move up, step by step. Bamboo is also very durable, showing persistence and perseverance. The green bamboo represents the significance of understanding; its hollowness also reflects the humbleness that an educated person should possess. For Chinese intellectuals, the bamboo is an ideal symbol, reflecting on those who are true to themselves. Su Dongpo, a Song dynasty poet, said, "I can eat without fish, but I cannot eat without seeing bamboo." In the hall, a pair of *duilian* (rhyming couplets or a pair of lines of verse written on the sides of a doorway) glide down: the door.

Zhu jie xin xu, xue ran hou zhi bu zu;
Shan you kui jin, wei ze bi yao qi cheng.

This duplet written by Cao Wenzhi explains how the name of the Bamboo Mountain Academy originated. It is interpreted as, "Bamboo understands the emptiness inside, and through learning, you are able to understand your deficiency. If you haul dirt and rocks basket by basket, you'll eventually create a mountain." Analogous to building a mountain, success is built up from your individual actions.

The art of the language of this poem is outstandingly impressive. The first sentence starts with *zhu*, or "bamboo" in translation; the second sentence starts with *shan*, or "mountain," so they combine together as Bamboo Mountain. The duplet implies that achievement is found in constant learning and continuous actions.

The academy is divided into two sections. The southern part is the lecture hall, and the northern part is the garden. Through a gate on the east side, you can enter the internal yard. Presiding over the garden are a small lecture hall, a study room, and a pavilion. Sitting in the pavilion, you can see boats sailing on the river through the window, emphasizing the peaceful environment created for the descendants to study in. This kind of man-made environment is very conducive for descendants to refresh ancient poems, compose new poems, create duplets, and draft essays, all of which are essential skills for students and scholars in the Confucian traditions.

The academy stands on a peach blossom embankment, facing the Xin An River, across the river from Bamboo Mountain. The architecture is traditional Hui style construction. "Bamboo Mountain Academy" is carved in calligraphy on the lintel of the door. The descendants of the Cao families studied here. Knowledge and learning accumulated generation by generation. Learning never stops as long as genealogy continues. Knowledge flows as blood.

We continued with our search for the secret of Chinese students' motivation. These cultural roots were fascinating to me.

When we arrived at Changxi Village, She County, we went to the Zhou Ancestral Hall. The ancestral hall has three main functions: to store all the family ancestral memorial tablets; for use as a family activity center; and to implement family rules along with announcing family precepts. The rules and precepts were posted inside the ancestral hall—a tradition since the Tang dynasty. Since the Song, Ming, and Qing dynasties, the concept of an ancestral hall has become very popular; almost every family has an ancestral hall, especially in the south of China.

The ancestral hall is an essential institution in Chinese society. Some large families have main halls and branch halls within their ancestral hall. This type of ancestral hall is a combination of the Confucian tradition and the commercial tradition. When families make money, they come back to their homes to build halls, refurbish halls, and expand halls. The halls have come to be an educational institute for the children. When the descendants of a family earn a reputation through the imperial examination system, which is the only way they can earn a reputation, their names are carved into tablets. Over the years, only those achievers who earn a reputation in examinations and public service are honored in the halls. When descendants step into the hall, they will only see the high achievers in the family, with their titles, rewards remarks, and accomplishments. All others have been forgotten.

The Zhou Ancestral Hall was built on Lai Long Mountain, surrounded by bamboo and pine trees, facing the Changyuan River, with gently flowing water moving downstream. The architecture of the hall is in a typical Hui style, commonly found in the Hui district area. The roof is built from carved ceramics, with *kylin* (a mythical beast, the Chinese unicorn) embellished on the roof. The kylin, aChinese symbol for fortune and luck, is a mythical, hooved, chimerical creature which is said to appear with the imminent arrival or passing of a wise sage or an illustrious ruler.

The walls are built of dark-blue bricks, with a stone foundation. The lintels are engraved with the words *En ci jinshi,* put there by the jinshi appointed by the emperor. From the middle of the Ming dynasty to the end of the Qing dynasty, the Zhou family had four jinshi, nine juren, and twenty-seven gongyuan, along with seventy-four xiucai. This is an extraordinary number of academic achievers in one family.

In the main hall, the different lintels have the title of jinshi carved into the wood, along with the title *Fu Zi Jinshi.* Once someone in the family has achieved high honors, he is inscribed in this pantheon of heroes. This is one of the deepest cultural traditions in China, especially in southern China.

Zhou Maoxiang assumed the position of a jinshi in 1829. He was appointed as an officer in the Interior Ministry by the *Keju*, the imperial examination system. After he died in Beijing, his wife brought his three sons and two daughters back to his home in Changxi. In the old, traditional society, the position of women was inferior to that of men. Women were expected only to take care of their husbands and children. In the 1900s, girls still weren't allowed to be educated and were expected to help their mothers with household work.

After Zhou Maoxiang died, his wife's only hope was her sons. Just like Mencius's mother, she continued the family legacy and educated her three sons. All three earned juren status. Her youngest son obtained the position of a jinshi. The jinshi lintel is for this branch of the family.

In the village, the Zhou family had to compete against the neighboring Wu family—a thriving family in terms of wealth and education in the town of Changxi. The amount of pressure on a family to thrive was enormous, and without hard work, families risked being looked down upon by others. The competition for education and wealth accumulation was vehement.

In the Zhou family hall, the main frame in the hall has many boards and tablets hanging from the ceiling inscribed with the words *jinshi* and *gongyuan*. It was a tradition that anybody in the family who took the imperial exam and became gongyuan, juren, or jinshi had a tablet made for them inside the hall, as well as flags for them displayed outside. In front of the ancestral hall, there is a town square that can hold 1,000 people, paved with egg-shaped marbles (symbols of thriving and prestige) to show the significance of the family.

This is where parents bring children to admonish them to show respect to their ancestors and to promise their ancestors they'll pursue an arduous life. Parents shame their children for wrongdoings, saying, "If you don't achieve, you will never live up to the hopes and expectations of your ancestors," or "If you don't achieve, your grandfather will be ashamed." Parents make their children read the precepts and the rules, embedding each one in their minds.

Construction of the hall began in 1497. The venue became a teaching hall and a Confucian learning center for the Zhou family, outliving the Ming dynasty (1368–1644) and the Qing dynasty (1644–1911). It has been maintained the way a basilica or cathedral is preserved in the West. Where the Bible was read in the sanctuaries of Western churches, the Confucian classics were rehearsed in China's ancestral halls and family academies.

To a large extent, learning and research of Confucian classics were institutionalized in the thousands of academies across China. These academies were the vehicles of Confucius' philosophy and teachings. China's first such classical learning institute, Yuelu Academy, is the most representative.

The Yuelu Academy is located on Yuelu Mountain in Changsha, Hunan Province, facing the Xiang River. It claims to be one of the three earliest universities in the world, founded in AD 976. The other two are Morocco's University of Al Karaouine, established in AD 959, and the Al-Azhar al-Sarif University in Egypt, established in AD 988. The earliest university in Europe is the Universita di Bologna in Italy, established in AD 1088. Yuelu Academy has survived through the Song, Yuan, Ming, and Qing dynasties. In 1903 it became the Hunan Institute of Higher Learning, then the Hunan Normal College, then the Hunan Public Polytechnic School, and finally, Hunan University in 1926. Despite the changes in the name, from the conversion of the Yuelu Academy to Hunan University, the transformation continued through the alternating phases of China's education system.

The Yuelu Academy is one of the most famous academies out of the thousands in China. The Yuelu Academy has three main functions: lectures, a library, and the practice of rituals. The purpose of the academy is to revive the Confucian tradition in a formal school system. The Yuelu Academy may be epitome for the Confucian tradition to be taught, practiced, honored, and expanded.

Stepping into the academy from the entrance, the couplet painted on the door says, *Wei chu you cai, yu si wei sheng*. This means, "Chu Guo, the area in which Yuelu Academy is located, possesses talents, and here, those talents excel." This couplet reveals the high aspiration of these Chinese intellectuals and scholars. The first part of the couplet comes from China's classic, *Zuo Zhuan*; the second part comes from Confucius' *Analects*.

The Yuelu Academy has five lecture halls. The famous Confucius scholars, Zhu Xi and Zhang Shi, neo-Confucianists of the Song dynasty, once jointly lectured here in AD 1167 became a tradition of exchanging viewpoints from different perspectives. Emperor Kang Xi famously wrote in calligraphy, *xue da xing tian*, promoting the Neo-Confucian Rationalistic School, and meaning "enhancing self cultivation through learning." The wall stones have student rules and reading methods engraved on them. The library contains all of the Confucian classics, along with the emperor's compilation of the classics, collected by the imperial court during the Qing dynasty and used by students and teachers. A temple was built inside the Yuelu Academy as a specific tribute to Confucius. Other great Confucian scholars in China's history have their own temples inside the academy. The "Da Cheng" gate and "Da Cheng" hall are the high-water marks of the academy, emphasizing that Confucius achieved to perfection.

Lian Xi Temple is a tribute to Zhou Dunyi, who conceptualized neo-Confucian cosmology, explaining the idea of the relationship between human conduct and universal forces, emphasizing the mastering of *qi*, and teaching his ideas to his students. Si Jian Pavilion is a tribute to Cheng Hao and Cheng Yi, brothers and also the students of Zhou Dunyi. The brothers were very different. The older, Cheng Hao, was very laid back, while the younger, Cheng Yi, was serious about his work. But both were well known for their contributions to philosophy.

Chong Dao Temple is a tribute to Zhu Xi, the leading figure of the School of Principle (*Li*), and Zhang Shi. The two were said to have argued for three days and three nights about the Doctrine of the Mean. Chuan Shan Temple is a tribute to Wang Fuzhi, who believed the Confucian teachings at the time had been distorted, so he wrote his own commentary on Confucius' philosophies. They were all neo-Confucianists.

Yuelu Academy became a center of Confucianism, furthering the development of Confucianism from the time of the Song dynasty. Generations of leading scholars came out of this academy. When students walk inside the Yuelu Academy, they feel as if they are experiencing thousands of years of history, philosophy, and culture. Chinese culture scholar, Yu Qiuyu, once said, "All the events that occurred in the Qing dynasty can be related to this academy on this mountain."

At Yuelu Academy, students are expected to follow strict rules. The students must frequently pay respect to their parents. Students must call on and pray to the sages. They must cultivate the habit of correcting their mistakes. Students must be earnest and solemn when they study. Students must also be very frugal and not excessive. Students must not become involved in other people's business, especially when it is irrelevant to them. When students sit, they must sit in order, respecting the elderly. A student must learn never to speak against someone's merit. He or she must never associate with inappropriate companions, chat, or waste time. Students must recite classics three times a day. Students must read outlines for classes and many pages of textbook material a day. They have to be up to date with current affairs and matters of the universe and nature. They have to read many classical essays and poems, and make notes when they read. When attending class, students must be on time. If a student studies late into the night, they cannot wake up late in the morning. If a student misses a class, he or she must make it up; if a student doubts something, they must resolve the doubt. All of this, the students must follow, and all of this is carved into the walls of the Academy. Aside from the precepts, in the Academy, there are numerous couplets meant to inspire students, following the Confucian tradition, to achieve their highest potential. The couplets are not only beautiful calligraphy, but they also teach the students morality, the ability to obtain knowledge, and self-cultivation. Out of the thousands of academies similar to the Yuelu Academy in China, this is the most visited academy of all.

The Yuelu Academy is a landmark in China's history of education. These monuments, couplets, and calligraphy give the visitors a picture of the evolution of China's education. These philosophies and principles of learning and advancing knowledge are as firm as those stone monuments and are inscribed on the memories of generations.

CHAPTER 13
School Competition

> If you want to be a political leader, go to Changsha First School.
>
> If you prepare to go abroad to study, go to Yali School.
>
> If you want to win a Nobel Prize, go to Shida Fuzhong.
>
> If you want to obtain high scores on gaokao, or go to Beijing University or Qinghua University, go to Chang Jun School.
>
> It's all that simple.

This was announced on a local TV educational program in Changsha, the capital city of Hunan Province. In this television program, the hosts tried to help parents select which high school would be the best fit for their children. Changsha First School, Yali School, Shida Fuzhong, and Chang Jun School are the four top, elite high schools in the province.

Changsha is the hometown of the four prestigious high schools, and it is claimed to be the cradle of China's renowned revolutionists and scholars since the 1850s. In the 1840s to the 1860s, Taiping's rebellion led by Hong Xiuquan swept through southern China, threatening the Qing dynasty's regime. Zeng Guofan was a Hunan military general and devout Confucian scholar. He organized the local army, suppressing the Taiping rebellion movement. Afterward, Zeng Guofan turned down every offer from the Qing emperor, and returned to Hunan Province. When he attacked the

Taiping rebellion movement, his generals collected a huge quantity of silver and gold from the rebels, which was then shipped back to Hunan. They didn't waste the money. Most of it went to academies, schools, and the education system, following the tradition of supporting the value of education. This makes Changsha, Hunan, an incubator of intellectuals and scholars.

Inside Shida Fuzhong is a monument with nineteen students' names carved into the stone. All of the students are winners of Olympiad gold medals. This school among all the schools in China has won the most gold medals in Olympiad competitions, which focuses on students competing in events geared towards a certain subject from math to physics to biology. In China, anyone who obtains an Olympiad gold medal can go to his or her school of choice anywhere in the nation.

Yali School sounds like Yale; and in actuality, a Yale alumnus established this high school. Yali School provides excellent foreign language and culture education, as well as regular contact with Yale University. Yale regularly sends teachers and visitors to Yali. In recent years, Beijing University, Qinghua University, and Fudan University were not the only the best choices for top students in Yali School: students were admitted to elite schools in Europe, the U.S., and Australia.

Changsha First School was the high school of many of China's leaders. It is the alma mater of Mao Zedong, the founding father of the People's Republic of China, and Zhu Rongji, the fifth prime minister of the People's Republic of China, along with many other leaders. In the Confucian tradition, obtaining a government post through the imperial examination system was a top goal for students. Changsha First School provided a very competitive advantage for students who pursued politics and public service.

Top scores in the gaokao always come from this school, and it produce smany zhuangyuan in the national entrance exam. In 2008 one student missed the test and did not get into a top school, but every other student in the class was accepted into elite schools. Can you imagine a school in which the entire class is accepted into elite schools except for one student who missed the test? Inside the school, essays written by famous alumni are displayed in glass cases, modeling the high motivation for the students to achieve.

Another elite school in the area, Changjun School, was the first high school in Hunan to be authorized by the College Board to offer Advanced Primer classes. The school selects first- and second-year high school students to focus on AP classes for three years, and second- and third-year high school students to focus on AP classes for two years. They have one goal: to get into American Ivy League colleges.

Changjun School has amassed over four hundred students selected from the four elite middle schools in Changsha so far. School competition is vehement and television, news media, micro-blogs, and the Internet amplify the competition. Parents believe that getting into the top four high schools is a guarantee for their children to be successful, and in Changsha parents try in every possible way to send their children to these four schools. But the acceptance rate is only 8.3 percent. They can only get into one high school, there are no options—thus the 8.3 percent means that the acceptance rate is 8.3 percent for all four of the schools, with no overlap.

One student said, "Getting into these schools does not mean that you are successful, it's just the beginning of three years of suffering in high school. Without strong perseverance and an iron will, a student shouldn't even consider these schools. We think that we work quite hard when we configure two or three ways to prove the Pythagorean theorem, but those students have to prove it in five or six different ways."

The competition among schools is expressed in the gaokao, and also on the high school entrance examinations, which are controlled by local education departments or bureaus. For example, Beijing Municipality Bureau of Education manages the high school entrance examinations. Zhongkao tests students in five subjects: Chinese (120 points), mathematics (120 points), English (120 points), physics (100 points), chemistry (80 points), and physical education (40 points) with a total 580 points.

The competition between high schools is cutthroat. In Beijing, the two schools that compete are Ren Da Fu Zhong and Beijing Number 4 School. The required points for acceptance to Ren Da Fu Zhong is 550 points, and for Beijing Number 4 School, 554 points. The next levels are Beijing Experiment School with 545 points, Qing Hua Fu Zhong (Affiliated School to Qinghua University) with 544 points, Bei Da Fu Zhong (Affiliated School to Beijing University) with 542 points, and Beijing Number 2 School with 542 points.

Top schools choose students strictly on these set requirements to guarantee they admit the highest caliber of students onto their campus. They allow a limited number of spots for students to choose their school. These students are called *ze xiao sheng*, or students selecting schools. Because these students are given the opportunity to select their intended or ideal school, they are allowed to have lower scores in the high school entrance examinations, but they need to pay a high cost. Even so, this difference is hair-thin. For example, the official acceptance line for Re Da Fu Zhong is 550 points; the score for students selecting schools is 548 points, only a two-point difference. The normal acceptance line for Beijing Experiment School is 545 points, while the score for students selecting schools is 544 points, a one-point difference. For Beijing No. 4 High School, the difference is zero. The normal acceptance line and the score for students selecting schools are identical.

To American students, this sounds absurd. What's the big deal if you miss one or two points out of 570 points? For my brother who took the MCAT, which is scored out of a total of forty-five points, one or two points might be a big deal. For the ACT test, which is scored out of thirty-six points, a couple of points may be meaningful, even significant. Beijing's zhongkao is a test with 570 points. This is in China, this is in Beijing, this is in Shanghai. They are the world's most competitive places for education. For students accepted into Beijing No. 4 High School, 40 percent—about 200 of its 500 students—will be accepted by Beijing University or Qinghua

University (China's Harvard and Stanford, students' and parents' dream schools).

For students who are accepted by ordinary high schools, their chances of getting into top universities are much slimmer. Although China's geography is dramatically different from north to south, east to west, this system for high school entrance examinations is the same across the country. In Nanjing, Nan Shi Da Fu Zhong (Affiliated School to Nanjing Normal University), Nanjing Foreign Language School, Shu Ren School, and Jin Ling School are in competition. In Changsha, Changsha First School, Hu Nan Shi Da Fu Zhong (Affiliated School to Hunan Normal University), Yali School, and Chang Jun School are embattled in fierce competition.

Leaving the Dragon School in Chengdu, we got into a taxi. We were flipping through the pages of the brochure from the Dragon School. On the cover, the registered trademark "479" was labeled in Chinese. The "4" represented Chengdu Fourth School. The "7" represented Chengdu Seventh School, and the "9" represented Chengdu Ninth School. The taxi driver noticed the numbers on the brochure, and suddenly burst into excited conversation. He told us that his daughter was in the Chengdu Fourth School. We told him why we went to the Dragon School—to learn about their traditional education—and from there he told us that he highly recommended that we visit the Fourth School.

Since that was only a few miles away, we decided to take his advice. He dropped us at the front gate of the Chengdu Fourth School, now known as "Shi Shi School." During the Cultural Revolution, all the schools changed their names to numbers, but afterward, the order was wrecked, and many schools returned to their traditional names. Shi Shi was a school brand for more than 2,000 years and now it was back to its original name.

Shi Shi School was established by Wen Weng, the former governor of Sichuan, in 143 BCE. It was the first public school in China. Although China evolved and changed from dynasty to dynasty, Shi Shi School was never interrupted. It has been in the same location for 2,155 years.

The architecture of the school is a combination of Han dynasty (roofs and walls) and modern technology (the newest and latest science labs, computers, electronics, and projection equipment). Shi Shi School is a national model school.

Walking into the school, we were pointed in the direction of the office. There we met Mr. Li, a staff member who was kind enough to give us a tour during his break. He talked about how the school emphasizes three main characteristics: tradition, basic education, and creative innovation, all heavily supported and enforced by the principal, the teachers, and the staff. The school is very internationally oriented, with prepared programs for students who plan to study abroad in the U.S. and Canada. They also have a China–New Zealand experimental class and a Cambridge experimental class. They hope to expand further in the future, and deal with more international venues.

There was a large red piece of paper hanging from the ceiling with many names printed in black ink. After Shi Shi School released the national exam scores in 2011, many top students were from Sichuan Province. In fact, there were an incredible number of students who passed the acceptance levels of the first-tier schools in science and humanities who were all from Sichuan.. The average English scores were also number one in Sichuan. Along with those names on the poster were all the names of students who scored above the acceptance level for the first-tier universities.

"At our school we have this legacy. There has never been a student who has gone through here who hasn't been accepted into college. With our school philosophy, we try to help every student in the best possible way, in the hope that we can shape their future, " remarked Mr. Li.

Shi Shi School's culture states that without education, you cannot thrive. To think that you can only become educated after you have become rich is wrong. Shi Shi School's motto has been alive for thousands of years, in their schools, and in the rest of China. I was reminded again: it doesn't matter what your background is, or your social status, or anything else, because everyone can learn. Education is the top priority whether you are rich or poor.

Before the system of modern education was introduced in the twentieth century in China, for 2,000 years, Shi Shi School consistently taught Confucius' classics, including *Classic of Poetry, Classic of Book Documents, The Classic of Rituals, Classic of Changes,* and *Spring and Autumn Annals,* compiled by Confucius and his followers. Civility and moral responsibility have been consistently advanced by education. Innovations, ideas, and technology have all come from the basic Confucian principles of education and have flourished into reality. For over 2,000 years, Confucian ideals have stood strong.

In Shanghai, Shanghai School (Shanghai Zhong Xue), High School Affiliated with Fudan University (Fu Dan Fu Zhong), High School Affiliated with Shanghai Jiaotong University (Jiao Da Fu Zhong), and High School Affiliated with China East Normal University (Shi Da Fu Zhong) compete for the students who are likely to be accepted into top colleges. In 2011, 98.9 percent of students from Shanghai School entered top colleges, 94 percent from Hua Shi Da Fu Zhong, 94 percent from Fu Dan Fu Zhong, and 91 percent from Jiao Da Fu Zhong.[1] Teachers read these numbers. Parents read these numbers. Students read these numbers. Principals read these numbers.

Shanghai School is a stand-alone school in terms of having no affiliation to any universities or colleges. The other three are all affiliated with top universities, Fudan University, Shanghai Jiaotong University, and China East Normal University. These schools are called "affiliated" because they were initially founded by the universities, although they later became independent from the universities so that they could recruit students form the whole metropolitan area. These schools are referred to as Shanghai's "big four" by the local Shanghaiese.

Dr. Li Zheng, my mom's schoolmate, told me in Shanghai, "Shanghai students compete to get into one of these four high schools. Parents are behind them. Families are behind them."

---

1 http://zhidao.baidu.com/question/294267783.html

Fu Dan Fu Zhong led the way in building a connection and pathway from high school education to college education. They advise students to select college classes. They invite university professors to teach advanced college-level classes. In this fervent competitive environment, every school wants to stand out. "These connections are seamless," claimed Principal Zheng Fangxian.

Competition also comes internally. Classes compete with each other and teachers' expectations get higher and higher. This expectation is reflected by the attitude regarding student scores—the goal is for everybody to get a perfect score.

A parent of a student in Jinan was called to the school his son attended. The teacher complained to the father, "Looking at your son's score—it is only 96 (out of 100) for his Chinese class, and 97 (out of 100) for the mathematics class." The father was confused.

The teacher continued, "All the other students in the class got 100 points in both Chinese class and mathematics class. If he continues to perform this poorly, what is his future?"

At the Affiliated School to Shanghai Jiaotong University after a physics test in junior high school, the top class averaged a score of 149.2 out of 150. These classes had about forty to fifty students in each class, with about ten to fifteen classes per grade. The teacher was infuriated with the average, and remarked that the class average should have been at least a 149.5. This class was the best class of the grade, but the expectation to do well involved more than simply being the best—there was also a minimum class score to be met. The teachers pushed their students even if the difference was only by an average of 0.3 points; the slightest difference marked the difference between approval and disappointment. American parents might consider this absolutely crazy. American teachers' glasses might fall off their noses as they consider this unbelievable pressure on students.

As the director of academic affairs at Shanghai Jiaotong University School of Medicine, Dr. Zhang Yanping participated in college admissions every year. Through the years, she experienced how aggressively each school promoted its students. Shanghai School emphasizes its solid foundation in basics of science, social studies, and humanities. The other three schools emphasize their students' readiness for college because of their institution's affiliation with top universities. China's model in having public schools affiliated with top universities. (In the United States, people may send their kids to private prep schools on the East Coast, such as Phillips Exeter Academy, Groton School, etc., and later their sons and daughters might attend Harvard, Yale, and Princeton, but these all are stand-alone schools.)

When I brought up the topic of memorization with a group of students from Shandong Province, China, who were attending the University of Minnesota, there was a pause in the room and some exchanged looks. They admitted they didn't like the tedious task of memorizing essay after essay, but they were forced to do it in school by their teachers back in Shandong. They knew they had to or else they would fall behind everyone else.

"Memorization is like a competition," said Jerry. "Who can memorize the most? Who can memorize the most mathematical formulas? Who can memorize the most chemical equations? Who can memorize the hardest material? Who can memorize the best? We would spend hours and hours clenching a book in our hands, reading and reading passages over and over. But deep down inside, while we were going to the bathroom, we knew that all the other students were memorizing more than us."

Recalling high school life a few years ago in Qingdao, Jeff admitted that there was some tension between the classes in his high school. Sometimes when students heard about another class in the same grade that was learning some things differently or obtaining some new materials, the students got suspicious, as did their parents. They were concerned that they might lose out on something, or that the students in other classes were getting ahead of them in their studies, or that students in other classes received exercises that made them better prepared for the national examinations. In fact, some teachers are better at guessing what questions will be on the national examinations than other teachers. This tension creates some strife among the classes. Jeff recalled a time when some teachers had such a fervent desire to produce better students that they stole students from other classes to make their own classes better. Jeff concluded that he wouldn't be surprised if other schools did the same.

When I read about the failures of the public schools in Washington, DC, I feel depressed. In 2007 only 12 percent of the incoming high school students could read at grade level; only 8 percent were at grade level in math; only 9 percent went on to graduate from college within five years of high school graduation. "The system in Washington, DC, was broken," concluded Michelle Rhee, the former chancellor of the District of Columbia Public Schools.[2]

Public schools in China's capital, Beijing, present a very different picture: In 2009 at the School Affiliated to China People's University (Ren Da Fu Zhong), the School Affiliated with Beijing University (Bei Da Fu Zhong), the School Affiliated with Qinghua University (Qing Hua Fu Zhong), the Beijing Eleventh School, the Beijing One Hundred-First School, and the School Affiliated with Capital Normal University (Shou Shi Da Fu Zhong), 100 percent of senior students entered four-year colleges.[3] In 2006, 76,375 students entered high schools; by 2009, 70,132 students graduated from high schools, with a graduation rate of 92 percent.[4]

What a tale of two capitals!

---

2 Carl Weber, *Waiting for "Superman": How Can We Save America's Failing Public Schools* . New York: Participant Media, 128.

3 "Acceptance Rates of Beijing High School Students," *Beijing Zhongkao Wang*, December 22 2012. http://www.beijing518.com/2010/1222/157377.html.

4 *China Education Yearbook*, 2007, and http://wenku.baidu.com/view/6ff9e1fb770bf78a652954db.html.

CHAPTER 14
A Soul with a Mission

While working on this book in March 2012, I signed on to my AOL account, and boostup.org (a student advocacy web site) popped up with some facts in an advertisement: "7,000 high school students drop out every school day. That's a line of desks four miles long." This type of headline is regularly seen in the American news media. But from the other side of the Pacific Ocean, we hear of different headlines.

A December 2010 headline about high school students in Shanghai occupied the news media in the West: "Top Test Scores from Shanghai Stun Educators" (*The New York Times*), "How Shanghai Topped PISA Rankings—And Why It's Not Big News in China" (*Washington Post*), "Shanghai Students Lead Global Results on PISA" (*Science*), "On Those 'Stunning' Shanghai Test Scores" (*The Atlantic*), "Japan Gets Pass Marks in OECD Test—But Trails Shanghai" (*Wall Street Journal*), "Shanghai Has the World's Smartest Teens" (*CNN International*), "Shanghai Students Ranked Best in the World at Math and Science" (*The Telegraph*), "'Wake-up Call': US Students Trail Global Leaders" (*Associated Press*) , "China Beats Out Finland for Top Marks in Education" (*Time*), "In International Report Card: Shanghai's School Students Out-Perform All Others" (*The Economist*). These headlines were the result of Shanghai's first-time participation in the Program for International Student Assessment (PISA) in 2009[1]. Shanghai students placed first in all three subjects: math, science, and reading. The

1 65 countries participated in the 2009 PISA ranging from the United States to Finland to Kyrgyzstan.

U.S. placed much farther down in the rankings: thirtieth in math, twenty-third in science, and seventeenth in reading.

China has made remarkable improvements in its education system. Chinese students outperform the world, at least in high schools. How is it that they achieve that? A look at Bella Zhou's schedule and plan described by Leslie Chang in *National Geographic*[2] is sufficient to help explain this phenomenon. Zhou Jiaying was enrolled in two classes at the age of four—Spoken American English and English Conversation. In the hope that she might go abroad for college, her parents gave her the English name Bella. When she was five, they enrolled her in an acting class. When she turned eight, she started piano lessons. During the summers she took swimming lessons, which her parents hoped would make her taller because Bella wanted to be a lawyer (height being an advantage for a lawyer). By age ten, Bella lived a fairly regimented life. She did homework unsupervised after school until her parents got home. After dinner, she had a bath and practiced piano. On the few occasions she was permitted to watch TV, she was only allowed to see the news. Saturdays meant a private essay class and Math Olympics, and Sundays were spent in a piano lesson and a prep class for her entrance exam to middle school. "The best moment of the week was Friday afternoon, when school let out early. Bella might take a deep breath and look around, like a man who discovers a glimpse of blue sky from the confines of the prison yard," wrote Chang.

Secondary education in the United States has received criticism from educators and entrepreneurs. Some private prep schools, such as Phillips Exeter Academy and Groton School, enjoy international popularity,. Equivalent to those prep schools stand several public schools, such as Boston Latin School, which are the best of the best in secondary education. But in general, America's secondary education is not compatible with the country's economic or military clout in the world, according to Bill Gates, Nicholas Kristof, and many commentators, some of whom consider

2 "Gilded Age Gilded Cage," Leslie T. Chang, *National Geographic*, Special Issue: China, Inside the Dragon, May 2008.

American secondary education a "failure." The World Economic Forum's "World Competitiveness Report" ranks China thirty-first out of 142 countries on the quality of its math and science education, well ahead of America's fifty-first position.[3] "If we keep the system as it is, millions of children will never get a chance to fulfill their promise," Gates said. "That is offensive to our values, and it's an insult to who we are." Warren Buffet said the failure to reverse the high-school dropout rate would have "devastating consequences for the nation."

Kerry Killinger, chairman and chief executive officer of Washington Mutual and former vice chairman of Achieve Inc., an organization focused on assuring high school graduates to be "college and career ready," said the nation must respond to growing competition from China and India as well as from more developed nations. "If we don't, we're positioning the United States to gradually become a less developed nation."[4]

More alarming data shows that the U.S. ranks sixteenth among twenty developed nations in the percentage of students who complete high school, and fourteenth among the top twenty in college graduation rates. Only eighteen of 100 students starting high school will go on to complete their college degree within six years of starting college. Ben Feller reports that the U.S. "has slipped from first to fifth internationally in the percentage of young people who hold a college degree." In math and science, American students are slipping behind the rest of the world between the fourth and twelfth grades, "starting among the top ranks and finishing near the bottom of industrialized nations," says Feller.[5] Bill Gates called for a reconstruction of the high schools in the United States declaring, "Our high schools were designed fifty years ago to meet the needs of another age. Until we design them to meet the needs of this century, we will keep

3 "How to Get a Date," *The Economist*. December 31, 2011.

4 Dan Balz, "Microsoft Gates Urges Governors to Restructure US High Schools." *Washington Post*. 27 February 2005.

5 Ben Feller, "Calling high schools obsolete, Microsoft chief urges restructuring." *The Boston Globe*. 27 February 2005.

limiting, even ruining, the lives of millions of Americans every year."[6]

A quote posted on the wall at Stowe Elementary in northwest Washington, DC, says, "There is nothing a teacher can do to overcome what a parent and a student will not do," stressing the key role of parents' responsibility in the education of children. In August of 2011 an issue of *The Economist* ran a column titled "No Child Left Behind, Testing Times," asserting that the main reason American schools do badly is "poor teaching." But is a student's success solely the teacher's responsibility? Perhaps we as a nation are performing poorly and blaming each other.

So whose responsibility is it? Who is to blame for the state of American students' education? The decline of American K-12 education causes enormous anxiety among parents, teachers, politicians, social entrepreneurs, and the general public. President Obama claimed this American education crisis was a wake-up call—"time for a Sputnik moment."[7] Bill Gates called for a complete restructure of the high school curriculum. What happened to our schools?

The direction we choose, the target we aim for, will determine whether we can turn this crisis around. We need to see the target and take precise aim. Imagine a cannon on a ship docked in port—to the right is the sea, to the left is the target. Our cannon is facing the sea at the moment, aiming at nothing specific. The vast sea provides plenty of area to shoot at, but no bull's eye. Education historian Diane Ravitch observed, "Every state should have a curriculum that is rich in knowledge, issues, and ideas, while leaving teachers free to use their own methods, with enough time to introduce topics and activities of their own choosing."[8]

Historian David McCullough began worrying about the gap in students' knowledge of history some twenty years ago when a college sophomore approached him after an appearance at "a very good university in the Midwest." She thanked him for coming and admitted, "Until I heard

6 Ibid.

7 State of the Union address, January 26, 2011.

8 Ravitch, 236.

your talk this morning, I never realized the original thirteen colonies were all on the East Coast." Remembering the incident, Mr. McCullough's snow-white eyebrows curled in pain. "I thought, *what have we been doing so wrong that this obviously bright young woman could get this far and not know that?*"[9]

The 2011 National Assessment of Educational Progress revealed that most fourth grade students were unable to say why Abraham Lincoln was an important figure. Few high school seniors were able to identify China as the North Korean ally that fought American troops during the Korean War, and fewer than a third of eighth graders could identify an important advantage American forces had over the British during the Revolution.[10] In other words, Americans don't know American history.

In Huantai Second High School, we met with a geography teacher, Song Lifeng. When I asked about what he covered in his geography class, he described three sections. One is natural geography, including rivers, valleys, mountains, and plateaus, patterns of weather, plants, and resources. The second section is the geography of humanity, including ethnic cultures and traditions. The third section is on climate change, global warming, and world catastrophes. One student's insightful grasp of African geography, the distribution of the African natural resources, and African cultural traditions of different tribes amazed me.

I admit my limited knowledge of geography. In elementary school, I learned the states and capitals. In middle school, each student was assigned a project on a place in the world. I chose Georgia, the country in Europe, not to be confused with the U.S. state of Georgia. I cannot claim that geography was excluded from the curriculum of my elementary school, middle school, and high school, but it was profoundly limited in my curriculum.

---

9 Brian Bolduc, "Don't Know Much About History" *Wall Street Journal*, June 18, 2011.

10 Sam Dillon. "US Students Remain Poor at History, Tests Show." *The New York Times*. 14 June 2011.

Zhang Zhaozhong's American experience caused me to cringe. Mr. Zhang is a commentator on world conflicts on China Central Television (CCTV). When he was a visiting scholar to the United States a few years ago, his American friend invited him to dinner at his home. His friend's son, who was in high school at the time, came down from upstairs, holding a globe. At first Mr. Zhang thought his friend's son wanted to give him a gift. But to his surprise, the boy asked Mr. Zhang to point out where China is on the globe![11]

Facebook created a game called "Traveler IQ Challenge" to entertain and enhance an average user's page and test the players' knowledge of world geography. In the game, users are provided with a map and a city or monument. The player needs to place a flag in the area where they think the named location is. The score is based on how close the guess was to the actual position of the city. With more than 65,000 Facebook users participating globally, the result showed that the U.S. was ranked 117th of 193 countries in terms of accuracy and knowledge of other nations. The United States has the most Facebook users, but its most rudimentary knowledge of world geography remains woefully underdeveloped.

The 2006 National Geographic-Roper Geographic Literacy Survey published statistics regarding U.S. citizens aged eighteen to twenty-four on their knowledge of geography. Fifty percent of Americans surveyed could not locate New York on a map; only 37 percent of Americans could find Iraq on a map, despite American troops having been stationed there for three years. Twenty percent of young Americans believed that Sudan is in Asia, although Sudan is the largest country in Africa and the Sudanese government has been continuously criticized in the news for its genocide.

Not only do American schools suffer from a lack of geographical knowledge, but also deficiency in foreign languages, which has caused many concerns. As a saying widely circulated among commentators: a person who knows two languages is bilingual. A a person who knows three languages is trilingual. A person who knows four languages is

11 *Focus*, July 20, 2011.

quadrilingual. The term for people who know only one language is "Americans," according to U.S. Trade Representative Ron Kirk in a description of his travels around the world.[12] And a more serious problem than speaking only one language is that our use of the only language we speak is declining in terms of students' reading and writing proficiency.

Certainly English is a world language. When my brother returned from a trip to Turkey, he said he realized that if had to choose only one language to know, it would definitely be English. He found it so wonderful to hear people in Turkey speak English, because that meant he could communicate with them.

Every student in China is learning English, with the expectation that in the future they will be able to put it to good use. English has become like the new "piano" in the country; learning English has reached a frenzy. When we were in Huantai, the county where my father was born in Shandong Province, we found a Cambridge Academy of English. English is embraced enthusiastically by parents and students at Dragon School (Wang Zi Chong Long School) in Chengdu, considered a major feeder school for Qinghua University and Beijing University, where they help students achieve the highest potential scores on the gaokao. In Loudi, Loudi First School wants to be the incubator of students for top elite schools. Mr. He, the English teacher, is one of the most honored and demanding teachers. In Shanghai, students and parents consider English and mathematics the core skills to hone from elementary school through high school. The United States may feel proud that the world is following in its footsteps, but how can we justify this pride when our own students can barely pass their mother-tongue language tests?

When his daughter was in third grade, Nicholas Kristof took her on a trip to China. Showing the Chinese students some of his daughter's homework from her school in New York, they saw that the level of study was similar to a first-grade level in a Shanghai school. Kristof noted that in

12 "There's a word for people who only know one language: American," In the Money Blog, October 20, 2011. http://blogs.app.com/inthemoney/2011/10/20/theres-a-word-for-people-who-only-know-one-language-american/

the schools of rural areas, which are far from being top-notch due to lack of funding, "it's normally impossible to hold even a primitive conversation in English with an English teacher. But the kids in the good schools in Chinese cities are leaving our children in the dust."[13]

Kristof remarked that during the summer, students in China spend hours each day completing homework, even before the added-on studies. In some schools, students spend all their time reading and writing book reports. Conversely, in the United States, "American students have to spend each September relearning what they forgot over the summer."

Though by now it is a cliché to repeat that we live in an age of globalization, it is fair to ask whether Americans are prepared to be global citizens. *Newsweek* journalist Rana Foroohar visited Qinghua University in 2010. At the end of her visit, she asked the students she met where they planned to settle after graduation. "Most said China. A handful said the United States; two had plans to go to Europe. But one, an engineer-to-be, gave what I thought was the most foresighted answer of all. 'West Africa,' he said. 'There's opportunity here, but China's very quickly becoming a normal country. I want to go where things are really happening.'"

Foroohar added, "The world has become their oyster."[14]

We Americans face a challenge in this globalization age.

Before my parents moved to the United States, they lived on the campus of Shandong University, Jinan. They had a neighbor who was also my mom's schoolmate. This neighbor now works in a medical school at a top university in Shanghai. His daughter graduated from Shanghai Jiaotong University in 2010. She applied to multiple American universities for her graduate studies, and decided to go to Georgia Institute of Technology for her PhD in computer science. After she settled and started school in Atlanta, my mom called her. She lived in a large apartment conveniently

13 Nicholas D. Kristof, "Chinese Medicine for American Schools" *New York Times*, June 27, 2008.

14 Rana Foroohar, "The World's Their Oyster," *The Daily Beast*, Oct 10, 2010.

located near the school. They chatted about her future. She impressed my mom with her plans. "I will take a few intern opportunities in Houston and Silicon Valley during my study years. After I graduate, I will work for Facebook or Microsoft for two years. Then I will go back to China for a professor position and start my own consulting company." It sounded as though she had already drawn her life map. Rana Foroohar reported the same story from Qinghua University students.[15] Leslie Chang reported similar stories in her National Geographic cover story, "Gilded Age Gilded Cage".[16] Is this mind-set attributable to national curriculum guidance? I think so.

Without a national curriculum, education inequality , poor standards and lack of consistency become obvious. Students in my school district and in some surrounding areas can be considered extremely lucky. Actually, I clearly remember the day we were told this. In tenth grade I took Enriched Biology, a class that involved quite a bit of lab work. We had just finished our gel electrophoresis unit and were about to complete our lab analyzing the DNA of lettuce and spinach by separating the DNA itself. Before we began our lab, my teacher told the class that we should feel very fortunate to be doing such labs. Many schools don't have the equipment that our school provides for us. Our high school provides a wide range of activities and subjects in classes, such as labs, art projects, extra literature (books), etc. that many schools don't have. And I appreciate that. But what about students in the rest of the nation? Taxes are quite high in our school district and that allows us to have high-quality equipment and opportunities.

Diane Ravitch reminds us why America's education must be built around a curriculum. "[A curriculum] is a road map. Without a road map, you are sure to drive in circles and get nowhere." She argues that with no curriculum, students are taught only generic skills, and not the knowledge needed for comprehension.

---

15 Ibid.

16 "Gilded Age Gilded Cage," Leslie T. Chang, *National Geographic*, Special Issue: China, Inside the Dragon, May 2008.

A clear depiction of the concern in regard to curriculum in the United States can be seen through my own experience. I have attended a Chinese-language school on Saturdays since I was five years old. Students in the class come from all districts of the metropolitan area: Roseville, Minnetonka, Wayzata, White Bear Lake, St. Paul, St. Louis Park, Edina, Eden Prairie, and Minneapolis. When we talked about our regular schoolwork, we were surprised at how different our experiences were. When discussing American history, it is hard for us to communicate about anything beyond the major chapters, such as the American Revolution, the Civil War, Reconstruction, World War I, and World War II. Some schools don't even teach the timeline of these events. My school provides in-depth coverage of certain topics that some other schools don't. Though our school districts were within minutes of each other, it may have been hundreds of miles given the contrast of our curriculum.

Diane Ravitch points out, "A typical middle-school history standard says that 'students will demonstrate an understanding of the chronology and concept of history and identify and explain historical relationships.' Or, 'explain, analyze and show connections among patterns of change and continuity by applying key historical concepts, such as time, chronology, causality, change, conflict, complexity, and movement.' Since these statements do not refer to any actual historical event, they do not require students to know any history. They contain no historical content that students might analyze, debate, or reflect on. Unfortunately, they are typical of most state standards in history."[17]

In China, I looked at my cousins' textbook for their Chinese class. Three of my cousins were seniors in high school. They had a 150-page textbook for each semester. Each textbook, though condensed, consisted of essays, selections from fiction, plays, and classical poems from Li Bai and Du Fu as well as modern poems from Yu Guangzhong and Ai Qing.

17 Ravitch, 19–20.

The essays included classical essays from Liu Zongyuan (a Tang dynasty essayist) and contemporary essays, such as "Mayor Chen Yi" by Sha Yexin. Other selections included Shakespeare's *The Merchant of Venice* and Charlotte Brontë's *Jane Eyre*. Students read parts of the book in class and were expected to read the whole book after class and select parts that expressed were significant to the students. Some pieces required being read aloud, rehearsing, and memorization. The teachers directed students in analyzing words, phrases, sentences, and the structure of the selections, as well as the main themes. For each textbook, from middle school to high school, the material covered more than 2,000 years. The textbooks included the best essays, poems, plays, and novels from both Eastern and Western civilizations.

China's national curriculum standard calls for specific requirements and recommendations. For example, the standard requires students from first grade to sixth grade to recite 160 poems and pieces of prose, and from seventh grade to the ninth grade they must recite eighty poems and pieces of prose. These 240 poems and pieces of prose are specifically identified. A long list of recommended after-class readings is included in the curriculum standard. For high school, forty classical essays and poems are listed. Chinese classics such as *Analects, Mencius, Zhuang Zi, Three Kingdoms*, and *A Dream of Red Mansions* are included. Foreign literature includes Cervantes' *Don Quixote*, Victor Hugo's *The Hunchback of Notre Dame*, Honoré de Balzac's *Eugénie Grandet*, Charles Dickens's *The Pickwick Papers*, Leo Tolstoy's *Resurrection*, Ernest Hemingway's *The Old Man and the Sea*, and William Shakespeare's *Hamlet*. Novellas from Guy de Maupassant, O. Henry, and Anton Chekhov are selected. Foreign poems from Russian poet Aleksandr Sergeyevich Pushkin and Indian poet Rabindranath Tagore are included. These selections are very broad. These gems of world literature are part of the core curriculum.

China adopted a nine-year voluntary education system, during which China's Ministry of Education made and updated the curriculum standards. The newly published standards cover nineteen subjects in Chinese, English, Japanese, Russian, mathematics, physics, chemistry, biology, history, geology, arts, music, drawing, and morality education.[18]

At Eden Prairie High School, the curriculum in my freshman year English class basically followed four subjects: grammar, vocabulary, writing, and reading comprehension. We spent a few weeks working on grammar, relearning everything students had forgotten from middle school, and then we did a few weeks of vocabulary, some small quizzes, and an essay project. For reading comprehension, we read *Romeo and Juliet* and *The Scarlet Letter*. With *Romeo and Juliet* we spent the class period reading from the play, acting out certain scenes. The teacher paused every so often to point out pieces of figurative language. With *The Scarlet Letter*, we were assigned a few chapters each night, and about ten questions per chapter. The next morning, if we finished our homework, we had it checked off. I also read *The Sun Also Rises* and *The Hobbit* as self-selected novels to complete book reports on.

That seems like a pretty basic routine not only for my high school, but for most high schools in our region. High schools and middle schools in China draw selections from a wide variety of literature and require students to be able to understand every piece thoroughly, which is one reason my parents sent me to the Great Books Summer Reading Camp in Amherst, Massachusetts, before starting my sophomore year.

For those two weeks, I read selections from a binder at night, in which each piece was carefully chosen by the staff to discuss the next morning. Our assignments consisted of three to four pieces each night, varying from selections such as Canto XXVI in Dante's *Inferno*, William Shakespeare's "Sonnet 130," Plato's *Symposium* (189a–193e), the Bible (Genesis 2–3, because we were talking about the theme of food), and Aristotle's *Nicomachean Ethics*. In addition to required classes, there were electives, in one of which I had to read Melville's *Bartleby, the*

18 Curriculum Standard by the Ministry of Education of People's Republic of China http://www.moe.edu.cn/publicfiles/business/htmlfiles/moe/moe_711/201201/xxgk_129268.html.

Scrivener and *Benito Cereno*.

We were lectured on the literature in the morning, filling our minds with new thoughts and ideas that were covered further during our discussion groups after the lecture. We could ask any question and talk about anything in reference to the piece. By the end of the day, we felt like we had really acquired an in-depth understanding of the piece, and the cycle then started again.

In the Great Books program, we were never required to memorize any major essay or a play. But in order to be mentally prepared for the next day, we had to read and reread the materials, enriching our brains with the content.

When my high school class read *Romeo and Juliet*, we read the whole book, and I could see that it would be difficult to read just one section of the play, because so much of its content is important. Reading entire books as opposed to small selections does have its advantages, depending on the significance of the particular book. The learning techniques stressed in the two countries (the U.S. and China) are both fulfilling for students. China emphasizes memorization for thoroughness in understanding, while in the U.S. memorization is a tool not required in the emphasis on individual creativity.

The U.S. and China have similar ambitions: the United States wants to stay on the top, and China wants to race to the top. But their approaches to their goals are different, and continuously changing. In the United States, most tests are designed to be multiple-choice Scantron sheets, with computer-fed grading. This format makes it quicker for teachers to grade them, and more accurate. But the practice of writing out answers and explanations in complete sentences, in full paragraphs, in written essays is fading away. Teachers are increasingly reluctant to take the time required to grade individual written work.

The 2001 book *Why Schools Matter* makes a comparison of countries across the world, along with their curricula and education system. A table inside the book, "Number of Mathematics Topics Included in the

Curriculum (Textbooks, Content Standards, and Teachers)," lists grades of each country using a scoring system. The U.S. has full points for Content Standards, Teacher Coverage, Topics Tested (Standards and Textbooks), and is just a few points off in Textbook Coverage. While China isn't listed as one of the countries, looking at Korea, Japan, and Russia, which have similar curricula, we can approximate where China stands. Scores for all three countries place them around last when it comes to Content Standards, Teacher Coverage, and Topics Tested (Standards and Textbooks). Looking at another table, "Eighth Grade Mathematics Textbooks Coverage for Countries (Including Only Topics with Some Coverage)," the U.S. is in second place after Switzerland, while Russia, Korea, and Japan hold the last few spots. In Diane Ravtich's book, *The Death and Life of the Great American School Stystem*, she states, "Other nations that outrank us on international assessments of mathematics and science do not concentrate obsessively on those subjects in their classrooms. Nations such as Japan and Finland have developed excellent curricula that spell out what students are supposed to learn in a wide variety of subjects. Their schools teach the major fields of study, including the arts and foreign languages, because they believe that this is the right education for their students, not because they will be tested. They do the right thing without rewards and sanctions. Their students excel in the tested subjects because they are well educated in many other subjects that teach them to use language well and to wrestle with important ideas."[19]

In the U.S., most textbooks are comprehensive when it comes to the *amount* of information they cover, whether in English, chemistry, math, or history, but that sheer volume is a problem. With 900+ pages, the hardcover textbooks we have to lug to school every day presents so much coverage and depth of material that it becomes a concern for thoughtful educators who have to wade through so much information. My mathematics textbook is 887 pages, my biology textbook is 907 pages, my chemistry textbook is 949 pages, my physics textbook is 974 pages, and

19 Diane Ravitch. *The Death and Life of the American School System*. 231.

my history textbook is 1,007 pages. My English textbook is an incredible 1,312 pages! Is it possible to absorb that much information effectively?

In light of such wide coverage and such thick textbooks, why is it that our report cards are ridiculously disappointing? As mentioned previously, in the 2009 PISA results, American students' math stands at thirty-first, science at twenty-third, and reading at seventeenth among the sixty-five participating countries and regions. In the 2007 Trends in International Mathematics and Science Study (TIMSS), which is an international assessment of the mathematics and science knowledge of nine and ten-year-old students (year five, or fourth grade), and thirteen and fourteen-year-old students (year nine, or eighth grade) around the world, American eighth-grade students were ranked ninth in math and eleventh in science among the forty-eight participating countries.

Big textbooks didn't necessarily produce the biggest results. Textbooks in China are very thin. Their covers consist of a small reflective paperback-like material, and the pages are thin, but packed with condensed information. The textbooks in physics, chemistry, history, etc., are regarded more as notebooks than textbooks, per se. It may seem that students in China cover less material than we American students do. Though their textbooks are smaller and thinner than our bulky textbooks, their concise and streamlined texts are effective in teaching those young students. "[Chinese] textbooks focus on a small number of key concepts by contrast with US textbooks, which cover a larger number of concepts superficially."[20] In the U.S., textbooks, curricula, and teaching methods go through quite a bit of variation. Many states have their own standards, and in order to meet the standards, the superficial aspect of the textbooks contributes to the diversity of expectations. On the other hand, in China, "Textbooks, materials, teacher preparation, and professional development are all clearly aligned to these (national) standards."[21]

My social studies teacher used to start classes with the words, "Back

---

20 *Education in China, Lessons for US Educators.*

21 *Math and Science Education in a Global Age.*

in the old days," referring to the fact my generation didn't capture our history and culture like his generation used to. We are caught up in moving forward so quickly that we don't take the time to reflect on where we came from. New technology is created every day, at lightning speed. The entire world is in a race toward the future. As Mr. Lu, the father of two twins he homeschools, told me, he preferred to restrict his own children from too much contact with new technology because it was simply corrupting children, threatening to distract them from more important endeavors.

Students are obsessed with the Internet, iPhones, iPads, games, and all kinds of electronics. China's parents, teachers, and schools are conscious of this issue. Chinese parents lock their computers, watch children when they are home, and prohibit wasting time on television in order to keep them focused on learning. They do not necessarily want to keep their children from any contact with technology; they simply do not want the distraction to lead their children away from the precious time they should be studying and preparing for their next tests.

Mr. Lu says, "The Internet is crap, television is crap, news isn't news; it's entertainment! If you want entertainment, read a book; that's where all the excitement is."

According to A.C. Nielsen Co., in one year, the average youth in America spends 900 hours in school, and in that same year watches 1,500 hours of television.[22] Though many parents are aware that kids watch too much television and may consider restricting the number of hours they watch, children are pretty powerful, both in the United States and in China. They have the power to resist, object, and think what they want to think. Parents can enforce rules on them, but that doesn't always work.

As the U.S. makes progress toward education reform in the twenty-first century, China is watching and learning along with us. This progress includes creating more open class debates and discussion, using more inquiry-oriented methods, and developing the concept of directing

---

22 Norman Herr, PhD, "Television and Health." http://www.csun.edu/science/health/docs/tv&health.html.

students toward more creative problem solving. Classrooms in China have tried to change, but it's hard to make sudden changes with the didactic curriculum. Parents, teachers, and other faculty members are afraid that such a change will weaken the curriculum standards, making the environment easy and playful, and less educational.

In China, the curriculum in math and science is quite unified—and largely controlled by the content of the university entrance exam. Teachers know what they're supposed to teach, and what other teachers are teaching. They can be sure that their students are being taught the exact same things. With the board curriculum in the U.S., and each state with different requirements for their standards, this order does not exist. Such flexibility is good for those regions and areas in which development is still in progress and some leverage is needed when it comes to education, but the lack of consistent order means that students do not receive a basic unified core education.

At my school, we have the option of enrolling in regular, enriched, or advanced placement classes for most subjects, such as English, social studies, physics, chemistry, biology, and math. This way, we students can choose what level of classes we want and learn at our own pace, which is something no one seems to complain about. But in China, every class is the same. There is the experimental class, but the curriculum is the same. It might vary slightly in Beijing, Shanghai, Guizhou, or Shanxi, but most students don't have options in their classes. There's no option for the type of gym class a student will enroll in, or the type of math class, or the difficulty level of other courses. There's less freedom.

If that were to be the case in the U.S., it would be difficult for many students to handle. Nicholas Kristof notes, "The magic of education in China could leave the U.S. playing catch-up."[23] Is that not a little bit frightening? He comments that "China has an enormous cultural respect for education, for its Confucian legacy, so governments and families alike pour resources into education." Have you noticed how often Confucius is

23 Nikolas Kristof, "The Education Giant," *New York Times*, May 28, 2008.

mentioned when referring to China's education? Confucius' philosophical concepts are a legacy, known by everyone from the youngest child to the oldest of the elderly.

Kristof makes an important note at the end of his article, suggesting that the U.S. should raise our standards to meet those of China. Looking at American education and Chinese education, I have to admit, the education system in the U.S. is at a crucial juncture. Teachers are often hired with little experience. We students talk about this in high school all the time. Students are not provided with the proper materials and information to fulfill certain standards. And speaking of standards, what are they? There are hundreds of textbooks that teachers use from all across the country, and some do not cover even a basic curriculum. Our teachers often complain about how horrid the textbooks are, when in all honestly, they just do not want to teach in a rigorous way. Harsh words, but true. I am not saying that in China it is necessarily any better, but at least in China there is a standard curriculum. I am not suggesting that the U.S. has to create a standard curriculum just like China's, but we should at least have some guideline that is accountable, measurable, specific, and forward-looking.

In the documentary film, *A Tale of Two Missions*, Kyle Olson and Juan Williams discovered that Noble School in Chicago had a 98 percent graduation rate compared to an average 56 percent graduation rate for all Chicago schools.[24] The reason is that the school can "dismiss underperforming teachers, reward good teachers with merit pay, specialize their curriculum, extend their school day, and more effectively deal with classroom discipline." This sounds to me like a version of the Chinese education experience.

---

24 Juan William, "Will Business Boost School Reform?" *Wall Street Journal*, February 28, 2012.

CHAPTER 15
Burning Ambitions

Please take a quiz:

1) There are nine trees, three trees in a row. You have to arrange ten rows, how do you make the arrangement?

2) Use these symbols (+, –, x, or /) to make the following equation hold true:

5 ( ) 5 ( ) 5 ( ) 5 = 2.

3) In a ratio, the denominator is 8, the nominator plus the quotient plus the residual equals 72. What is the nominator?

You may suspect that these are SAT test questions. Well, they might be in the United States of America, but they are not in China. The first question was a winter break homework assignment for first-grade students in some Shenzhen schools. The second question was a winter break homework question for second-grade students. The third problem was a winter break homework question for third-grade students. During the Shenzhen school winter break in February 2011, parents in Shenzhen were bewildered by these questions, discussing with other parents and students solutions for many homework problems. The three questions above were just a few of examples.

Students were paranoid. Parents were paranoid. One of the parents had graduated from a top college in China, and when he saw the problems he pondered, "Did I really graduate from a top college, or even a college at all?

Who wrote these questions for first- and second-grade students? Are they expecting all of our children to be mathematician Hua Luogeng?" (Hua Luogeng was one of the top mathematicians of the twentieth century in China.)

Many parents liked the challenging questions. One parent said, "Our children's generation is not like ours. 'One plus one is equal to two,' or simple arithmetic, is Epipaleolithic Age mathematics. Challenging questions help develop the children's intellectual capacity."

The answer to the first question:

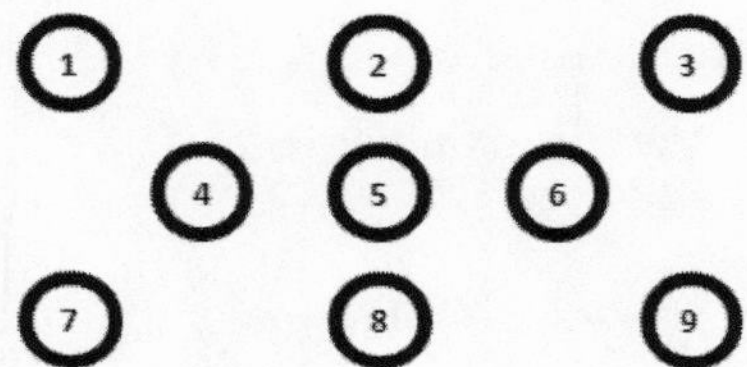

The answer to the second question:
[5 (/) 5] (+) [5 (/) 5] = 2

The answer to the third question: 64.
64 + [64 (/) 8] (+) 0 = 72

Education in Shenzhen follows the inspirational story of its economy. Shenzhen, located directly north of Hong Kong, has been named possibly China's most successful Special Economic Zone. A photo of Shenzhen in the 1970s shows low houses, farmland, and a couple of shabby buildings. A photo of the same area in 2010 shows a city full of highrise buildings. There are no farmlands or open areas of that sort; highways run in every direction. In the last thirty years, the city has developed at rocket speed, showcasing its achievement to the world—development that occurred so quickly, it seems unreal to many.

Shenzhen was designated a Special Economic Zone in 1980 and was China's experimental laboratory for its economy's reform and restructuring. People immigrated from all around China to turn the area from a rice field into a metropolis like New York within twenty years. Shenzhen has flourished tremendously, thanks to millions of dollars from overseas Chinese and foreign companies invested in the economy.

Everything is new about the now vast city of Shenzhen, with towering skyscrapers and gigantic apartment buildings with glass windows. Shenzhen stands as a "miracle" of the Chinese economy and a model for other developing cities.

This "Shenzhen Miracle" can be attributed to the "factory girls"[1] who worked ten to twelve hours a day, seven days a week. The manufacturing workers in Shenzhen toil beyond the legal limit of forty-nine hours a week in the "world factory"—where the creativity of workers is pushed to the limit. Miracles happen at the limit.

No one in Shenzhen wants to fall behind. Parents and educators in Shenzhen apply that same mentality to children, creating high expectations from everyone involved. Teachers in Shenzhen use manufacturing protocols with their students, expecting miracles from their industrious students. In a survey conducted by Shenzhen Educational TV Channel, 40 percent of the students thought their summer and winter breaks entailed more work than normal school days because the amount of homework was so much heavier.

Students in Shenzhen have a one-month winter break during the Chinese lunar New Year. But, rather than being a break from school work, this is the time for most students to attend review sessions, English classes, math classes, Chinese classes, and art classes. Li Xiaohui, an eighth-grade student, says, "My plan for the winter break is class, homework, and sleep." Her English assignments included reading twelve pages in the English newspaper, memorizing two essays from the textbook *New Concept English* every week, reading one selection from *New Concept English* five times every day, watching CCTV-9 English channel news at 12:00 p.m.,

1 Leslie T. Chang, *Factory Girls: From Village to City in a Changing China*, Spiegal & Grau, November 2009.

5:00 p.m., or 7:00 p.m. every day, watching *BBC World International News*, watching two English movies every week, singing two English songs every week, reading selections from *The Complete Analysis Textbook* and writing summaries for each selection every day, and transcribing English essays every day. For Chinese class, her teacher assigned her five books. She needed to transcribe twenty essays from these five books, write two book reports, and transcribe forty-eight pages in calligraphy. For mathematics class, Ms. Li earned 100 points, thus she didn't have any winter break homework from that class. But students who had ninety-five to ninety-nine points had to do five sets of a simulation test. Students who received below ninety-five points had to do more work—the five simulation sets, plus more for each point they lost below ninety-five (six sets for ninety-four points—and 100 sets for zero points). Ms. Li's parents sent her to review classes every morning—two hours for math class and two hours for science class.

The week before the Spring Festival, Ms. Li had to spend three hours each afternoon studying for her English verbal class. In addition, her parents paid a Chinese teacher to come to her house and tutor her in the subject of Chinese for two-and-a-half hours each Saturday and Sunday.

What a winter break!

On February 17, 2011, venture capitalist John Doerr hosted a dinner for President Barack Obama at his Silicon Valley home. Guests invited included Carol Bartz, president and CEO of Yahoo; John Chamber, CEO of Cisco Systems; Dick Costolo, CEO of Twitter; Larry Ellison, CEO of Oracle; Reed Hastings, CEO of Netflix; Steve Jobs, chairman and CEO of Apple; Art Levinson, chairman and former CEO of Genentech; Eric Schmidt, CEO of Google; Mark Zuckerberg, founder and CEO of Facebook; and Stanford University President John Hennessy. Steve Jobs was seated to the left of the president. Mark Zuckerberg was seated to the right of the president. The topic of the dinner meeting was job creation and education. Each guest was asked to come up with a question for the president.

Apple CEO Steve Jobs spoke. Apple produced seventy million iPhones, thirty million iPads, and fifty-nine million other products in 2011. Almost all Apple products were manufactured overseas. Apple became the most valuable company in the world as of August 9, 2011. President Obama interrupted Jobs to ask how those manufacturing jobs could be brought back to the United States.

"Those jobs aren't coming back," Steve Jobs answered.

Most of those jobs went to China, and there is a reason for that. The *New York Times* reported that Apple redesigned the iPhone's screen and revamped iPhone manufacturing at the last minute in 2007. This was only a month from the time the new iPhone was scheduled to appear in stores. The assembly line had to be overhauled. The new screen design arrived at the Foxconn plant in Shenzhen at about midnight. Eight thousand workers were immediately awakened and guided to the workstations. Within half an hour they started a twelve-hour shift, fitting glass screens into beveled frames. Within ninety-six hours, over 10,000 iPhones were produced. Within three months, Apple sold one million iPhones. Foxconn has assembled more than 200 million iPhones since then. The Foxconn facility has 230,000 employees. They work six days a week, up to twelve hours a day. Over a quarter of Foxconn's workers live in the company's dormitories. They are available twenty-four hours a day. Work has become a habitual action.

The scale, flexibility, and diligence of Foxconn amazed the American executives. "What US plant can find 3,000 people overnight and convince them to live in dorms?" asked Jennifer Rigoni, Apple's worldwide supply demand manager at the time.

This scene of colossal magnitude is not only seen in China's manufacturing sector. In China's education, we saw the same picture. On March 29, 2008, it was raining hard in Chongqing, China, and a public speech was scheduled at Chongqing University the same day. The speaker was Kai-Fu Lee, founder of Google China. (He is known as an inspiration to college students in China and enjoys the popularity of a movie star.) The title of the speech was "I Study. I Grow. Five Questions Concerning

College Students." The rain didn't stop the attendees from coming. The university prepared 7,000 raincoats for them. More than 10,000 students showed up for this public event. Students from other colleges in Chongqing also rushed to event. Mr. Lee talked about technological innovations, research-based study, and scientific breakthroughs.

In Huantai Second High School, which is walking distance from my grandfather's apartment, a recital session of Confucian classics was conducted. Five thousand students lined up and synchronously recited Di Zi Gui (Rules for Students) and selections from Confucius' *Analects*. These Confucian classics drive them to study hard, respect their parents, and take moral responsibility for their country. In the morning exercise sessions, teachers run with the students in their classes. The school principal, Gao Daquan, stood on a high platform to supervise the students and his teachers. They looked like they were in military training. Student activities are highly structured and efficiently organized; in harmony with Confucian principles. They applied this mentality to their homework assignments, to their classics recitals, to their preparation for national examinations, and to their learning activities.

In light of China's national ambition, the Ministry of Education made an intentional commitment to expand upon the ongoing commitment to education and offer an elite education that is the best in the world. That intention is reflected by three grand programs. The first, Project 863, was initiated in 1983 to promote science and engineering in China. Project 211 (initiated in 1996) and Project 985 (initiated in 1998) were each created with the goal of establishing "world class" universities around the country. The central government provides funding for the top colleges to court the best professors from the U.S. and bring them into their schools. With the government's heavily targeted funding, the selected universities are bound to rise to the top, leading China to greater innovation. The government selects top schools from each school district, city, and county; and top students are selected from each class, school, district, city, and province. The selection processes are not conducted by a peer review or commercial activity. China is creating model middle schools, high schools, and universities.

China's central government has a "Thousand People Plan" and every province has a "Hundred People Plan." Under these plans, Chinese schools and research institutes target American and European professors. They attract those who have achieved breakthroughs or have the potential to excel in their fields. They provide funding, labs, and all the facilities and conveniences for these professors to advance science and technology in China.

Shi Yigong, the youngest tenured professor in the history of Princeton University, was a rising star in cellular biology, determining the crystal structure of several critical apoptotic proteins. He was courted by Qinghua University, and appointed dean of the Life Science Institute of Qinghua University. Xiao Yi, a former Northwestern University professor, was a rising star in neurobiology. Dr. Xiao Yi was courted by Beijing University and appointed dean of the Life Science Institute of Beijing University. Both professors had excellent reputations in the United States.

Yale University President Richard C. Levin is a keen observer of the trends in global higher education, especially in China. He confirmed that China and India have an ambitious agenda. "Both seek to expand their higher education systems; and since the late 1990s, China has done so dramatically. They are also aspiring to create a limited number of world-class universities. In China, the nine universities that receive the most supplemental government funding recently self-identified as the C9—China's Ivy League."[2]

When Levin delivered a speech to the Royal Society in London, England, he said, "One of our most distinguished geneticists at Yale and members of his team now split their time between laboratories in New Haven and Fudan University in Shanghai. Another distinguished Yale professor, a plant biologist, has a similar arrangement at Peking University. In both cases, the Chinese provide abundant space and research staff to

2 *Foreign Affairs*, May/June 2010.

support the efforts of Yale scientists, while collaboration with the Yale scientists upgrades the skills of young Chinese professors and graduate students. Both sides benefit."

He continued, "In the 1990s only 10 percent of Chinese who received PhDs in science and engineering in the U.S. returned home. That number is now rising; and, increasingly, China has been able to repatriate mid-career scholars and scientists from tenured positions in the United States and the United Kingdom, who are attracted by the greatly improved working conditions and the opportunities to participate in China's rise."[3]

In 1995 China started an ambitious initiative, attempting to establish 1,000 model high schools. Each school had at least eighteen different classrooms; every class was limited to fifty students. The teacher-to-student ratio was required to be less than one in ten. Schools needed to have demonstration labs, a computer lab, a linguistic lab, and a multimedia lab. As a result, a flood of model schools rose in every province and municipality. Government funding poured into these schools. Parents chose these schools for their children.

Class size in the U.S., even in large public schools, is usually around thirty students. The teacher-to-student ratio isn't even close to China's; but ancillary staff such as counselors, assistants, and volunteer parents, add to the number of interested others.

China's plan is ambitious and may have far-reaching consequences for academia in the U.S. As they implement their plans, they are, in the process, luring some of the best academic talent from the United States. If China is able to sustain to pay the high price of this recruitment, and the commensurate salaries, what academic talent will be left in the U.S. over the next few generations?

Now led by China's State Council, Project 211 is currently the highest

---

3 Richard Levin, "The Rise of Asia's University, Seventh Annual Lecture of the Higher Education Policy Institute. Center for Human Resources Development. Speech to Royal Society, London, January 31, 2010. http://chrd.edu.vn/site/en/?p=806.

administrative organ of education in the country. In the mid-1990s, the top thirty universities in China were not thought to be comparable with the top international universities, thus the project aimed to boost top schools to the bar of international standards. It was a national effort led by the Chinese government. The number "211" was chosen as the project name: "21" representing the twenty-first century, and "1" representing the one hundred universities to be transformed.

In the first ten years of the program, the capacity for training doctorate students increased by five times, funding increased by seven times, publications by the Scientific Citation Index (SCI) standard increased by seven times, and the number of advisers of doctoral students increased by five times. The definition of "transformation" is training four-fifths of the doctoral students, two-thirds of graduate students, half the students from abroad, and one third of undergraduates, strengthening the students by providing them with higher education in key disciplinary areas. The project has already chosen the 602 disciplines, including humanities, social science, economics, law, basic science, high technology, environmental sciences, medicine, etc. The hope is that, for each of the 602 disciplines, there will be world-class Chinese researchers, scientists, and experimenters in the field.

Project 985 was created in the month of May (so named for the year 1998 and the fifth month) in an attempt to transform the top ten universities of China into "world first-class" universities. When the former president, Jiang Zemin, delivered a speech on the 100-year anniversary of Beijing University, he declared the goal for China to have the most elite first-class university in the world, and the mechanism for meeting this goal: starting in 1998, and continuing for three years, the Chinese government would allocate 1 percent of the national budget to funding universities. This is the equivalent to about RMB 30 billion. Qinghua University and Beijing University were the targets for the first stage of the project. Each of them received RMB 1.8. Through 2006 the project expanded to total thirty-nine universities, the second stage of the project. The 985 project created many national labs and research centers, courting world experts to help China reach the top level. Billions of government dollars have gone into this program that turned Beijing University and Qinghua University into first-class world universities—the best of the best; and other Chinese universities have achieved national and international acclaim. China is influencing the future of education throughout the world.

The oldest among the three projects is the 863 Program, created during March of 1986. The idea was first proposed by four Chinese government engineers endorsed by the former Chinese leader, Deng Xiaoping. This became Deng Xiaoping's flagship program. The goal was to advance seven technological fields to the very frontier: biotechnology, space, IT, laser technology, automation, energy, and new materials, with a budget of about RMB 200 billion of government funding to spend on communication technology and information. In 2001 it was reported that 2,000 patents had resulted so far. The Loongson computer processor family and Shenzhou spacecraft have been results of the program.

The initial goal of the 863 Program was to match the world's best strategic technology, but it evolved quickly to surpass the performance of Europe and the United States (and anyone else) in technology and development. From a technology perspective, China moved onto the world's frontier. Achievements have included the Computer Integrated Manufacturing System (CIMS), robotic deep-ocean diving (excelling the depth attained by the U.S.), the super computer, nickel-metal hydride batteries (green batteries), etc.

China targets newly emerging technology and uses a collective operation to speed up modernization and maintain and express a strategic frontier outlook. With government funding, the project hopes to continue to help students excel in areas of scientific research, management, and institutional efficiency, reforming the management industry, and trying to solve the country's struggles in social and economic development.

After China's leading rocket scientist, Qian Xuesen, passed away, the Mount Everest Program was created, an experimental program for selected top students in basic science: mathematics, physics, chemistry, biology, and computer science. The program selected sixteen universities, including Beijing University, Qinghua University, Zhejiang University, Nanjin University, and Fudan University. Each university built a special residential college to implement the program. Taishan Academy is the program created with Shandong University. Their goals are highly focused: for these extremely talented young people to operate on the cutting edge of science and technology, compete globally with their peers, publish leading papers, and obtain top honors. The president of Shandong University said, "Twenty years later, if Taishan Academy can produce a Nobel Prize winner, that means our exploration is successful."

Entrepreneurs, educators, and commentators in the United States feel the heat of this competition. China is catching up quickly. Thomas Friedman acknowledged, "For now, the United States still excels at teaching science and engineering at the graduate level, and also in university-based research." However, as the "feeder stock" comes through improved Chinese high schools and universities, "they will get to the same level as us after a decade," said Intel chairman Craig Barrett. "We are not graduating the volume, we do not have a lock on the infrastructure, we do not have a lock on the new ideas, and we are either flat-lining, or in real dollars cutting back, our investments in physical science."[4]

Richard Levin pointed out what it takes to build universities capable of world-class status in research. "First and foremost, it requires the capacity to attract scholars and scientists of the highest quality. In the sciences, this means first-class research facilities, adequate funding to support research, and competitive salaries and benefits. China is making substantial investments on all three fronts. Shanghai's top universities—Fudan, Shanghai Jiaotong, and Tongji—have each developed whole new campuses within the past few years, with outstanding research facilities, located close to industrial partners. Research funding has grown in parallel with the expansion of enrollment, and Chinese universities now

4 Thomas Friedman, *The World is Flat*, 347.

compete much more effectively for faculty talent."[5]

China is not just catching up quickly, but in an unparalleled scale. Thomas Friedman sees a large gap in the interest of young people in America for the study of advanced math, science, and engineering. He referred to the annual worldwide Intel International Science and Engineering Fair that attracts participants from forty countries as, "nominating talent through local affiliate affairs." Intel reported that the 2004 Intel Fair attracted around 65,000 American kids. Friedman spoke with the president of Intel in Beijing and asked Wee Theng Tan about participation in China. Tan described the national affiliate science fair that acts as a feeder system to select kids for the global Intel fair, saying that "Almost every single province has students going to one of these affiliate fairs. We have as many as six million kids competing, although not all are competing for the top levels . . . [But] you know how seriously they take it. Those selected to go to the international [Intel] fair are immediately exempted from college entrance exams,' and basically get their choice of any top university in China. In the 2004 Intel Science Fair, China came home with thirty-five awards, more than any other country in Asia, including one of the top three global awards."[6]

As China is integrated into the world economy, its industries move up from low-end commodities to high value-added products and services. "Recognizing that the country needs a better-trained workforce in order to move up the economic value chain, the central government committed itself to boosting scholarships and other types of aid in 2008 to $2.7 billion, up from $240 million in 2006. Officials expanded overall government spending on education, which was a measly 2.8 percent of GDP in 2006, to 4 percent in 2010, a large portion of which is devoted to a small number of globally competitive elite institutions," observed Fareed Zakaria in *The Post-American World*.

5 Richard Levin, The Rise of Asia's Universities, Speech to Royal Society, London, January 31, 2010.

6 Thomas Friedman, *The World is Flat*, 335.

The Chinese economy seems to have climbed to the top of the world economy in a short time. Since Beijing University and Qinghua University are now close in ranking with Harvard, Yale, Cambridge, and Oxford, there should be no surprise. Clearly, China does not lack the ambition to achieve this position. Richard Levin, Thomas Friedman, and Fareed Zakaria have already recognized that eventuality.

Qinghua University's publications on material science have ascended to number one in the world among universities and research institutes. Beijing University's publications on chemistry have swelled to number one among universities. These achievements have caused some optimists to predict that within five to seven years, mainland China will finally have its first Nobel Prize winner, most likely in material science or chemistry. That will be the moment the Chinese have dreamt about. China is anxiously awaiting her time. During the more than one hundred years of Nobel Prize history, the first fifty winners were European. The recent fifty years have been dominated by the United States. Could China be next? Every year in October, the Chinese listen for news released from the Royal Swedish Academy of Sciences. A Chinese winner of the Nobel Prize will prompt an uproarious celebration for 1.4 billion people.

CHAPTER 16
On Top of the World

June 22, 2011
United States Institute of Peace
Washington DC

"*Gong xi! Zhu he ni*" (Congratulations!) When Dr. Richard Solomon, director of the United States Institute of Peace, former assistant secretary of state for East Asian and Pacific affairs and ambassador to the Philippines, handed the Peace Essay Award to me, he used his standard Mandarin to congratulate me. On the same night, he used his Chinese to express congratulations to Katherine Hsu from California, Daway Chou-Ren from New Jersey, Connie Zhou from Ohio, Lily Zhang from Pennsylvania, Victoria Gu from Rhode Island, and Bryant Yang from South Dakota. We were seven of the forty-two winners of the 2010–11 Peace Essay contest. Chinese students in America haven't demonstrated an overwhelming advantage in essay competitions. They have more advantages in science, math, and technology.

Numbers talk. And these numbers may stun some. Asian-Americans make up 4 percent of the entirepopulation.[1] As of 2006, 42 percent of students at the University of California at Berkeley were Asian, 25 percent at Columbia, 24 percent at Stanford, 23 percent at the University of Pennsylvania, 18 percent at Harvard, 17 percent at Northwestern, and 15

1 Dr. Soo Kim Abboud and Jane Kim, Top of the Class: How Asian Parents Raise High Achievers-and How You Can Too, 2006.

percent at Johns Hopkins. Are you surprised?

If we look at the country's top high schools, the enrollment of Asian students is completely out of proportion relative to the country's Asian population, or even the local Asian population. Thomas Jefferson High School for Science and Technology has enrolled 40 percent Asian students, Oxford Academy 71 percent, New York's two well-known public high schools, Stuyvesant High School 65 percent, Bronx High School of Science 60 percent, and Whitney High School 85 percent![2]

On March 16, 2011, the forty winners of America's oldest and most prestigious pre-college science competition in the 2010 Intel Science Talent Search were announced in Washington, DC. Almost 40 percent of the winners were of Asian ethnicity. They were either new immigrants or descendents of Chinese immigrants. In the 2011 Intel Science Talent Search, more than 3,000 students submitted applications and more than 1,000 students entered the semifinal competition. Three hundred students out of this 1,000 are Chinese. More than seventy percent of the 300 students were newly immigrated from mainland China within the last three years.[3]

In the 2012 Intel Science Talent Search, 1,839 students submitted applications, and 300 students were selected as semifinalists; among them, 103 were Chinese students.

Fox Business Network correspondent Connell McShane wrote, "It's taken me a month of traveling on assignment, but I think I've figured out how America stays competitive with China and the rest of the world. The answer is actually somewhat simple and self-evident: we think it, and they make it. They understand that in Kannapolis, North Carolina, and San Jose, California. The folks in Burton, Michigan, still need some convincing. As for Shanghai and Beijing, well that's a story in and of itself.

---

2 *US News and World Report*, "Best High Schools in the US." 2012. http://education.usnews.rankingsandreviews.com/best-high-schools/rankings/highest-asian-american-enrollment-list.

3 http://blog.sina.com.cn/s/blog_9ec6cf980100ywj5.html?tj=1.

I'm just wrapping up my month of globetrotting here in San Jose at the Intel Science and Engineering Fair. The giant chipmaker brought together 1,600 high school students from fifty-nine different countries. You're probably thinking these kids are all from places like India and China, threats to America's place in the world. Well, the winner, fifteen-year-old Amy Chyao, is Chinese. She's Chinese-American. Her parents were born in China. She was born here. In fact, more than 40 percent of the students in the competition are American. Intel CEO Paul Otellini says we need more families like the Chyaos. He went so far as to suggest we should 'staple a visa' to overseas students who come to study in our colleges. How's that for an immigration policy!"

There's no doubt that people in cities like Shanghai and Beijing are motivated and hungry to take jobs from Americans in North Carolina, Michigan, and California. I met many of them when we were there. One of the locals told me that a lot of Chinese kids are coming to America to study, but plan to return to China to start a business. In the past, a ticket from China to the USA was more often one-way. As Paul Otellini of Intel suggests, maybe the United States needs to staple a visa on the incoming students if we want to keep their talent in the U.S.[4]

In the Dragon School in Chengdu, banners to congratulate the international Olympiad winners hung on the entrance doors and in the hallways. The Dragon School offers Olympiad training courses across their nineteen campuses. I got the strong impression that the Olympiads were a major event in Chengdu. When my family visited my brother's fiancée during the Christmas season, her brother, Jason Zhang, was practicing math for his Olympiad. Their family is originally from Shanghai, but they carried their Shanghai tradition to Dallas.

On July 19–28, 2010, the 42nd International Chemistry Olympiad was held in Waseda University and at the University of Toyko, Japan. All

4 Connell McShane, "How America Competes With China and the Rest of the Globe," Fox Business. 14 May 2010. http://www.foxbusiness.com/markets/2010/05/14/america-competes-china-rest-globe/#ixzz1kihe1BSH.

members of the Chinese team, Xianghang Shangguan, Qilei Zhu, Zhiyao Zhou, and Ruyi Wang, received gold medals. Among the four members of the Chinese Taibei team, two of them, Yu-Chi Kuo, and Ming-Ko Cho received gold medals; and two of them, Wei-Che Tsai and Bo-Yun Gu, received silver medals. Among the four members of the Singapore team, two members, Fong Jie Ming Nigel and Lum Jian Yang, received gold medals; and two, Tng Jia Hao Barry and Khu Boon Hou Derek, received silver medals. Colin Lu obtained a gold medal, and Richard Li obtained a silver medal for the US team. Connie Zhao, Brian Bi, and Richard Liu received silver medals for the Canada team. Pilkeun Jang, Hyeonjae Lee, and Jaehyun Lim were gold medalists, and Won Jae Kim was a silver medalist for the South Korea team.[5]

In the 52nd International Mathematics Olympiad held in Amsterdam in July 16–24, 2010, all members of the Chinese team, Lin Chen, Tianyou Zhou, Bowen Yao, Zichao Long, Zhaorong Jin, and Mengxi Wu, received gold medals. Chinese teams earned the first position for the seventeenth time among the twenty-five times that China participated in the competition (since 1985).

All six members of the US team received gold medals. Four of them, David Yang, Xiaoyu He, Mitchell Lee, and Wenyu Cao, were Chinese immigrants. They helped the US team obtain second position among the groups. Jeck Lim, Jun Jie Joseph Kuan, Jie Jun Ang, and Yue Ding grasped gold medals. Yan Sheng Ang received a silver medal, and Chong Luck Ryan Kor obtained a bronze medal for the Singapore team.[6]

In July 11–17, 2010, the 42nd International Physics Olympiad was held in Bangkok, Thailand. All five contestants from Taiwan, Tzu-Ming Hsu, Hung-I Yang, Yun-Cheng Lin, Hung-Jui Huang, and Su-Kuan Chu, received gold medals. And all five contestants from mainland China,

5 "42nd International Chemistry Olympiad," Chemistry the Key to Our Future. July 2010. http://www.icho2010.org/en/results.html.

6 "International Mathematics Olympiad." http://official.imo2011.nl/results.aspx.

Lanqing Li, Chongyuan Xiong, Kexin Yi, Yifei Wang, and Fan Yang, received gold medals. All five contestants from Singapore, Zi Yang Kang, Kewei Li, Sen Lin, Jiahuang Lin, and Zong Xuan Tan, received gold medals. All five contestants from South Korea, Jaeik Oh, Jinil Choi, Min Woo Jung, Sunjin Choi, and Yubin Nam, received gold medals. For the five-member Hong Kong team, Andy Loo, Tsz Ki Chau, and Hil Fung Harry Cheung received gold medals; Yu Fu Wong and Yuk Fai Wong received silver medals. Brian Zhang and Ante Qu obtained gold medals, and Lucy Chen received a silver medal for the US team.[7]

In July 10–17, 2011, the 22nd International Biology Olympiad was held in Taipei, Taiwan, China. All participants from Taiwan, Chang Je-rui, Lu Hsiao-hung, Lin Yu-min, and Tung Yu-hung, won gold medals. Three contestants from mainland China, Zidong Zhang, Yao Xiao, and Kemeng Wu, received gold medals; and one contestant, Jin Yang, received a silver medal. Rebecca Doris Shi from the US obtained the highest score in the competition.[8]

Education Week, which is read by teachers all over America, ran an article (July 28, 2004), with the headline "Immigrants' Children Inhabit the Top Ranks of Math, Science Meets." The article states, "Research conducted by the National Foundation for American Policy shows that 60 percent of the nation's top science students and 65 percent of the top mathematics students are children of recent immigrants, according to an analysis of award winners in three scholastic competitions . . . the Intel Science Talent Search, the US team for the International Mathematical Olympiad, and the US Physics Team." The study's author and executive director of the foundation, Stuart Anderson, attributed the immigrant students' success "partly to their parents' insistence that they manage study time wisely." He noted that "Many immigrant parents encourage

7 "International Physics Olympiad," Gold Medals. Bangkok, Thailand. 2011. http://www.ipho2011.org/contents/gold_medals.

8 http://www.ibo2011.org.tw/main/IBO/userfiles/file/IBO2011%20final%20result.pdf.

their children to pursue mathematics and science interests, believing those skills would lead to strong career opportunities and insulate them from bias and lack of connections in the workplace . . . A strong percentage of the students surveyed had parents who arrived in the United States on H-1B visas, reserved for professional workers. US policymakers who back overly restrictive immigration policies do so at the risk of cutting off a steady infusion of technological and scientific skill."[9]

No one argues with the fact that Chinese students work hard. They practice their musical instruments more hours as their Western counterparts. They do three to ten times as many math exercises and homework problems than Western students. They memorize classical essays, even without that requirement in the Western world, specifically the U.S. and certain places in Europe. They have twice as many classroom hours than their Western peers. They spend more hours in review sessions, which Western countries do not typically offer. All these activities consume their time. How do they stay awake and alert in order to be efficient in their study?

Confucian tradition provides a clue. This is the first part of a classical essay found in every high school textbook in China, written by Xun Zi, an educator, philosopher, and thinker.

Gentleman said, learning is not allowed to stop. Dark blue comes from blue, but it's deeper than the color blue. Ice is made of water, but it is colder than water. Wood can make a straight ruler, but it can also be made into round wheels through a bending process. Straight wood can be made into round circles, but when it has dried, it cannot be straight again for it has been processed. Through measurements and instruments, any wood can be straightened. Swords and knives can be sharpened by rubbing them against stone. By studying and reflecting, a gentleman can be intelligent and not make mistakes. If you don't climb high mountains, you don't know how high the sky is. If you don't go into the deep valleys,

9 Thomas Friedman, *The World is Flat*, 335–36.

you don't know how deep the earth is. If you don't learn the teachings of the previous sages, you don't know how broad and deep their knowledge is. Everyone is the same when they are born, but habit can make a difference. This is the essence of education.[10]

Xun Zi was one of the Confucian scholars during the late Warring States Period. In China, every student can recite this essay. The purpose isn't for the beauty of the language, but rather for the importance of the meaning.

"Dark blue comes from blue, but it's deeper than the color blue." This is the ancient sage's way of saying that students are trained by their teachers, and they should work to be better than their teachers. The sage advises teachers to expect their students to be brighter and more intelligent. This sentiment has been deeply embedded into the history of China, and teachers take it to heart.

Yin ren shi jiao, or "Teach according to the individual," is a fundamental teaching philosophy from Confucius. Ouyang Ruirui told us at the airport that day, "I have found that every student has his or her own way of learning. Being a piano teacher, the thing that parents do not understand is that piano is not for everyone. If the student does not love it, they should give it up now, or as early as they can. You have to have a thriving passion for something in order to succeed in it. Once I asked a student who was Chinese and was about five years old. I asked him, 'How many times do you want to practice this piece this week?' When I ask my American students, they would say about five times, or sometimes ten times a week. But he responded, 'Until I am satisfied. Until my mom is satisfied. Until my teacher is satisfied.'"

Walker Rowe wrote, "Many of us have run into the Chinese affinity for classical music firsthand. I took my oldest son to Suzuki piano classes when he was a boy. He squirmed on the piano stool, refused to practice, and generally was not prepared for lessons when we arrived. The piano

10 *Advising Learning* by Xun Zi.

studio was filled with Chinese girls who behaved like angels, sat up straight, and played the piano note-perfect. My son and I quit the class and I crawled away feeling somewhat humiliated. I believe the teacher was glad to see us go."[11]

Elvis Presley sang, "It's Now or Never." Is it true that we either take actions now or never? What if there is a circumstance where giving up is the only thing that will save you? Ouyang Ruirui was right. If a student does not have a passion for something, how will that person ever be able to achieve anything? Most people who take piano lessons do so for enjoyment, or because their parents want or force them to. The few who take piano lessons because they seek a professional future in piano are the ones who ought to play piano, right?

Thinking back to the story of Lang Lang, I wondered about all the people who auditioned for spots in conservatories, performances, recitals, etc. Why was it that those who did not make it did not make it?

Ouyang Ruirui said, "You are always given an amount of genius. Some people decide to waste it, but some expand it; it just matters how you use it. That is how prodigies and miracles are made."

"I don't understand what you mean," I responded.

She went on, "It is like that saying, if life gives you lemons, make lemonade. But not everyone does."

"Why not? I thought that was what you are supposed to do with the lemons."

"Because it takes time, effort, will, and strength. But those who do make lemonade, and those who do make the effort are rewarded in the end. People who do make it gave it everything they could."

"But do they all deserve their success? What about the cheaters—those who don't put in the time practicing?"

"Yes, there are cases in which some people succeed due to other reasons; but the ones that get in deserve it, because they tried as hard as

---

11 "Do the Chinese Make Better Parents?" February 9, 2012. http://www.gringolandiasantiago.com/2012/02/09/do-the-chinese-make-better-parents/.

they could and expanded themselves."

I asked Ouyang Ruirui about some experiences she had during her studies—certain moments in her life when something truly memorable occurred.

"I remember a Russian pianist who came to Oklahoma City a few years ago. He played beautifully, and truly put the audience in awe. When he finished his performance, as fans rushed toward him, he said, 'No handshakes or photos, please.' A few months afterward, Midori, a very famous Japanese violinist had just finished yet another amazing performance. Afterward, she stood on the bottom of the stage for two hours, as she took photos with the hundreds of fans who rushed up to her. Two people with great talent, but they expressed their actions differently. Midori's humility and willingness to spend time with her fans was memorable, whereas the Russian pianist gave his fans the cold shoulder after his performance—which I now think of as having been mediocre.

"Geniuses are the ones who are modest, as Confucius says. But the thing is, modesty has to be bestowed upon oneself by one's self, not by someone else such as parents or teachers."

The rise of China's education is being observed around the world. Chief executive of the Royal Society of Chemistry, Dr. Richard Pike, thinks that the future of England's schools and students will require a new direction. School staff discourages their students from even taking math after the age of sixteen due to the difficulty level and the risk of examination failures. However, they now see that this has negatively affected British commerce and industry due to the performance level of students at university in the field of science. The study of chemistry and physics relies heavily on the knowledge of mathematics, and Pike says that the incoming students have such limited math skills that they require "remedial sessions" to make up for the halted curriculum. Before the remedial sessions, simplistic math tests recorded the level of the students, demonstrating that they were two years behind in the General Certificate of Secondary Education level.

"This contrasts starkly with countries like China in which mathematics is seen as integral to the sciences and to the nation's economy, and is taught to all up to the age of eighteen. There, the concept of remedial courses at university would be inconceivable," said Pike.

Pike does not want another report done about the situation; he wants a focused plan of action to embrace the endangered principles of learning, so that his country is placed at the forefront of education. "Our future depends on it," he said.[12]

Du Runze from the University of Minnesota noted the difference in his educational experiences between China and the U.S. In China, classes don't have syllabi; teachers follow the textbooks. When Chinese students first started their classes at US universities, their English wasn't very fluent; they were not used to using a syllabus as a guide to class. The teacher often rambled on during lectures, paused and wrote down the homework, and then resumed the lecture.

One new Chinese student observed, "It was hard writing down so much stuff because we were still thinking about the lecture when he mentioned it. After class we asked students all around us to find out what the homework was. Then one night, we finally discovered that the syllabus was so helpful. Often the teacher added on more reading and homework to the syllabus, so we still had to keep our eye out for that."

Many newcomers have a hard time, but they persevere and survive, according to Margaret Wang, the director of international students at Breck School, a private high school in Minnesota. "Schools love Chinese students! They study hard. They come in with good study habits, and they become role models for our American students."

Jack Wang, a senior at my school, studied at Breck his junior year. When he came to Breck as a freshman, his English was not very fluent. But by the end of his junior year, he was number one in his English class.

---

12 "Chinese maths level embarrasses English system," RFC Advancing The Chemical Sciences. 27 April 2007. http://www.rsc.org/AboutUs/News/PressReleases/2007/ChineseMaths.asp.

In the state of Minnesota where I currently reside, I see students from China everywhere. During Chinese New Year's Eve last year, my parents invited Xu Fangzhou from the University of Minnesota to join us for the celebration. He came from Jinan, where my parents come from. His father is a friend of my mother's classmate, Uncle Wang.

Xu Fangzhou was a transfer student when he came to the University of Minnesota in January 2010, along with forty-five students from Shandong University of Finance and Economics in Jinan in China. There were five groups preceding his group. Following his group, a seventh group, including thirty-eight students, came in the fall of 2011; and an eighth group with forty-eight students came in the winter of 2012. The University of Minnesota has an office in Beijing for student recruitment and houses more Chinese students than any other college or university in the U.S.

Hundreds of Chinese students study at Mankato State University in southern Minnesota. Carleton College in Northfield (a small liberal arts school that is ranked as one of the nation's best colleges) recruits students from China. Breck School, the K-12 private institute, aggressively recruits students from China.

A report of Open Doors 2010 from the International Institute of Education showed that the number of international students studying in the U.S. has only kept growing. The growth was primarily driven by a 30 percent increase in Chinese student enrollment in the U.S. to a total of nearly 128,000 students, or more than 18 percent of the total international student population, making China the leading "sending" country.[13] That momentum did not subside in 2011 when 157,558 Chinese students enrolled in American universities and colleges, a 23 percent increase over the previous year. Chinese students accounted for 22 percent of total

13 Alliance for International Educational and Cultural Exchange. "Open Doors 2010 Report Showes Foreign Students Up, Study Abroad Down," by Lisa Heyn. 11.15.2010. http://www.alliance-exchange.org/policy-monitor/11/15/2010/open-doors-2010-report-shows-foreign-students-study-abroad-down.

international student population in 2011.[14]

Jacques Steinberg, in his *New York Times* article, said that 10 percent of the applications to Grinnell College, a liberal arts college in rural Iowa, are from students in China. Colleges and universities throughout the U.S. have begun advertising and marketing their schools in China, to achieve more diversification in their schools, and to attract students who are willing to pay full tuition. But the problem is, when faced with 200 or so applications from students in China, how do schools decide whom to accept? SAT scores often show a very narrow difference between students. Most have perfect scores on the math portion, and trail close behind in the other sections. Their grades are usually in the 70s or 80s range, since schools in China offer a "far less generous curve"[15] than American schools. Students in China don't have the opportunity to take AP or honor classes simply because they are not offered in their schools.

Before my father came to the University of Minnesota to study economics in 1989, Chinese students came to the U.S. to study only a handful of subjects: mathematics, physics, chemistry, and biology. Chinese students now enroll in "a full range of US higher education," said Peggy Blumenthal, senior counselor to the president of the Institute of International Education, the organization that compiled the Open Doors report.[16] "Ten, twenty years ago, students from China only knew of a handful of US institutions; but now, they are enrolling in our community colleges, in our small liberal arts institutions, in the research universities--

---

14 "Open Doors 2011 Briefing Presentation." Pdf. http://www.iie.org/en/Research-and-Publications/~/media/Files/Corporate/Open-Doors/Open-Doors-2011-Briefing-Presentation.ashx.

15 Jacques Steinberg, "Recruiting in China Pays off for US Colleges." *The New York Times*, February 11, 2011. http://www.nytimes.com/2011/02/12/education/12college.html?_r=1&scp=1&sq=Jacques%20Steinberg%20China&st=cse.

16 Ira Mellman, "Chinese Top List of International Students in US," *Voice of America.* November 13, 2011. http://www.voanews.com/english/news/asia/China-Tops-List-of-International-Students-in-US-133841133.html.

really spread across the country."

As part of the financial crisis that started in 2008, charity donations to private universities shrank and public funding was cut to public schools. Jobs were jeopardized, so family support for education was reduced in the U.S. The robust Chinese economy allowed Chinese students to fill this gap. Jiang Xueqin wrote in *The Diplomat* blog, "It's something US colleges and high schools have discovered to their delight, with at least 100,000 Chinese students currently enrolled in the United States, many of whom are paying around 50,000 dollars a year for the privilege. That's probably why the US embassy in Beijing seems keen to rush through student visa applications, and why Chinese education fairs draw so many foreign participants."[17]

In our family, we often talk about how my father's coming to the University of Minnesota might very well have been due to a miscommunication some years earlier between China's paramount leader, Deng Xiao Ping, and the former US president, Jimmy Carter. On the eve of resuming the formal diplomatic relationship between the People's Republic of China and the United States of America, President Jimmy Carter sent a private emissary to China to discuss the details of the diplomatic relationship. A direct communication was arranged between Jimmy Carter and his emissary in Beijing to discuss an important issue.

The emissary was meeting with Deng Xiaoping about issues involved in sending Chinese students/scholars to the U.S. Mr. Deng asked if the U.S. would accept 5,000 students to study in US universities and colleges. The issue was significant, the number involved was huge, and the result could have decided the fate of the relationship between China and the United States.

The story goes that due to the fifteen-hour time difference between Washington, DC, and Beijing, the telephone rang in the White House at

17 Jiang Xueqin, "China's Education Golden Rush," *The Diplomat*, November 3, 2010. http://the-diplomat.com/china-power/2010/11/03/china%e2%80%99s-education-gold-rush/.

3:00 a.m., waking President Carter. He was apparently not happy being awakened in the middle of a dream. When the president picked up the phone, he answered the question abruptly, saying, "Yes, yes, tell Mr. Deng he can even send 100,000 students."

Just months later in January 1979, fifty-two scholars/students landed in the U.S., just before the new school term commenced. When Mr. Deng Xiaoping visited the U.S. that month, all fifty-two scholars were invited to the White House to attend the welcome party hosted by former first lady, Rosalyn Carter. Ten years later, in 1989, my father came to the U.S., along with 8,500 other Chinese students.

By 2012 more than 150,000 Chinese students, way beyond the 5,000 Mr. Deng requested and even more than President Carter's "unintentional" 100,000 students, had enrolled in colleges and universities in the U.S. Chinese students have been placed in academic institutions all across the nation, studying majors such as math and computer science, engineering, and physical and life sciences. Now, 28 percent of Chinese students study business and management. They are aggressively entering fields of social sciences, fine arts, health professions, and humanities.[18]

If a welcome party were now held for all the Chinese students in the U.S., the White House would not be big enough to hold them all. Times Square might be the more apt space to hold the largest foreign student body in the United States.

18 PDF "2011 Open Doors Briefing Presentation." http://www.iie.org/en/Research-and-Publications/~/media/Files/Corporate/Open-Doors/Open-Doors-2011-Briefing-Presentation.ashx.

CHAPTER 17
Another Voice

Education in China has reached "a dead end," said one of China's most famous professors, Gu Mingyuan,[1] when he met my brother Dan in Beijing in June of 2005. "Although our basic education (primary education) is good, we are suppressing our children's creativity and imagination. We aren't expanding the capacity of their thinking. Our students retain much knowledge, but how do we obtain innovation from the knowledge? This aspect is what we lack in our education system. This is why, when our students come to the United States, they can't raise good questions to the teacher or to the classroom. But our traditional education system also has some good aspects to it: morality, social responsibility, unity of the human and nature, etc. But on the downside, it's these things that hinder the lack of individuality. The amount of space for free development is restrained. Traditional education values conformity, and scorns anomaly. It respects its authorities and has contempt for challenges to authorities. Students favor one answer to one question, and are befuddled by a multiplicity of answers to one question."

As I see it, China's success story is based on:

- A diligent and dedicated student
- A coherent national curriculum
- A devoted well-trained teaching team
- An extremely involved parent

---

1 Gu Mingyuan is the president of the China Education Association and a professor at Beijing Normal University.

- A vehement competition among students
- A feverish competition among schools
- A national agenda for excellence in education
- An excessive focus on the national entrance exams

This system has produced:

- Successful kids
- Super academic performance
- High capability to take tests
- High conformity

But some of these characteristics invite certain criticism, as we learned from the uproar over Amy Chua's "tiger mom" role. Acclaimed by many Chinese people as a "superior" mother, Amy Chua produced two super-achiever kids with a parenting approach that seemed extreme to many Americans. But during her visit to China, parents asked her for parenting advice.

Chua suggested play dates and sleepovers. She felt that China's intensive education left students with "no freedom, no choice, and no creativity." Students need some room for relaxation. They need to take some deep breaths.

I met Amy Chua when she gave a presentation at the University of Minnesota, and she shared this story: *Newsweek* magazine asked her to write a cover article about the four most successful women in China. During her interviews with these extraordinary women, each asked Amy Chua the same exact question. They wanted to know how to send their kids to an Ivy League school in the United States.

English historian and biochemist, Joseph Needham, is the highest authority in the research of Chinese science and civilization. He compiled twenty-four volumes on this topic. He documented how China led the world in almost every area related to science and technology before the sixteenth century. But after the seven trips around the world by explorer

Zheng He,[2] China closed its doors to international travel. Joseph Needham asked why modern science has not developed in China. His question remains unanswered.

China's leading rocket scientist, Qian Xuesen, made a similar observation in 2005 when Premier Wen Jiabao met him. "China is not yet developed. One important reason is because we don't have a university to train innovative scientists. We don't have any independent innovations. Thus, we cannot produce extraordinary talent."

For basic education, China is the top winner in the Olympiads and PISA. On almost any international tests, Chinese students have earned top positions. But when it comes to innovative ideas in universities and top researchers leading scientific frontiers, China is not competing.

Echoing Qian Xueshen's observation, Premier Wen Jiabao agreed that China has trained many scientists since the People's Republic of China was established, but that current Chinese scientists do not inhabit the top positions in the world. In comparison, he pointed out a small country, England, where one university, Cambridge, produced eighty Nobel Prize winners. "They are very proud of that. I feel that if we want to train top experts, we must have advanced education ideals, break the constraint of the traditional ideas, aggressively explore and reform the education system, curriculum, education methodology, and evaluations. We need true educators to manage education,"[3] he said. Wen Jiabao is worried.

The dilemma described by Qian Xuesen and Wen Jiabao is a concern for those in power in China. Government leaders are paying attention to education reform. While Americans criticize China's percieved failures in education, China is quietly taking the best parts from the American education paradigm and integrating them into its curricula.

On August 22, 2006, in Zhong Nan Hai, headquarters of the central Chinese government, Premier Wen Jiabao invited a group of educators to

2 *Voyages of Zheng He* took place from 1405 to 1433.

3 "Wen Jiabo Talked to Students and Teachers at Beijing No. 35 School," September 4, 2010. http://politics.people.com.cn/GB/8198/10173498.html.

discuss education reforms. One of the guests was Professor Gu Mingyuan who presented the premier with two books authored by my brother, Dan Gong.

My brother's books documented his study experience at the Central Middle School in Eden Prairie and Eden Prairie High School in Minnesota. One project he described was a history class assignment intended to be the single most important project in his American History course: the project was called Historical Portfolio: 1898–1945. The assignment included a cover page, timeline, choosing a famous/infamous person to write an obituary about and delivering a eulogy in the first person, interviewing a historical figure, writing a movie review, writing a book review, a main event during the period, providing a historical snapshot, and writing a dedication. For this project, Dan picked the South-East Theater of World War II. He chose Claire L. Chennault (leader of the Flying Tigers) as the historical figure. He chose Madame Chiang Kai-shek for the obituary and eulogy. He reviewed Thomas Hart Benson's *Arts of the South* and the movie *Citizen Kane*. He reviewed *The Jungle* and *All Quiet on the Western Front*. One assignment from his art class and one from his science class in middle school were also presented to Premier Wen Jiabao.

Professor Gu Mingyuan was clearly impressed. He told the group that this was the kind of thing he is aware of and has talked about. He felt that "these free capitalist countries" have curricula that are "well designed to tap students' creativity and initiative. They broaden the students' knowledge base. If the students are motivated to study, how is their basic education not firm?"

Premier Wen Jiabao also commented positively about Dan's books and the study methods used at Eden Prairie High School to induce or direct students to think creatively. "They take a heuristic approach, not an indoctrinate approach," he observed.

A report from the *Education Guide* on March 15, 2011, made the front page with a headline, "Say 'Bye Bye' to the Inculcating Education." The report talked about an eighth-grade student in China, Tong Xiaolin, whose school had adopted education reform methods. When he got home each day, he spent only a half hour on homework. After that half hour, he went outside to play with his friends. Two weeks later, his observant grandmother thought something was suspicious, and told Tong Xiaolin's father, who worked in the city. His father called the class advisor, Tan Wenze, asking why his son was given so little homework.

Tan Wenze patiently explained that most of the homework was completed during the class period. The father then asked, "Isn't the classroom time when the teacher lectures? How do the students have time to do homework?"

The teacher explained how recently they had changed the instruction format, now using a heuristic approach. The teachers now teach less, but the students must complete more independent study.

So his father asked whether his son understood the concepts being taught.

Mr. Tan Wenze replied, "Of course! His scores are going up, and he has also won an award!"

However, this transition had actually worried the principal of the school who said, "We talk about quality education in China. The teaching pressure is reduced; teachers like it. Play time has increased and after-school homework has been reduced; students like that. But if we only pursue quality education, our student's futures will be damaged and hindered." Last generation educators still believe in China's traditional indoctrinate approach. For them, feeding students knowledge and achieving high performance in tests are important goals.

In the face of criticism for "mindless" rote learning, China has explored different options. One of these explorations entailed research-based education, which Chinese educators call the "American model." Integrating this approach into their teaching is not easy for Chinese teachers. He Li Na, the English teacher we met at the Affiliated School to Shanxi Normal University, observed, "The new education system creates new problems and questions for students. Students have to work hard on these new problems, harder than just memorizing facts. This transformation is not easy. It actually appears to be harder for students to adapt to the new educational system, compared to just using the old one. The traditional system is a top-down system. Teachers are the authority; they disseminate their knowledge among the students and cannot be challenged. Everything the teacher says is true, and the teachers and students are clearly on a different level. Students who accumulate the most knowledge are the best of the best. But in the new system, it's bottom-up. If we let the students' creativity prevail, they must challenge authority. They must doubt their authorities and search for the truth. Now there is a question about which level the teachers are on, and which level the students are on. Thus it's not just rewriting for new problems, but it's also that the evaluation system has been completely changed."

A Chinese blogger and former mathematics teacher at the School Affiliated to China People's University, Wang Jinzhan, wrote in his blog that the culture of Wang Zi Cheng Long (a Chinese proverb meaning parents expect their children to be dragons), where parents expect their children to be outstanding, is common in China. "But children are not parents' accessories; parents shouldn't put their dreams, their will, onto their children. Students are individuals; they are all different. They should have different goals, different objectives. Parents should understand their children's advantage and respect their children's choice. Parents may design or plan their children's future, but parents must understand their child first," wrote Wang.

Favoritism also created problems for students. Lin Lin, who we spoke to at her high school, had gone to a local school in Jiangxi Province before she was transferred to Beijing Fifth High School. She admitted that the teachers there were biased toward students with better academic performances. They paid more attention to the good students that excelled in class, treating them favorably, and ignored the students at the bottom. This wasn't uncommon.

Many schools in China extend help to students on the lower levels, but many others try to push the top students the most, and focus on the few to excel and be accepted into top schools. They are satisfied to have the other students understand basic concepts.

Lin Lin told me, "This created psychological problems among those students who didn't perform as well academically."

When the University of Minnesota PhD student, Jackie, visited my home, she said, "Something that many students in China lack is imagination." (This is the most common criticism of China's education.) "For students in China, their creativity is killed by the time they are in kindergarten. My little brother drew a tree in class one day and colored it purple, and the teacher yelled at him and told him it couldn't be purple! It should be green. They are so young, and the teachers will not even let their children's imagination run," says Jackie. "And this is only the start. Children are criticized in school about their lack of discipline even when they are only in kindergarten. They learn to memorize and read stories and learn about history while they should be playing and running around; at least that is what I think. When I was in daycare, I loved drawing. I loved drawing because then I would get to take home loads and loads of paper on which I had marked on."

This caused serious concerns for educators with international perspectives. Jiang Xueqin, a graduate form Yale University and now director of an international program in China asked, "Do Chinese schools make learning so unpleasant for students that they don't want to learn anymore after they leave school? Anecdotal evidence suggests that's the case: After they finish the national examination, Chinese students burn their textbooks, spend four years in college playing video games, and enter the workforce unprepared for the re-learning that their job requires."

A fifth-grade student in Nanjing, Qiu Jiachen, did a survey[4] of twenty-one students in his class about how they spent their winter break. Fifteen of the twenty-one students planned to spend more than ten full days in classes such as Little Science Doctors, Olympic Mathematics, and

4 http://edu.sina.com.cn/zxx/2012-01-21/1012324710.shtml.

Bookman English. That is 71 percent of the students and more than half of the winter break time. Asked why they would attend winter break classes, sixteen students responded they were asked to do so by their parents, and seventeen students said they wanted to improve their test performance so a top middle school would accept them. Asked about which school they wanted to attend, all of them selected Nanjing Foreign Language School, Shu Ren School, and Jin Ling School; all of which are elite schools in Nanjing. When they were asked what they would want to do if the winter break plans were their choice, all answered, "Play!"

In the Beijing Huangchenggen Elementary School, the average student has five after-school classes such as art, calligraphy, music, computer, etc. On the weekends, every science museum is jammed. Not only do parents bring their children to the museum, but every review class, special class, and after-school session also brings their students.

In the U.S., most students participate in some after-school sporting activity. We are permitted to enjoy life.

When educators and commentators in China called for reducing students' burdens, nobody paid attention. Students' school bags became heavier and heavier. Study hours became longer and longer. The high pressure extended from high schools to middle schools, elementary schools, preschools, and kindergartens. The competitive examinations traditionally offered for college entrance were then applied to high schools. The pressure mounted and radiated to every student in China.

In Huantai Second School, we saw 5,000 students rehearsing the *Di Zi Gui* (a Confucian classic). This kind of ritual has been sweeping the whole country in recent years. Mencius Mother Hall is a well-known advocate of this kind of practice. This academy is not a formal school, but an after-school program dedicated mainly to three areas: rehearsing the classics, practicing rituals, and cultivating art. These programs are attempting to revive Confucius-based education. The classics include *Great Learning, Analects, Dao De Qing, Zhuang Zi,* and classical poetry such as, *Yi Jing, Three Hundred Tang Poems*, and selected essays. English classics are also included, such as Shakespeare's *Midsummer's Night Dream* and sonnets, the *Bible*, Plato, and Socrates, and Aristotle. The students' age range is from one to thirteen, and their principal wants them to learn these classics, believing that memorization and simulation are a good fit with the nature of children. But the result of this practice is apprehension in children.

The current debate continues in China. On one side are those who support the renaissance of traditional education—the desire to revive all that was created in the past few thousand years, and bring back what made China so successful. The classics are the foundation of Chinese civilization. One side asks, "If a Chinese person does not have an understanding of Chinese history and culture, how can we define ourselves as a society?" This viewpoint holds that the recovery of traditional Chinese education will propel China toward a successful future.

On the other side of the argument are those who recognize that modern society is technology based. Some argue, "Why should we force students in the twenty-first century to carry the huge burden of history? Why must students fill their minds with thousands of years' worth of information? Technology makes it possible for students to access whatever information they need, so why memorize things that they can just look up on the Internet?"

Most schools in China have embraced technology despite any resistance. The top public schools are well equipped with the most advanced technological tools.

Though, on the surface, technology may appear to offer a challenge to the most conservative parents and teachers in China, access to technology is not necessarily a threat to advanced or complex learning. Just as the introduction of the concepts of individuality and the questioning of authority have allowed some students in China to compete more effectively on a global scale, so too must some accommodations be made for confronting the rigidity of some aspects of the traditional approach in order to make the most of all resources available now and in the future. Students in China must be as well informed and well versed in the use of new technologies as will be all students throughout the world. Certainly, covering the "blank slate" that is a child with information gleaned from the classics of the world will provide a strong foundation and assist in the grounding of character and integrity.

Learning is the job of every child, whether or not it is proactively enforced by parents and others from infancy. That complex and difficult learnings can be introduced to and absorbed by a small child before those learnings are labeled "complex and difficult" suggests that in supportive circumstances, children may be capable of magnificent achievements, miracles of learning. To find the balance of discipline and individual creativity is the challenge of all parents and educators in China. And parents and educators throughout the world would do well to apply a similarly balanced approach.

"I am not one who was born in the possession of knowledge;

I am one who is fond of antiquity, and earnest in seeking it there."

~ Confucius, *The Analects*

ACKNOWLEDGMENTS

This book would not have come together without the support of the following people: my editors, Marly Cornell and Leila Nielson, whose time and patience guided me through the editing process; my father who offered his insight and his own wise words when I needed them the most; my mother who always expressed her faith in me and my project; and my friends who understood the importance of this project to me and offered their intelligence and their cooperation.

I would also like to thank the principals, teachers, parents, and students who participated in interviews and conversations during the research process: Gao Daquan, Gong Maolin, and Dai Qun, principals who expressed their care and feelings toward the subject of education in their schools and in China; Margaret Wong, Chen Haiyan, Yu Jun, Ma Jiansheng, Ms. Tang, Bi Junhua, and Song Lifeng, teachers who offered insight into their experiences and viewpoints about the gaokao, the school systems, and their students; He Yixin, Ms. Liu, Lin Lin, Mr. Du, Wang Qing, Zhang Yong, and Ouyang Ruirui who taught me about the culture and education system of China through their eyes, whether as a tour guide or a student just out of high school; Mr. Wang, Mr. Wu, Ms. Zhang, and Dr. Zhang, parents who shared their viewpoints about the education system in China while their own children were living through it; Wang Jiayi, Annie Jiao, Su Rui, Wang Jinghan, Wang Mengxiao, Geng Liping, and Deng Yan, students who told me their own stories and views as the current generation involved in Chinese education. Thank you to Mr. Lu and his two sons, who introduced me to the most interesting story of homeschooling his twin boys, and for his perspective on the education system in China. And to all the schools, including my very own in Eden Prairie, thank you for giving me the opportunity to meet with your students, teachers, and principals.

ABOUT THE AUTHOR

Yanna Gong is a student at Eden Prairie High School in Eden Prairie, Minnesota. She is the 2011 state winner of the National Peace Essay Competition, two-time first place winner of the annual International Chinese Youth Essay Competition, and third place winner of the 2010 Second Amendment Essay Competition. Gong enjoys traveling with her family, giving back to her community through volunteering, and pursuing her education outside of class through academic competitions and papers.

GLOSSARY

211 Project—A project of National Key Universities and Colleges initiated in 1995 by China's Ministry of Education, with the intent of raising the research standards of high-level universities and cultivating strategies for socioeconomic development.

863 Project—State High-Tech Development Plan funded and administered by the government of the People's Republic of China intended to stimulate the development of advanced technologies in biotechnology, space, information technology, laser technology, automation, energy, new materials, telecommunications, and marine technology. The Project is associated with China's major universities and research institutes.

973 Project—China's National Basic Research Program initiated to achieve a technological and strategic edge in various scientific fields, especially in the development of the rare-earth minerals industry. The Project is associated with China's major universities and research institutes.

985 Project—A project involving both the national and local governments allocating significant amounts of funding to certain universities for building new research centers, improving facilities, holding international conferences, attracting world-renowned faculty and visiting scholars, and helping Chinese faculty attend conferences abroad. Initially, the Project included nine universities, later it expanded to thirty-nine universities. The Project has not admitted other universities since 2011.

C-9 League—The Chinese equivalent of the US Ivy League, an alliance of nine prestigious Chinese universities established in 2009. These nine universities include Fudan University, Harbin Institute of Technology, Nanjing University, Beijing University, Shanghai Jiao Tong University, Tsinghua University, University of Science and Technology of China, Xi'an Jiao Tong University, and Zhejiang University.

Cheng Hao (AD 1032–1085) and Cheng Yi (AD 1033–1107)—Brothers and scholars of neo-Confucian philosophy during the Song dynasty; students of Zhou Dunyi.

Chinese Revolution—The Communist Party of China, led by Mao Zedong, defeated the Nationalists, led by Chiang Kai-shek, and won the civil war (1946–1949), taking over China in 1949.

Confucius Classics—A term for Confucius' texts including four books (Great Learning, Doctrine of the Mean, Analects, and Mencius) compiled by Zhu Xi in the Song dynasty, and five classics (Classic of Poetry, Book of Documents, Book of Rites, Classic of Changes, and Spring and Autumn Annals) compiled by Confucius. They have been used as the primary tests in China for more than a thousand years.

Confucius (551–479 BC)—Chinese educator and philosopher of the Spring and Autumn Period of Chinese history. Confucius emphasized personal and governmental morality, correctness of social relationships, justice, and sincerity. Confucius' thoughts and philosophy was China's official ideology from the Han dynasty to the end of Qin dynasty (AD 220–905).

Cultural Revolution—Also known as the Great Proletarian Cultural Revolution; a social-political movement that took place in China from 1966 through 1976. Mao Zedong, then chairman of the Communist Party of China, launched the movement with its goal of enforcing communism by removing capitalism, eliminating traditional and cultural elements from Chinese society, and imposing Mao's doctrine across the country. The movement paralyzed China economically and politically and significantly affected the country socially.

Di Zi Gui—Translated as "Rules for Students" or "Standards for Being a Good Pupil"; an education primer following Confucian tradition written during the seventeenth century by Li Yu Xiu. It is based on the teachings of Confucius that emphasize the basic requisites for being a good person and guidelines for living in harmony with others.

Dianshi—The national examination administered directly by the emperor or by a special delegate of the emperor. This was the highest level of imperial examinations in the Keju system.

Du Fu (AD 618–907)—One of China's most famous poets, also considered a Confucian scholar. He lived in the Tang dynasty (AD 618–907), an era considered the pinnacle of China's poetic literature.

Gaokao—China's annual national college entrance examinations, which started in the 1950s, was suspended during the Cultural Revolution (1966–76), and resumed in 1977.

Gongyuan (also called Gongsheng)—Title and honor awarded to senior xiucai who are qualified to take advanced imperial examinations.

Gongshi—Title and honor awarded to juren who passed the prequalification examination.

Han Yu (768–824 BC)—A precursor of neo-Confucianism as well as an essayist and poet during the Tang dynasty. Han Yu wrote the famous essay, "On Teachers."

Huishi—The examination administered by the imperial Department of Rituals in the spring following the xiangshi; it was offered once every three years. This was the second level of the imperial examinations.

Jinshi—The title and honor awarded to those who passed the huishi in China's imperial examination.

Juren—The title and honor awarded to those who passed the xiangshi examination in China's imperial examination.

Keju System—China's imperial examination system, which was initiated in AD 605 and ended in AD 1905, lasting thirteen hundred years. The examinations were held at the provincial level, ministerial level, and the highest level, which was administered directly by the emperor.

Mao Zedong (1893–1976)—Commonly referred to as Chairman Mao, Mao Zedong was a Chinese communist revolutionary, political theorist, politician, and poet. He led the Chinese Revolution to victory in 1949 and stayed in power until his death.

Mencius (Meng Zi) (372–289 BC)—A founder of Confucianism and Chinese philosopher who was arguably the most famous Confucian after Confucius himself. Mencius believed that man was innately good.

Neo-Confucianism—A philosophical movement of the twelfth to the sixteenth centuries in China, incorporating Taoism and Buddhism with an adaptation of Confucianism.

San Zi Jing—Translated as "Three Character Classic"; a classical primer of home education written in the thirteenth century; a distillation of the essentials of Confucianism expressed in a way suitable for teaching young children; as a Confucian catechism, it was written in couplets of three Chinese characters for easy memorization.

Thousand Model High School—A program to establish 1,000 model high schools across China. Each school requires having demonstration labs, computer labs, linguistic labs, and multimedia labs.

Thousand People Plan—A program administrated by China's central government for Chinese universities and research institutes to attract talent who has achieved or have potential to achieve in their fields. They provide funding, labs, and all the facilities and conveniences for them to advance science and technology in China.

Wang Fuzhi (1619–92)—A Chinese philosopher of the late Ming and early Qing dynasties. Wang Fuzhi was a follower of Confucius but criticized the neo-Confucian philosophy. He wrote his own commentaries on the Confucian classics and many other topics, including metaphysics, epistemology, moral philosophy, poetry, and politics.

Wang Zi Cheng Long—"Expecting children to be dragons"; a deeply rooted Chinese family education tradition.

Xiangshi—The examination held in the capital city of provinces in the Keju ystem; it was offered once every three years. This was the first level of the imperial examinations.

Xiucai—The title and honor awarded to those who passed the local yuanshi test in the qualification test for China's imperial examination.

Xun Zi (312–230 BC)—An educator and Confucian philosopher who lived during the turbulent Warring States Period. Xunzi believed that man's inborn tendencies need to be curbed through education and ritual. He also believed that ethical norms had to be invented to rectify mankind.

Yuanshi—The local examination administered by the provincial minister of education; a qualification test for taking formal tests in the Keju system. Yuanshi was held at the county level.

Zeng Zi (505–436 BC)—A Chinese philosopher and student of Confucius. He was credited with having authored a major portion of Great Learning.

Zhongkao—China's annual regional high-school entrance examinations administered by the local bureaus of education.

Zhou Dunyi (AD 1017–73)—A Chinese neo-Confucian philosopher and cosmologist during the Song dynasty and one of the architects of neo-Confucian cosmology.

Zhu Xi (AD 1130–1200)—A Song dynasty Confucian philosopher who became the leading figure of the School of Principle (Li) and the most influential rationalist neo-Confucian in China.

Zhuangyuan—The title awarded to the student with the highest score in dianshi in China's imperial examination.